Theatres of Democracy

Between the Epic and the Everyday

Selected Essays

SHIV VISVANATHAN

Edited by

CHANDAN GOWDA

HarperCollins *Publishers* India

First published in hardback in India in 2016 by
HarperCollins *Publishers* India
4th Floor, Tower A, Building No. 10, Phase II
DLF Cyber City, Gurugram, Haryana -122002
www.harpercollins.co.in

P-ISBN: 978-93-5177-562-1
E-ISBN: 978-93-5177-563-8

2 4 6 8 10 9 7 5 3 1

Typeset in 10.5/14.2 Berling LT Std
by Jojy Philip, New Delhi 110 015

Printed and bound at
Manipal Technologies Limited, Manipal

To

The friendship of SEMINAR magazine, New Delhi
The hospitality of the NINASAM theatre community, Heggodu
The happy eccentricity of the COMPOST HEAP, Gandhi Nagar

Contents

Part 6: Elections as Soap Opera

Part 7: The Necessity of Dissent

Part 8: Taking Policy Seriously

Editor's Introduction

During a phone conversation in late 2012, I had asked Shiv Visvanathan what he wished his newspaper writings to do. He had written four or five op-eds just about every week over the previous couple of months.

'I'm trying to create a different kind of social science.'

'You should bring them out as a book then.'

'Why don't *you* do it?'

This is how the book came to be started.

In the academic world, Shiv Visvanathan is known for his work on the culture of science in modern India. His reflections on the violence of development have been justly influential even among social activists. Alongside these writings, a large body of his exciting work lies inside the pages of newspapers and magazines.

Taking on subjects as diverse as the media, middle-class culture, cities, cinema, elections, political parties, cricket, social movements, to name a few, Visvanathan's essays in the popular media form a vibrant archive of the complexity of contemporary India. They almost always offer inventive readings and nudge us to think differently. In their hyper alertness to the distinctness of a predicament or an episode or a personality, the impulse is less that of a contrarian, and more that of someone keen on interpretive justice. They also hold out a distinct way of looking at Indian society.

'Mine is especially an oral imagination', Visvanathan clarifies in a chance self-referential remark. 'One recites an event and in reciting an event, in all its sonorous beauty, the narrative unfolds.'[1] Reciting an event allows it to be relived, an effect not guaranteed in print. Marked by a spoken quality, his essays create an unusual image of the social analyst: a modern-day storyteller with a large narrative canvas and clear commitments to the well-being of society. Drawing from wide ranging sources, the interpretive aims of his essays are leavened with aphorisms, anecdotes, hypotheses and normative passions. In addition, he has a fondness for putting down 'wish lists and scenarios of "What if"'.[2] His essays bristle, as a result, with a strange unruliness and stand apart from the staid analyses of the self-styled specialist.

As storyteller, Visvanathan expects much from his audience by way of preparedness: modern history, politics, social theory, popular culture, science, sports, international politics, all should matter to them.

Suffused with metaphors and analogies, his essays keep feeling and intellect together. Their wit, irony and occasional sarcasm imbue the commentary with vitality and warmth. Moral seriousness though is never at risk anywhere. Consider a few instances: Prime Minister Manmohan Singh 'seemed like the cartoonist R.K. Laxman's Common Man but with a Ph.D'; 'M.N. Srinivas's *The Remembered Village* (is) the closest equivalent to Malgudi in social science'; 'The metaphors of war are catwalking happily through our society'; 'Politicians might make money but their real currency is the symbol'.

Visvanathan loves to bring together categories normally

kept apart and shake up settled thought; the conversation as a result takes surprising directions. A few favourite instances of mine in this regard: 'Patriotism is a theory of hospitality'; 'A mistake is an incomplete conversation with the world'; 'Public policy has to be an intellectual commons'.

Visvanathan never fails to bring new things to the table. His essay, 'The Necessity of Corruption', for instance, disaggregates what everyone loathes, i.e., corruption, to show that it works as 'a knowledge of survival' for poor urban migrants. Elsewhere, he points out that Sachin Tendulkar's discipline, professionalism and proper social manners made him a middle-class model of 'guiltless success' with full rights of conspicuous consumption.

Steadfastly non-partisan, and non-ideological, whether of the left, liberal, or right variety, unswayed by political correctness and always life-affirming, Visvanathan's writings reveal, at bottom, a quest to understand modern India. This search is often moored in abstract normative commitments: democracy, pluralism and justice are non-negotiable ideals, even as the forms they might take remain open. The conviction that creativity in knowledge and ethics in informal social arenas can enrich the democratic experience also runs deep.

The mimicry of the West in contemporary intellectual work in India is deplored again and again. In contrast, intellectuals in colonial India exhibited self-confidence and playfulness in their ideas. The essay, 'A Celebration of Difference', offers an exciting account of this creative phase in Indian science.

For Visvanathan, the eccentric and dissenting minds seen in independent India also constitute a precious cultural legacy. Social movements like the Narmada Bachao Andolan and the anti-nuclear protests challenged the country's development priorities and raised fundamental issues for debate. The creativity of individuals like P.K. Sethi, the designer of the Jaipur Foot, Nek Chand, the creator of a rock garden, and Yellappa, the indigo-dyer, are cherished episodes in India's democratic culture.

The passion for renewing India's intellectual life, in Visvanathan, does not lead to a search for local concepts, or a foray into the world of Indian languages. He has put down his preferred idea of 'the South Asian Intellectual': 'a person sure of his identity, at home in diversity, ironic about the West, critical of his own traditions and yet deeply inventive of new possibilities.'[3]

It is no surprise that Visvanathan has on occasion called himself 'a social science nomad': his interests and inspirations exhibit an exuberant range. He regrets, for instance, that Indian cities are yet to find their Thomas Pynchon or Walter Benjamin. References from around the world dart through his sentences as well: Steve Biko, Eliza Doolittle, Gustavo Esteva, Patrick Geddes, Ivan Illich, the Punch and Judy Show, Rasputin, Rumplestiltskin, Valhalla. And his political concerns often extend beyond India. Sharing his enthusiasm for the Arab Spring protests, he recalls, 'People born in the 1950s are honorary Egyptians who understood the dreams of Nasser and the Non-Aligned Movement.' And India's support for Tibet, for him, is integral to its tradition of idealism.

Unlike writers, journalists and Bollywood filmmakers, Visvanathan never tires of reminding us that the social sciences have not succeeded in bringing alive the realities of India. As he remarks icily, 'it is as if society has seceded from the social sciences'.[4] In striving to be objective, he points out, the latter remained indifferent to the sensoriness of social life, i.e., the colours, sounds and smells, and to the varieties of time in it. Further, their analytical vocabulary derived heavily from Western social theory. Understanding the dimensions of violence and evil was low among their priorities too. The essays in this book hold up the value of being attentive to these.

Visvanathan's worries are apparent: the rise of a security-based idea of nation-state, religious fundamentalisms, the mediocrity in higher education, the power of the market, the lure of technocratic governance, among others. Several of the essays disclose the subtle and not-so-subtle harms posed by these forces. Steering clear of cynicism, however, Visvanathan stays fully alert to turns of event and action that aid in, to borrow his phrase, 'the democratization of democracy'.

Politics and ethics, it will become obvious, do not exhaust his preoccupations. The impulse to understand for understanding's sake is impossible to miss. His comparisons of the Maruti and Ambassador cars, the Independence Day and the Republic Day celebrations, Sachin Tendulkar and Viswanathan Anand, among many others, are scintillating illustrations here.

While Visvanathan's mercurial prose allows one to speed through the sentences, a fast reading will almost certainly risk glossing over the provocations that come in quick succession, most of which demand close consideration. Then there are the telegraphic phrases that ask to be elaborated. On one occasion, Visvanathan asks Indians to 'by heart China', as that would make them better Indians. On another, he asks that the scientists whose innovations displace existing technologies work with 'an ethics of memory'. Less aimed at providing clarity, they work more to provoke pathways to new thought.

Social thought should aid, Visvanathan believes, the creation of new theories of peace, justice, pluralism; it is key to work with a sense of the possibilities for the future. He writes that 'the tribal, the nomad might also present a case arguing that the evolution of Indian society has to be plural, that the oral, the digital and the literate worlds have to exist together. This is the only framework for democracy and knowledge in the 21st century.'[5]

The essays for this anthology have been picked from over a thousand that Visvanathan has published in newspapers and magazines over the last two decades. I chose those that help convey the astonishing range of his concerns and commitments as a public intellectual. The section themes remain an ironic attempt, of course, to classify writings that resist classification at their core.

In the pages that follow, India, and indeed the world, appear in ways not usually seen.

References

1. 'The Bhopal Gas Tragedy Should Never Be Forgotten', *Daily O*, 12 December 2014.
2. 'The Cynical State of Telangana', *The Asian Age*, 14 January 2011.
3. 'Alternative Histories, Alternative Futures', *New Indian Express*, 16 August 2009.
4. 'The Coming Decline of the Social Sciences', *The Tribune*, 9 February 2015.
5. 'Silly Ideas on Knowledge, Choice Are Destroying Us', *Deccan Chronicle*, 29 June 2009.

Part 1

Reading Society

The Necessity of Corruption

Dear Acharya Kripalani, I read your article on corruption in *Seminar* (No. 8, April 1960). I was moved by its clarity, its integrity and its sense of history. Like you, I believe in an ethical universe. Like your generation, I believe character building and nation building go together. And yet, I find that a lot of what you wrote seems archaic. It also gets banalized when articulated as policy by 'idiot' bureaucrats and World Bank officials. Let me state my disagreement. Like you I want to fight corruption, but my sense of sociology is rather different.

Imagine you are a villager entering a city. You enter it and realize you have to survive. Even to live at subsistence, you need surplus. To sleep at night on the pavements, you have to pay the land sharks. To live you have to pay the policeman. You need a job quickly in a *chai dhaba*, at a railway station, at a construction site. To connect, you need a middleman. He makes survival possible. He initiates you into the literacy of a city. Only connect. Your first model of success is the clerk, cop and middleman. No wonder you want to be like these magicians of the city extracting miraculous surplus out of nothing. You suddenly discover that the rules of the city are all wrong. Right is left. Up is down. You realize that the city is a strange classificatory system. Your intuitive sense of life won't do. To enter, to survive, to subsist, to sustain, you need a map.

A city is a knowledge economy and many of its knowledges are not open. They are tacit, monopolized, secret, changing and manipulative. To enter modernity, development, urbanization, you need to know three things. First, that they are forms of knowledge, rule games. Second, to play these games you need access, entry, membership, which too are forms of knowledge. Third, a city is a classification; it's full of lethal dualisms like formal and informal, white economy–black economy, official and unofficial. Success is the art of being on the right side of these dualisms.

Unfortunately, in terms of these taxonomies, you are by definition illegal, informal and unofficial. You also realize that citizenship is for the formal, legal and the official. You know you live beyond contract, in the crevices between the informal and the unofficial. Rights are a privilege of the abstract citizen. As a migrant, you are outside the law. Therefore, you are prey to the law. Every migrant is a potential victim in the Hobbesian system created by law. As squatter, poacher, hawker, scavenger, forager, as a creature without a ration card, you lack the first semblance of citizenship. Remember, all you are is a potential source of surplus. It is the poor who have to pay and that is the first rule of the extractive economy called the city.

What every entrant needs are rules of thumb, a sense of prohibitions of whom to evade, whom to avoid, whom to beg from. These are the rules of coping and out of them emerge the strategies of corruption.

Corruption is the recognition of a dual city. It is based on the understanding that the social contract that binds modernity is between the official and the unofficial, the formal and the informal, the front stage and the back stage of a city. The contract is not universal; it is not a charter of rights but a domain of negotiated possibilities. A modern city is a tragedy of taxonomies; the drama begins as you negotiate this world. The first axiom of knowledge is that the social is negotiable. You can be reclassified for the day, the hour. Behind such a rule game is uncertainty, a lack of insurance.

Survival as security comes from knowing someone. Sustainability comes from knowing who to pay. There is no central sovereign in the city. Every door has its leviathan, every street its tyrant. He commands absolute power over a limited domain. A nukkad (street corner) could be a Gulag.

A nomad, a squatter, a hawker, a rickshaw-wallah realizes corruption is the knowledge of survival, the fundamental rules of coping. He realizes that the city is not just a collection of rule games. It is an aggregation of rules called a bureaucracy. A municipal committee, a police station, a ration shop are bureaucracies. All of them thrive on the informal sector. All bureaucracies are forms of exclusion that perpetually threaten openings, opportunities, entries and exits.

The squatter, the migrant is perpetually accessing or avoiding these bureaucracies which demand two forms of payment. Payment because you are not a member. And payment to become one.

Corruption is not an identity tag or a label on an object or person. Corruption is that relation between official and unofficial, formal and informal, public and private that the city as architectonic creates. Corruption stems from taxonomy, the power to classify and declassify which is coded deeply into the city.

Ironically the classification has a lovely ethnocentricity of colour that only modernity and enlightenment can produce. A city is free, or open, or understandable as rational design according to its visuality and transparency. So it is divided into a black and a white economy with a grey zone. A red light is equally accessible, equally barred. There is a front stage visually open and a back stage visually obfuscated, barred and covered.

Corruption is the world of grey and black. Corruption in official narratives needs to be exposed to light and revealed in reform narratives.

One has to understand that the social does not begin with gigantism of the state but with an enormous array of these micro-narratives of life. We could summon an Erving Goffman from the other side of sociology to understand it.

Let us be clear that one is talking of two kinds of relationships. Let us christen the first 'The Hummock'. It is an idea I borrowed from Gustavo Esteva. The hummock is the rubric for all relationships of conviviality among the poor, all their attempts to enrich life within the informal sector. Corruption can then refer to all rules, relationships between these entrants and the structures of modernity, development and urban life. Corruption is that ethnoscience, the rules of coping, the body language, the tacit knowledge that copes, confronts and domesticates the rules of state, the corporation, and the structures of modern life. It summons both the middleman and the relative as kinsman or caste man.

Corruption is the first great ethnoscience. Unfortunately, the word 'ethnoscience' is used to refer to native systems of knowledge. I would instead use that word to refer to how the native as migrant, squatter, poacher, smuggler, copes with modernity. Corruption begins as anti- or contra-management science that combats the managerialism, the power and planning, the physical and symbolic threats of a city.

Corruption uses the language of the gift and the hummock to speak to modernity. It has at its centre the middleman as expert. It is not accidental that he is the most reviled creature in the modernity saga.

What corruption as enthnoscience also does is that it sustains agency for the squatter, the migrant. He is not a helpless victim, an object acted upon. He has agency. This is important for this letter still hopes that one day urban planning will begin with the hawker or squatter and build around him, understand his ethnoscience to re-liberate the city. Once we realize that corruption is a great management science, we can redo the city as a form of knowledge.

Corruption is not just a liberatory or coping exercise. There is equally a pathology, a bowdlerization that we must understand. Maybe we can call it the tragedy of the inverted commons.

The bureaucracy is converted to an enclosure. Every rule becomes a turf. Every file is a sovereign domain of a clerk, who as gatekeeper may or may not grant entry. Corruption recolonizes the grammar of a bureaucracy. A rational sequence of laws becomes a labyrinth. It is a process of strip-mining the state, or turning it into an extractive economy for personal ends. The bureaucracy becomes a collection of private domains, or public domains for private benefit. The tout and the middleman take over the system, thereby regrammatizing it.

There are pluses or minuses to such an activity. The bureaucracy demands a literacy which an oral or ethnic community may not have. Corruption then becomes a form of reskilling, a travelogue, a catalogue of how to access the system – whom to meet, what to give, how to converse, what to ask and when. It becomes a package of performative rituals without which a bureaucracy is inaccessible.

There is something about the impersonality, the suffocating demand for expertise, in filling forms, for example, that people find alien. It is a confrontation of strangers without the rules of hospitality. It is contra-culture. People feel insecure about it. One is always asked if one has 'contacts' or an 'approach to someone'. A presence inside domesticates and revives an alien place. Rules give way to rituals. You meet a body, a person, a relative, a friend of a friend. It almost becomes a home away from home. Nepotism gives one a sense of temporary dwelling, of being in touch with someone in control. Corruption, in this sense, recolonizes a bureaucracy. From impersonality, rationality and expertise, one moves to the conviviality of a patron–client relationship. It provides an umbilical guarantee, a sense of security, and a prospect of translation. A bureaucracy nepotized is truly in Pidgin English a 'service' economy, playing on both meanings of the term. Corruption is a recognition that every economy is a knowledge economy by definition.

Let me tell you that it is not just the poor tribal or migrant to a city who suffers the above syndrome. I felt the same way when I was hunting for a house and settling down in America. I had a visiting professorship in Arizona at a delightful research centre for science policy. But settling down was a nightmare.

I walked all over examining flats meant more for students doing postgraduate research, stumbling from pillar to post, getting nowhere, tired, helpless and clueless about where anything was. Yes, status back home helps. You are someone who knows someone who knows someone else. At the end of a tired day, all I could say was that I wished I could have bribed someone. A bribe is an act of problem solving even for those who want to do it the right way.

The Third World scenario would have been different. People would have dropped in, asked, offered information, rung up other people like gossipy worker ants. I didn't want a starchy American colleague next door asking me about my 'significant other' and promising a lunch whenever she turns up. I felt he was doing his Christian duty or reading me my rights.

I needed a car and a team to help me out. Impersonality and anonymity might spell freedom but sometimes what one needs is security or the guarantee of negotiability of concessions. A Third Worlder would have asked, '*Kuchh* contact *hai?*'

Contact. It is actually a lovely Hindi word, which guarantees humans one can plug into, who electrify life. Corruption is a warm organism, a wonderful term from a Hanklyn-Janklin, promising translations which guarantee movements across difference. One distorts the world, not only to subvert it but to seduce it to one's own way of life. Words must be made life-giving before they freeze their initial openness.

Let us look at this other world as a normative process and understand it. The best way is to look at what are called the proverbs of corruption. I have assembled some of them.

- Everything is negotiable.
- Obstacles are created so that someone can surmount them.
- Every rule is an opportunity. The more rules, the greater the opportunity.
- Each reform is an attempt to test a rule game.
- Never say Yes. Never say No either. A windfall of opportunity lies between them.
- Transparency is an illusion. Transparency International is a bigger illusion.
- Two things the liberal West won't allow: an attack on property and a defence of corruption.
- Corruption is not about an open society. It is about openings in a society.
- Corruption is unsanctified expertise and therefore must be paid for twice, first as expertise and second for the lack of recognition.
- Corruption recognizes that delay is money, but too much delay is inflationary.
- Corruption does not demand that you be in power, merely that you know someone who is powerful.
- What a minister can do, his PA can do too. Probably better.
- For a corrupt society, the labyrinth is paradise.
- I didn't pay a bribe. I knew someone who knew someone.
- Corruption shows you that rules are constructed twice, once by the rule-giver, once by the man who applies the rules.
- Corruption is not about the rule of property; it is about rules as property.

Rather than seeing them as cynical statements, what one needs to do is to model them as a heuristics. Corruption must be mimicked and modelled as the basis of a new system. The boss, the tout, the pimp must be the triad around which the new system must be constructed.

Please don't think I am being cynical. Corruption is a site which has to be seen as an imagination, a conspiracy of verb and noun plotting sentences and paragraphs. In fact, I often think of Kekule's dream, of how the chemist is supposed to have dreamt the chemistry of the benzene ring as a snake swallowing its own tail. The chemistry of corruption is slightly different. It is an organism that uses reform as compost. Every reform recycles corruption in a renewed form. In fact, I was reminded of two small anecdotes in this context.

I was once on TV with a World Bank expert who was advocating summer schools for bureaucrats on corruption. I laughed at the corruptibility of the idea and the expert was displeased. He contended people like me should not be on TV and I agreed.

Contrast this with a Bulgarian social scientist I met in Berlin. He came to me and said, 'I loved your book'.* I asked him, 'How did you get it? It is an Indian edition and not easily available.' He said, 'I stole it from a library.' He added, 'Watching India, I understand Europe. Corruption is a form of entrepreneurship. We need to model it, build it into our institutions.'

Corruption answers a need, creates a conviviality we must understand. To fight it, we must simulate it, understand its heuristics of action. It is like recreating an ecology for a different purpose. We need the pragmatism of my Bulgarian friend.

Let me list out my sense of how to fight corruption. Understand the state first, understand that for people it is an

* Shiv Visvanathan and Harsh Sethi (eds), 1998. *Foul Play: Chronicles of Corruption, 1947–97*, Banyan Books, Delhi.

obstacle course and for officials, a labyrinth they must sustain. The state is the inverted commons, an availability of resources, skills that a society needs. As a rule game it is dense. The clerk and tout domesticate the insensitivity of the bureaucracy, make it user-friendly. What the clerk and tout also make sure is that the state remains a labyrinth. You can call it baroquization.

The social scientist, Mary Kaldor, talked of Baroque arsenals. She argued that every general replicates the last war and the tank was the great weapon of World War II. Today's generals want every weapon to look like a tank. So what was once a great weapon became unnecessarily complex, brittle, ornamental and expensive. More and more was spent to achieve less and less. What we are confronting is two things. One, corruption as a response to felt need and two, the baroquization of the state by the corrupt.

To simplify, we have to fix the circuits of the state. To do that effectively we have to reset the taxonomies of the state. The dualism of formal and informal is lethal with the former policing the latter and creating an extractive economy. Two things are clear in a subsistence economy. Corruption is the tax the oral pays to the literate economy of the file and the contract, and it is the price of subsistence the informal pays the officialdom of the formal. We need to break this classification. It is not life affirming.

Look at the sites of the economy. To the opposition of formal and informal, we have the world of the parallel economies of smuggling, aid, disasters, tourism, prohibition and terror. You can add defence to it for all practical purposes. The parallel economy and the informal economy are service economies. They cover a huge part of the map where corruption is a way of life. To alter a way of life, you have to affect conceptions of that life and its livelihood. The clerk, the cop, the tout, the pimp, the prostitute are all sustained by us. We feel they deliver a service, possess modes of knowledge that we do not have. Use the information revolution to challenge that fragment of the older knowledge society. Once you widen the hummock, simplify the rules of subsistence, you can challenge the construction of the state.

For most people the state is either what Shalini Randeria called a 'cunning state' pretending to give a guarantee of well-being, or a shamiana state which creates the trappings of governance around events like aid, disasters and doles. We need to pre-empt the corruption of states by restoring and returning work back to communities. Only communities can decentre a bureaucracy.

Begin by creating smaller corruptions, changing rule games in favour of the citizens. A computer giving all the dates in a court, a website announcing all exam results, a shop announcing all prices, development projects announcing dates of projects and a map of resources and benefits – all goes a long way. Corruption is the old information revolution that baroquized the state. Now one needs a new information revolution to redo the state, which then hands over problem solving to the community. The community, especially women, as problem solvers can go a long way in re-weaving corruption.

We talked of corruption as a subsistence-cum-migratory tactic. But there is also the corruption of corporations, defence departments and pharmaceutical companies. Treat that as criminal. It is a taxonomic problem again. A society has to know what to criminalize and decriminalize. Imagine an information department with the commitment of an NGO and the knowledge and enthusiasm of a tout. We can go far in reworking the state.

Once corruption is built in heuristically, treat the squatter, scavenger, the hawker as our prime citizens. Build cities around them after seeing how they build cities. It is a model of reciprocal problem solving which should be the basis of a new society.

There is nothing arcane to it. It is an older model of medicine.

Instead of the iatrogeny (expert-induced illness) of allopathy which creates more of corruption, let us reset the logic of classification to fight contexts. We need a new connectivity to fight old definitions. Ethics is also an imagination and for too long we have either outsourced or hypothecated our imagination to the World Bank or Transparency International. By reworking corruption we can be the first society to move from subsistence to true sustainability.

Seminar
October 2008

In the Name of Terror

Times of terror often become times of intolerance. A diversified society suddenly behaves in terms of homogeneous scripts. Security becomes the key word around which a temporary social contract is built. A society in its attempt to hold together forsakes the very thing that makes it secure, its sense of difference and its tolerance for disorder. Disorder offers a sense of debate, the possibility of negotiation; it eliminates a sense of a final doctrine and a final solution. Fear unravels the threads of diversity by reordering a society around order, uniformity and homogeneity. Fear and the sense of helplessness against terror allow it to tolerate forms of intrusion, modes of violence that it would not normally countenance. The greater good of the whole makes a society ready to sacrifice a part. National security allows one to sin and violate in a way a democracy would deem impermissible. Yet, oddly and ironically, national security has become one of the guiding tenets of our democracy.

The first casualty of terror is human rights. The second victim is everydayness, the third, diversity. But it is these things that make a society livable, create the forms of well-being we cherish. We face an apparent paradox. To protect the society and the social order we have created, we destroy the very things we value. What creates this rite of passage or this reversal from peace to a simpler form of order is security as a response to terror. It transforms a protean society celebrating diversity, fluidity and border crossing to a Procrustean one, with monolithic centres and monolingual definitions. Terror destroys the dialects of difference which make dialogue possible. Society speaks in a single voice and without a hearing aid. Between the megaphone and silence, there is no possibility for the worlds we call noise.

Security militarizes civil society into a set of disciplinary structures. It sees no major differences between controlling traffic and controlling thought. To put it differently, it wishes to see thought as mere traffic so that its channels can be easily blocked. In emphasizing order, stability, control, it revalidates authoritarianism in the name of democracy, a syllogism that the middle class in particular is susceptible to. Finally human rights become a luxury, a conspicuous consumption we can ill afford.

Rights are not merely a set of protective devices against harassments or a set of entitlements guaranteeing access to forms of competence. They make spaces for forms of life, forms of thought, forms of difference. Rights protect difference against threat. Security protects a monolithic order against the right to be different. But rights are only a guarantee of a framework of plural thoughts. Rights to survive against the pressures of security or terror need to be animated by dissent.

Dissent is a label that includes a variety of celebration of difference. Dissent includes the radical rebel, the eccentric, the deviant, the pluralist and the seeker of alternatives. Terror and security need all of them as an antidote to the very instability or false stability they create. Eccentricity is a question of style, a way of doing things differently. It focuses more on the odd or the quixotic. It is individual. Amplified to the level of collectivity, we confront ethnicity. Meanwhile, the rebel challenges authority, especially its authoritarianism or corruption. Whistle-blowing is one well known form of rebellion. Radicalism demands system transformation. NGOs can be rebellious while Naxalites can threaten a radical alteration of the social structure. Dissent involves a critique of society at every level of texture. It differs in thought and in action because a way of thinking is frequently accompanied by a change in lifestyle. It can move from suspicion and scepticism to an advocacy of more differences within the frame or an alternative frame. Unless security, rights, sustainability play themselves out within the tenor of life, they will remain un-nuanced. Security then will set the stage for that worst of tyrannies, the monoculture of the mind.

Indian Express
8 August 2008

Silly Ideas on Knowledge, Choice Are Destroying Us

C Wright Mills, an American sociologist, once described America in the 1950s as the 'great celebration'. While the United States was becoming a military-industrial complex, its middle class was celebrating its sense of power and opportunity, crass about its cost in terms of freedom. India is in a similar position today and the great celebration is enacted in the works of management experts like Nandan Nilekani, C.K. Prahlad. They are works of great intelligence, both thoughtful and positive. Yet somehow one feels that theirs is a restricted story confined to a sector of the middle class. They are acute about innovation but innocent about violence, evil and the problems of social justice. Their idea of India is a vision of a global secretariat. One does not have to be a card-carrying Leftist to provide an alternative imagination to the New Macaulayism where English and IT have become a sign of grace and success.

Watching India, listening to the shrill voice of electronic media, one senses that the country is being 'out thought' and 'out fought' in the battles of the twenty-first century. We are forced into idiot comparisons with China or we become suckers to our own brand-building game about this being the 'Indian century'. Academics wax eloquent about how India can be a hub for education as it is becoming for medical tourism when most of our universities don't even have a decent library. These celebratory sentiments cater to some deep unconscious need of Indians for recognition and certificates from the First World.

We are a society where the importance of information is destroying knowledge and livelihoods that go with it. Imagine a tribal listening to a TV story after his life of forced migration. He would argue that his life, livelihood and the knowledge systems that accompany it are declared as non-knowledge. Soon this society of non-knowledge will become a form of non-being either by being 'developed' or eliminated.

A tribal with cosmopolitan experience might even ask why innovation in scientific terms is a privileged form of knowledge. He might point out that the squatter, the hawker, the scavenger all live by using 'make dos'. Yet this form of survival is dismissed as mere coping. The knowledge systems most of India lives by are not even treated as forms of knowing.

Secondly, the tribal, the nomad, might also present a case arguing that the evolution of Indian society has to be plural, that the oral, the digital and the literate worlds have to exist together. This is the only framework for democracy and knowledge in the twenty-first century.

The argument is not just that our systems of knowledge destroy the context around them. What one is arguing is that the elite operate with forms of restricted knowledge. Our ideas of management and science embody little of the new and exciting ideas of complexity, diversity and uncertainty. We pretend that science is still a Newtonian domain, thus leaving us deaf to the idea of 'risk'. Risk is a framework defining the uncertainty and unpredictability, depriving governance of the certainties it once provided. The very existence of the precautionary principle in law was an effort to affix responsibility in this age when knowledge remains uncertain and science remains unpredictable.

Subsistence societies had their own modes of prudence, their rituals of sustainability. But industrial India needs a new ecology of responsibility. It is in probing this that we realize that the key terms we operate with – security, predictability, federalism, innovation, sovereignty – condemn us to an outdated world. What is true of generals is also true of our policymakers. We are either fighting the last war or an older crisis. We can't handle climate change with the vocabulary of the relief code.

The only dissenting academics of knowledge were our NGOs and the movements which challenged both science and government to explore alternatives. But sadly, we are more concerned with knowledge systems for choice than for alternatives. Choice is located in terms of individual preferences whereas alternatives deal with the plural ecologies of culture and livelihoods. The latter emphasize the community. We read diversity through the logic of individual consumption, not through the logic of alternatives which speaks through the prism of culture. For example, biotechnology cannot be understood in terms of market preferences of farmers but in terms of the future of agricultural diversity.

With the emergence of print, our notion of memory, which involved retelling and reinvention, has become rote, marked by cliché. What was dubbed illiterate, was actually a different form of sensibility which emphasized memory as invention and storytelling as record and which was open to all the different senses. A society which has an inventive idea of memory builds its own safeguards against obsolescence and erasure. As India turns officially to census and history, forms of knowledge which occur in print are valued over orality. Ironically, we store information by erasing knowledge. Many forms of our knowledge are too tacit to be coded in discs.

We are a society that is so caught in the immediate and the

practical that we have lost our sense of the future. The future is a site for imaginaries, for possibilities other than the present. But our elite is too enamoured with the present. Between our official sense of history and our narrowness of market time, we are losing the sense of long-run strategy. We plan roads for five years, our syllabi are outdated by the time they are accepted – we can't think through the long run.

Consider our Constitution. It claims its Directive Principles are futuristic when they are virtually Victorian. We have no scenarios or heuristics for the future. Our notion of science fiction is limited to the image of America as the future. Ours is an information society destroying a community of knowledges.

In an oddly tragic way, our elite is museumizing our society in the name of innovation, rendering ways of life obsolescent in the name of history. Ours is a society where, to modify what John Maynard Keynes the economist once said, it is in the short run that a lot of us may be dead, or obsolescent, thanks to our idiot ideas about knowledge and innovation.

Deccan Chronicle
29 July 2009

Saints of the Paranoid

Language is such a beautiful system in its logic, its variability, its sense of order and its ability to surprise. What is logical and what is pathological is sometimes so difficult to pin down. One is reminded of a story about the great Irish writer James Joyce, whose *Ulysses* was a work of genius for its sense of the English language. Joyce once visited the psychologist Carl Jung. He had taken his son along. Joyce spoke, talking rapturously of his son's adventures with words claiming that he was also a genius with language. Jung listened quietly to the young man and turned to Joyce and said, 'You might be a genius but your son is a schizophrenic.' Something of the double sidedness of this story follows the debates of language. One part is haunted by diversity, while on the other stands the tyranny of uniformity and standardization.

Linguistic chauvinism is a craving for homogeneity as a form of exclusion. It is an ultimatum that only those who speak a language can belong to a community. It becomes, at one blow, a mark of identity, uniformity and exclusion. It refuses diversity, translation and pidginization. In fact, it attempts to freeze language in amber.

Linguistic chauvinism is the tyranny of language which

destroys its own plurality. It appears in times of economic crisis or political hostility. It becomes a way of creating an artificial community which can claim to be pure. Linguistic chauvinism is the sibling of electoral democracy, where the dominant or majoritarian group uses language as a strategy of exclusion. The likes of Raj Thackeray argue that they represent social interests. But more than their violence, it is the illiteracy of their bullyboy sociology that is pathetic.

Prabodh Pandit then a professor of linguistics at the University of Delhi observed in a lecture, 'Consider the language routines of a Gujarati businessman, a spice merchant, 50 years ago, settled in Bombay, how many languages would he use in the course of a day and in what contexts? Our Gujarati businessman, who was more likely to have hailed from Saurashtra coast, spoke his variety of Gujarati at home. He probably lived in Ghatkopar, a suburb of North Bombay; when he went out in the morning to buy vegetables, since the vegetable vendors spoke in colloquial Marathi (spoken in the coastal district of Colaba), he spoke colloquial Marathi with them; he caught the 9:35 suburban train to the city. To buy his ticket or transact any business with the officers of the railway, who were more likely to be Anglo-Indians rather than speakers of Gujarati or Marathi, he spoke in colloquial Hindustani. As a spice merchant his sphere of activity was in the spice market around Masjid Bunder; because the merchants in the spice trade were mainly speakers of Gujarati, Kutchi and Konkani, our merchant spent his business hours speaking and listening to these three languages. If he was educated in English, say up to matriculation, he might occasionally read an English newspaper; he might also see a Hindustani film with his family. The number of languages he used in a day's routine was about six; but note that he used them in limited and specific contexts only.'

Pandit's argument needs attention because he shows that the unilingual man is rare. In fact, in India, he is an oxymoron.

Pandit observes that such languages, to use the idiom of the Pepsi advertisement, have nothing official about them. They are not acquired through any formal channel of education, nor are they a burden on the speaker. In fact, the speaker rather than being an outsider adds to the richness and diversity of the local language, providing playful variations that celebrate the openness of a city like Mumbai. Such a variety of mixes and of hybridities is often portrayed in Bollywood movies providing both occasions for humour and celebrations of hospitality.

In terms of the logic of language, Raj Thackeray understands neither the diversity of language nor the dynamism of the city. In fact, his claims to understand culture are a caricature. The question one has to then ask: if the Shiv Sena and its extensions are linguistically illiterate, what is their source of power and popularity?

Linguistic chauvinism is an ode to economics, politics and the anxieties it creates. It is a symptom of the fear of the outsider. In this case the outsider is the migrant. Here one must emphasize that a lot of migration is internal. But what becomes the focus is either the south Indian as the Tamilian or the UP migrant as taxi and auto driver or as a part of the informal economy. The outsider becomes the scapegoat because he is seen as depriving the native of jobs. Ironically the cultural vibrancy which adds to the economic dynamism is seen as the source of deprivation. Language becomes the means to eliminate the outsider. In electoral politics, populism always caters to public fears and anxieties. Fear gets overblown by the politician to provide impetus for vote banks. Parties like the Shiv Sena become saints of the paranoid. The sadness is that electoral democracies thrive on populism, and populism in turn survives on the language of the paranoid. It is easy to beat up a few taxi drivers as a panacea to this imaginary economy. The sadness is that the people of Mumbai fail to realize that Raj Thackeray and family threaten Mumbai in the long run.

One must realize that when the word 'culture' is mentioned, the new Goebbels of propaganda reach for the scapegoat and then the gun. Without scapegoats as fodder, chauvinism cannot survive. Without the alleged outsider, Raj Thackeray would have no raj to rule.

In an ironic way, linguistic chauvinism focuses on superficials like city names, oaths for office. But there is a deeper politics of dialects and marginal languages it hides. Officially dominant languages destroy dialects. The languages of the marginalized and nomads are not protected. The three-language formula is too strait-laced to sustain a dialect.

There is a failure of the official here. Raj Thackeray has not been confronted by the Knowledge Commission or the commission on the unorganized sector. My argument is that he goes beyond the violation of rights. His political mind is a truncated one. Like most bullies who survive on fear and create fear, his is a failure of the imagination, revealing the limits of a cultural understanding that the future will find hard to forgive. But by that time, language would have created a new Hobson-Jobson of words around him, a thesaurus of new metaphors for those who bind language and scar democracy. In fact, the name Raj could become ironic. It would refer to a new model of linguistic colonialism. His linguistic chauvinism is illiteracy about language combined with an illegitimacy of politics, a populism that uses electoral politics to create the taproots of tyranny.

New Indian Express
20 November 2009

The Ambassador and Maruti 800

An Affair to Remember

My childhood centred on the Morris Minor, the Baby Hindustan and the Ambassador cars. There was something dumpy about all three. I remember especially the Ambassador which conveyed the spirit of the 1960s. It smelt of the joint family, the public sector and the proliferating Congressman. Each conveyed an enormous respectability. The Ambassador was a wonderful beast of burden. It was a stand-in for a bus carrying at least fourteen children stuffed like harassed toys to school. The local repair shops swore by it as it legitimized their native skill. But for all its proliferation, the Ambassador was a piece of nostalgia and has acquired an honoured place at the Smithsonian museum.

The Ambassador was a period piece. It belonged to the 1960s and reflected a Nehruvian confidence and optimism. The Emergency changed the symbolic locus of the car. Through its black visions of demolition, the Emergency suggested that the Ambassador, like parliamentary politics, was slow and inefficient. It failed to convey a sense of speed. The main perpetrator of the Emergency dreamt of a car that fitted his new political vision.

Trained for a while in British workshops, Sanjay Gandhi dreamt of a new car. But his skills were expressed in the car which ran forty miles before the door fell off. The original Maruti was a pathetic specimen reflecting the engineering illiteracy of its inventor. Even after the Emergency was lifted and democracy returned, the idea of the new car remained alive. The Neanderthal inventions of Sanjay were quickly forgotten. But the idea of a car consonant with post-Emergency imagination was an idea whose time had come. Created with Japanese help, embodying new ideas of a workforce, Maruti 800 took pride of place on Indian roads. It was an icon of fashion, a small family car. The company thought of it as a modest invention, a hybrid not quite American, not quite Japanese. Maruti Udyog Ltd was heralded in the post-Emergency era as the ideal firm and it became an absolute hit. It was as if modernity had come of age in India. Not quite erotic, not quite functional, the Maruti car reflected new norms of efficiency, something petit, a family car that did not look perpetually portly like the Ambassador. The Ambassador was dethroned.

The Maruti 800 evoked an entirely different semiotics. It was an aspirational car, a family vehicle that conveyed a sense of youth and individualism. It evoked mobility. It signified even speed. Bollywood movies could no longer employ an Ambassador. A horse could race an Ambassador, but not outrace a Maruti even in its imagination. Maruti Jeeps became symbols of police speed and efficiency. It was as if the law itself had speeded up.

The one public domain that the Maruti could not touch was the taxi. The Fiat and the Ambassador looked more capacious and affable. They indicated a familiarity with Indian luggage. Taxi drivers had deep loyalties to the Ambassador. They felt that while the Maruti saved petrol, it was not quite a taxi. They suggested that it lacked a sense of feudal qualities found in the Ambassador.

But beyond such caveats, the Maruti was king. The Maruti was a woman-friendly car both in design and manoeuvrability. It allowed for change inside. It started the wave for seeking car accessories. The Fiat was too family-like, the Ambassador too official. The Maruti allowed the individualization of each family member. Women, students, young executives, all felt it bore their personal signature. The Maruti 800 allowed for individual identity while still remaining anchored in the family.

Its semiotic message was different. The Ambassador was affably functional. The Maruti was elegant for its time, signalled efficiency and competence. It evoked professionalism, conveying a sense of design, aesthetics, engineering innovation, properties that the earlier cars could not match. Its size conveyed a message of compactness, intimacy, control; it celebrated a 'juniority' of a particular kind. It was a car for teenagers, children and young girls turning professional. In that sense it evoked many stages in a life cycle.

If the Ambassador dressed in uniforms, the Maruti suggested a bazaar of colours. Colour was so rare in socialist modernity that the Maruti 800 looked profligate, even promiscuous. It added colour to a public imagination that had gone grim on ration cards, shortages and a socialist uniformity. The Maruti by its playfulness prepared a middle class for consumerism, the magic of choice, a sense of change but all with a sense of intimacy, familiarity and colour.

The historian Aditi Sarkar claimed Kolkata did not welcome the Maruti with the same warmth as Delhi or Mumbai. The Maruti still evoked Emergency and the tyranny of the Gandhis. It acquired a local nickname. It was called a *chharpoka*, a bed bug. The Maruti could dart across streets with startling efficiency at an unexpected speed. But one must confess that the Bengali nickname was not quite as endearing as the Beetle. Bengal could have used a better term of endearment.

As liberalization invaded India, and foreign cars proliferated, the Maruti started appearing outdated. It held its place in the market but without the earlier lustre. A new generation of technology and design was upsetting loyalties. Aspirations shifted to superior machines but the Maruti 800 still commanded fierce loyalties. Friends said that it marked a rite of passage from the scooter to the affordability of a car. Where could you get a machine where a woman could change tyres and shatter the image of dependency?

Fun was a crucial word. When India emerged from the grimness of Emergency, one needed a fun car which provided more than fun. The Maruti occupied that niche superbly for decades. It was an aspirational car without VIP hang-ups.

The Maruti did not grow old. It did not convey the middle-agedness of the Ambassadorial bulk. It exuded youthfulness but India now needed a different sense of renewal. New words like sustainability and carbon credit were entering our vocabulary and one sensed a need for a new vision of the city of the future. The car which once heralded the future no longer seemed cost-effective given the new demands for emission control. The decision was not to retire it, but phase it out, signalling that the Maruti itself was a flow of time. It was time to move on with pride and dignity, holding on to a sense of intimacy and loyalty. The harbinger of the new had to yield to a new newness. But it knew it had held its own. A farewell to the Maruti 800 could never be an obituary. It could only be an ode, a salute to a piece of technology which is now a friend, a memory, an epic, a legend and a car to remember and race again through the streets of memory.

New Indian Express
5 April 2010

Caste Is Information in Knowledge Society

Mary, Mary, quite contrary,
Tell me how does governance grow?
With Casteist Bells in World Bank Shells,
And pretty Khaps all in a row.

This is not a Brahmanic essay defending the superiority or necessity of caste. This is a contrarian essay, which argues that without a sense of contraries we cannot or will not understand the power of caste and its survival. Contrariness is necessary especially when hypocrisy is official and the government piously refuses to include caste in the census. This is as cowardly and as illiterate as its refusal to carry out a linguistic survey of India. Caste and language, along with religion, constitute the glue of our society. Condemning caste drives it underground or creates distortions that are more difficult to erase.

In an age when individuality is something we are not used to and at a time when modern and secular forces are seeing caste as backward, we have to understand the power of caste. Caste is a code of behaviour. It enforces a range of behaviours including rules of marriage as in a Khap panchayat. Caste is an index of solidarity when it creates the grammar of interaction for people who are migrating to the city. To a new migrant, caste is the grid of familiarity and of survival. The division of labour present in caste, particularly craft communities, creates the diversity that India is famous for. It took first-rate biologists like J.B.S. Haldane and Madhav Gadgil to realize the ability of caste to create diversity.

In a political sense, caste is no longer a horizontal group. It represents the vertical solidarity of caste agglomerations, which use caste to create the grammar of electoral democracy. Acronyms like AJGAR (Ahir, Jat, Gujjar and Rajput) or KHAM (Kshatriya, Harijan, Adivasi and Muslim) are caste solidarities that are part of the logic of electoralism. As a sociologist, one realizes caste can be a Procrustean entity imposing constraints on the individual citizen. But the same Janus-faced entity as a collective self produces identity, solidarity and mobility. In disasters, as in Gujarat in 2002, caste communities could come to the rescue arranging for relief that no NGO can match.

It is the protean nature of caste, its adaptability and inventiveness that we have to grasp. There is something cognitive about caste that we must analyze. Anthropologically, caste is intriguing. Read a colonial gazetteer, a caste census after J.H. Hutton (census commissioner during the 1931 census), a Kayasth directory, or even Levi-Strauss's essay on the role of caste, and one will have to realize that the *Homo Equalis* has competition. No social scientist can deny the intellectual fascination of these documents. Equality has to contend with the power of hierarchy in a modernizing world. Caste enforces ambivalence on democracy. It demands to be heard. Its message is simple. It argues that the modern and the secular are not inventive enough. They have to learn to mimic the inventiveness of caste. It creates solidarities and adaptabilities that we need to understand. Face it, everyone from the Yadavs to Mayawati speak caste. Even their occasional objections are that other groups use caste as they please.

To fight caste, one needs an anthropological understanding of it. Governance has to have a sense of its logic, an understanding of its dynamism. One cannot fight it by refusing to allow caste as a category in a census. While looking it in the eye, one can create timelines of change, be pragmatic about reforms and trim the privileges of the creamy layer. One has to move caste from its locus in a moral economy to its location in a political economy.

Caste is information, and to hide information in a knowledge society is silly. Open it up because by being analytical, we realize that caste is a part of our collective unconscious. By being open to the caste identity in us, we might understand the perverse logic of change. When the way you cook, your mode of travel, your sense of security and your idea of marriage depends on caste, you need information on each and every intricacy and nuance of this proliferative institution. Calling it names will not help. The rhetoric of modernity has to be culturally sensitive. Only then can we slowly understand the humus of caste and create a different kind of soil.

Let us face it, the great reform movements of India were not the modernist, communist, socialist or liberal democratic ones. The great reform movement was the bhakti tradition. Nanak, Kabir, Mirabai did more to dent caste than *The Communist Manifesto*. Once one realizes the wisdom and potential of this fact, the ironies of caste become more obvious. Then contraries can move to other domains and to other stories. Till then the die is never cast in the way modernists hysterically wish it to be. Rhetoric is bad sociology, poor ethics and lousy governance. This much caste can teach you.

The Times of India
16 May 2010

Indian God-men and the Sacred Complex

Our sacred complex in India demands a scrutiny much like the military industrial complex in the USA. The sacred complex constitutes the fourth estate far more powerful than the media or the NGOs.

Our sacred complex has two parts. The first is Hinduism as a way of life, a religion without a church, or a central text, syncretic in its orientation and invertebrate in its organization. The second is the collection of god-men who are singular as individuals and impressive in their diversity.

The god-men are masters in organization theory. Their religious organization is Semitic. As organizational geniuses, they combine the charisma of the leader, the traditional modes of community around the *darshan* and the *satsang* and the discourse with the best of management theory. The best-run organizations in India like the Sai ashram or the Swaminarayan sect can make the Tatas and Infosys sound like management amateurs. Their idea of corporate spiritual responsibility makes corporate social responsibility seem superficial. For example, Sai Baba has to only wish for water and the ashram makes sure that four hundred villages in Andhra obtain access to drinking water. The leader's wish becomes the community's command. Oddly, no IIM has a reliable case study of the god-men as an organizational phenomenon.

Three things mark the god-man phenomenon. It is anchored in a middle-class search for meaning and faith as the class turns competitive and mobile. The god-man provides both the collective message and individual advice in anxious times. His spiritual therapy, as Art of Living, or any other message, combines religion, psychoanalysis and good career tactics – in effective packages. Each god-man has a tremendous diasporic following turning each leader into a global player. Thirdly, the Indian god-man sees little contradiction between science and religion and is usually tech-savvy. Ashrams usually have the best information technologies, the latest innovations and the best marketing techniques.

As fourth estate, each god-man controls a community, a constituency, a spiritual electorate which can be converted to secular purposes. But the politics is more subtle. Our elite is affiliated to a variety of god-men. Our politicians and bureaucrats, our corporate dons go to them for advice. As those involved in risk, they seek reassurance. They are also shrewd enough to realize that god-men shape orientations to politics. Closeness to a god-man creates legitimation and adds to the power of the politician. A politician without a god-man is a losing proposition. As a result, each god-man is an influence peddler in a spiritual guise. As corporate complexes, they wield enormous power. As one Swamiji confessed, political parties come and go, our power is permanent. This matter-of-factness hides one part of political decision making we have not scrutinized. Consider just two simple events. When the Supreme Court silenced the anti-Narmada critics and as the waters flowed down Sabarmati, Narendra Modi was accompanied by Pramukh Swamiji. The Anna Hazare movement received tremendous support from

Ramdev and the Art of Living movement. The god-men today collect political followers like confetti. Their advice, their role as middlemen needs scrutiny in any electoral system. They influence politics without being politically accountable. One is not suggesting conspiracy, only just asking for information.

Think of a simple project. Just as you have an annual review of B-schools, why not have an annual review of god-men in terms of followers, especially VIPs, good works, branded products, land owned, money acquired, nature of message? Here is a sociological world whose political power we have not grasped. What is native, what is spiritual or authoritarian or fundamentalist has to be unravelled. The spiritual one understands and respects but when spirituality creates a corporate style, a political constituency, one needs to understand it further. Politicians realize this. It is time social science follows their intuitive sense of power and legitimacy.

IBN Live
2 May 2011

Dreams of Childhood

Every time I pass by a school, I shudder. I feel schools are institutions meant to destroy childhood. I remember my years as a child in a small town called Jamshedpur. It was a snooty, well-heeled company town but it allowed for innocence and dream time. I remember only little things. One of them is walking home in the rain collecting red rain bugs, stroking their velvet coats. When you touched them, the insects withdrew their feet like red mimosas.

Childhood was dream time and it allowed for hours of boredom where you did nothing and yet something creative happened to you.

The teacher was law and you felt your first sense of tyranny and injustice as one wrote 'I will not talk in class' 500 times. It is strange how all those years of penal writing did not improve quality of penmanship. I was lousy at sport and average in studies. All I did was climb trees, eat guavas and search for raw mangoes. All one needed was a dog, a younger sister and a story book and life felt gloriously open and happily complete.

One was a glutton about books and a friend of Dell Comics. Bugs Bunny and Mickey Mouse were characters, like Hamlet and Macbeth. The beauty was one could discuss them in the same breath. Summers meant mangoes and salt with a gorgeous touch of chilli powder and winter summoned guavas, deeply and lusciously pink inside.

The only art form I mastered was street cricket played with a tennis ball. I keep wondering where all the geniuses of the game disappeared – many of my heroes were the riff-raff of the class, the poets of anarchy.

I sense the sadness of growing up. I remember I met one of them years later. He was working in a bank, hiding in the shadows, hoping I would not see him.

There is a poignancy and emptiness in meeting a school friend years later with nothing to say. Memories look like castaways from a different world. So little of childhood survives into the future.

The Indian reality begins too early and competition destroys the sense of play. Exams and failure in exams becomes the first catastrophe. If agriculture in India was a gamble with the rains and monsoons, education is a wager on exams.

I think childhood is a sensorium, a gift of smells, sounds, memories, touch, fables and all this gets lost in the search for information. I think information destroys knowledge. You lose the sense of craft and the freedom and curiosity to be foolish. An exam becomes an act of tyranny and years are lost in simulated preparation, in coaching schools which corrupt knowledge. There was no celebration of a text. Education never allowed for play or fantasy. That was exiled to the world of films. Think of a place like Kota, a town created to train one for exams and you realize what a tragedy our IITs are as heartbreak houses. I still hear scholars confess sadly that they missed IIT by three marks.

I sometimes see brilliant students and engineers who claim that they have not read a storybook in years. There was one guy who said he could not even bring himself to read newspapers. It all seemed purposeless in a world where you xerox ideas and download information. I realize many of them download pornography as matter of information. What gets lost is the world of the body, the sense of the erotic which is so much a part of knowledge, the high of learning.

I sometimes wonder whether India would benefit by declaring a ban on IITs and the like and allow students to enjoy education in the same way we enjoyed plays, good food, music and friendship. I think our addas and our tea shops teach us more about culture than our formal schools.

I am a teacher and I think what made me a teacher was the joy of childhood, the need to share the way I learnt. I sense this missing now. When I hear about Knowledge Commissions and education reports, I wonder what new idiocy they are piling on us.

I think our rituals of transition from childhood to adulthood are not evocative enough. Boys do not really grow up. The exams cannot be the rite of passage to a man's world. Our men are adolescents at forty with many of the teenage repressions. There is a claim to masculinity but little sense of manhood. Our education with its linear ode to professionalism destroys diversity. Firstly, many among the young are forced into careers they do not want. Secondly, the straitjacket model of careers destroys the imagination. The burnout rate is high and little attention is paid to the reasons for it. Few recognize the agony of a life of regret at thirty. Oddly, by the forties, men look like clones of each other and, more and more, it is the women who are interesting, with their idea of autonomy, their feeling about companionship.

I know I might sound irrelevant. However, I must stick my neck out and say that the destruction of childhood, of the worlds of boredom and dream time, are serious charges against any society.

We talk of our demographic dividend, our youthful society as if it is a plus point in a Darwinian world, where knowledge replaces tooth and claw as the new fangs of a society. This idea is philistine. We need to ask what we have done to our youth and ask them to dream beyond consumerism and competition. India needs to explore this rather than worry about competitive advantage in an increasingly arid world.

Deccan Chronicle
10 January 2013

Maggi Adulterated My Memory, Not Food

Memory and sentiment often go together. Memory is a sensorium, a vista of smells and sounds, a nostalgia for the touch, taste or texture of an object or event. Memory can be sublime as one remembers a place of pilgrimage or a piece of music or it can carry the fables of everydayness, the joys of childhood.

Today when I hear that Maggi noodle packets are banned from stores, I feel a sense of sadness. Maggi was not just a food, it was a way of life, a celebration, a marker of some of the best moments of childhood and college life. Maggi noodles could have been a chapter in many an autobiography.

I remember at school there was nothing like Maggi. The closest to instant food was the samosa, or a bouquet of pakodas which one wolfed down with chutney. Our chutneys not only added spice to food but to our expectation of life. Samosa and chai were the ideal snacks and no school, no street corner was complete without it. In our socialist world with its ascetic dribbles of pocket money, chai and samosa spelt luxury.

The advent of Maggi was thus a triple conquest. A conquest

that came in several stages. The first Trojan Horse, the warning sign was the ubiquitous bread pakoda. It was an industrial product, sliced bread filled with potato and chutney yielding reluctantly to sauce. Sauce, tomato sauce, deprived chutney of its mystique. Sauce like comic books never got full parental approval, so sauce, tomato sauce, smelt of freedom. Instead of the spiciness of chutneys, we preferred the freedom in sauce.

The Walls of Jericho crumbled further when chow mein entered our universities. Chow mein was a world of its own served by Tibetan refugees and Nepali assistants. It was seductively cheap, a compost heap of spices and smells. It was a distant cousin to the Chinese food served in sophisticated restaurants. This chow mein was proletarian, cheap, piled in huge quantities, so students who were broke could share it. This chow mein was desi, Indian, as local as anything, the perfect challenge to idli-vada or the bread pakoda. It verged on the unhealthy but filled happy stomachs.

Maggi noodles followed chow mein. It was more antiseptic, more industrial. After instant coffee, it was my first introduction to instant food. In fact, for me globalization began with Maggi noodles. It represented instantaneity more visibly than finance capital or the Internet. Maggi noodles graduated from materiality to mentality. Someone called it the Mother Teresa of foods. One mother explained, 'My son survived IIT Madras and the US, thanks to Maggi noodles.' In those days she even carried packets from India for her son.

Maggi entered and transformed our lives in myriad ways. It was the first advertisement beyond Surf and Hamam that we internalized. Cooking Maggi was sacramental because it was so ridiculously simple. Mothers' cookbooks were unnecessary. It was the illiterate cook's discovery of skill.

Maggi was sheer solace. If you worked hard and returned from work late at night, food was ready before one could spell ajinomoto. Maggi in those moments was a salve, soothing hunger and tiredness, in a way no other food could. With its flavours also came a sense of choice and Maggi and tomato sauce were the food of the year, an indestructible pair no cook could rend asunder. One realized it lacked vitamins, the healthy nutrition, but one did not care. Maggi was a Linus blanket. No student, no hiker could go hungry as long as Maggi was there.

Maggi was never seen as a multinational product. There was something desi about it. Maggi sounded like a desi name. Maggi referred to all noodles. The way the name Tommy referred to all dogs. Brand and genre merged to create household folklore. More than Boost, Bournvita or Horlicks, Maggi became a self-sustaining world for the young. It was so unpretentious that anyone could adopt it, so humble that all could eat it, and yet, so modern that it felt absolutely contemporary. Eating Maggi was like going to Sunday school or attending church. It evoked a community of sharing.

I somehow dropped the Maggi habit after college. One almost felt pious about it. I even pretended to look disapprovingly at Maggi consumers, not that it made a difference. Fortress Maggi was impregnable.

Thinking back, Maggi was one of the first non-socialist products. It was not public sector. It was not individualistic. One shared it. It suggested cottage industry though it behaved as a multinational. Maggi was the lingua franca of a new generation. Maggi went with TV serials, school food and late-night breaks from tedious homework. It even came to be an answer to boredom nibbling at your entrails. Maggi noodles became the open sesame to the modern world like Amul butter. It was no longer a brand. It had acquired mythic proportions. One felt Maggi was here to stay.

In fact when the controversy happened, I did not think it would go so far, or be treated so seriously. Adulteration marks many an Indian product. Our fruits have chemicals, our vegetable hormones and our milk water. I thought Maggi would recover.

I think controlling Maggi gave the government – especially when it cannot control pollution, corruption or radiation – a sense of vindication. Our new regulatory economy needed a minor victory and suddenly Maggi acquired an instant demonology. The media turned pious, our consumer groups became vigilante, but my nostalgia makes me sad. I miss Maggi though I know I won't eat it again. What Maggi adulterated was not food but memory. It contaminated nostalgia and disfigured the immaculate myth of instant cooking. It was a fall from Eden where a new generation was thrust into the world of health food. But I guess I am a sucker for ads.

As I watch Madhuri Dixit advertise Maggi oats noodles, I realize an era has ended. Both Madhuri and Maggi will disappear together. I have to mourn and say goodbye. They marked a life and a lifetime. One will miss them. I think I will buy myself a new cookbook, a classy one or return to my dosa and idli.

Deccan Chronicle
11 June 2015

Part 2

An Invitation to Politics

The Yogi and the Commissar's Wife

The Ramdev controversy is one of the most delightful encounters in the politics of culture. It demands a set of playful reflections not just in terms of events and facts but also in the categories in which the latter were constructed.

The main characters are important, but the chorus of responses is equally important. The two together show that predictable dualisms can produce unpredictable dialectics in Indian culture.

Consider the cast of the play. Brinda Karat presents a symbolically arrogant Marxism. There is nothing in her record to show that folklore can have its own idea of false consciousness. She accuses Ramdev's pharmacy of making preparations with human bones.

Enter Ramdev. Most Marxists would see in the hirsute yogi, a character out of Tsarist Russia. More Rumplestiltskin than Rasputin he throws a tantrum at Karat's critique about the purity of his medicines. He is convinced that a challenge to the purity of his medicines is a challenge to the purity of his intentions.

At first sight, this promises to be a stereotypical confrontation. A westernized, feminist, Marxist, party activist confronting a

Hindu guru practising Ayurveda and popularizing yoga through the television channel Astha. Both are telegenic personalities.

Yet the drama goes beyond the standard dualisms of modern and non-modern, scientific and unscientific. Despite the chorus of demonologies by Mahendra Singh Tikait, CPI(M) and Shiv Sena, the drama is an endearing one because it has no real villains or heroes.

Effigies are burnt but even protestors realize that rather than burning Karat's effigy, they should greet it with laughter.

It should be clear that this is not a standard science versus anti-science script. Ramdev is a man who wants to see yoga and Ayurveda as world systems.

He sees Ayurveda as scientific and wants to create an archive with all the paraphernalia of modern science: testimony, proof, standards and institutes of research. For him, only science can put the status of Ayurveda beyond doubt. Yet he is clear that Ayurveda is not a reductionist science but rooted like all holisms in a cosmology, a religion, a civilization.

Ironically, Ayurveda's battle for scientific recognition reminds one of another defeated science, Marxism. Marxism today is seen as a dead science and a defeated ideology, yet Karat shows no consciousness of this.

Poignantly, Karat and Ramdev emerge as siblings in this quest, each contending to save a fragment of knowledge.

Of course Karat carries all the trappings of modernity, feminism, secularism, Marxism. Yet she appears less reflective about knowledge than Ramdev, the folk hero. It is at the cognitive level that Karat's performance falls short. But there is more to it.

The language and politics of Ramdev's discourse, Mandalist in tenor, does not concern itself with English. Ramdev's politics is a dialect spoken by Lalu and Mulayam that seeks to challenge and absorb the world on its own terms. They are not too bothered if science appears as a formula or a proverb as long as it is available. In fact, it is interesting that all the regional socialist parties support him.

The two great modernizing parties, CPI(M) and Congress, are stuck with Karat while Ramdev gets away happily talking about 'hurry, worry and curry' being the ruin of India. Yet Ramdev without Karat does not seem complete.

The dramatic movement is not one of Karat's isolation but of the possibility of further encounters. Karat adds to Ramdev a notion of feminism and trade union rights which Ramdev's world may not be sensitive to.

In a sense, both realize that they are not complete without each other. She, in fact, presents herself as a native of Kerala where Ayurvedic norms are more stringent. Now it is like two dialects talking to each other.

Ramdev offers to teach her pranayama. Both know they have to fight the language of the market as a mentality and the coercive power of the multinational companies.

There is high semiotics to the drama. Karat is a poster girl for the CPI(M), more flamboyant and human than the dour ideologists on display.

Ramdev, rustic, populist, tele-savvy, is a truly glocal character. He shows a different confidence, a mix of attitudes that official Nehruvians may not approve. Ramdev's story has shades of Bollywood, so improbable that even the urbane Karat has a role in it.

Yet there are worrying elements in this politics of street theatre. Our cosmologies, our ethnic selves still necessitate testimonials, kangaroo courts, touch-me-not protests.

The Ramdev episode shows that this part of the public sphere needs looking at. Karat by pointing to the nature of debates here makes an important contribution to democracy.

Only in India can Ayurveda and Marxism combine to add

to the democratic imagination. Years ago, Bertolt Brecht wrote *Life of Galileo,* a remarkable play about the so-called conflict of science and religion. *Life of Ramdev* may one day be a more polymorphous play written by a future Brechtian mind.

The Times of India
11 January 2006

Hijacking the Sardar

I love Indian politics not merely for its lessons on democracy but for the fact that the same story can be read Rashomon-like at different levels. I want to read the Jaswant Singh episode within such a perspective.

Sometime ago, L.K. Advani described Jinnah as a decent man, a true leader, a nationalist. The silencing was swift and Advani's return to political correctness complete. His reaction was explained away as Sindhi nostalgia. The impact of his guru or the emotionalism of a Bollywood movie lover was added as extenuating circumstance.

A plethora of ifs and buts connect the narratives of Partition in different ways. But history soon goes into deep freeze, rigid like an Old Testament diktat. History also sustains the rationale for political parties and the iconography of politicians creating aspirations for future behaviour. More importantly when ideology is weak, it is these idols that provide the focus for politics.

As a party the Congress got into the icon trade rather early. In fact, for a long time it controlled the trade, possessing a huge pantheon of leaders including Nehru, Gandhi, Patel, Ghaffar Khan, Rajaji, Rajendra Prasad. These icons created a virtual surplus of symbolic capital that the Congress thrived on. They worked overtime for the Congress as an official civics, a moral code paraded from police stations to barber shops. The only two unexpected characters in the picture were Subhash Bose and Bhagat Singh. They represented two kinds of machismo which could be evoked to accuse the Congress of a touch of weakness. Early opposition to the Congress did use these figures to create a microclimate of decisiveness and urgency. But while Bose and Bhagat Singh worked at the level of popular culture, they were tokens that were not convertible into hard political currency.

The Congress was also reworking its act, aware that too many leaders gave one a feeling of confusion. An official party needed the clarity of an official icon. It soon settled for Nehru. Nehru was apt as our first prime minister, patriarch of a dynasty that has ruled India with almost absent-minded confidence. In fact, Nehru is back in mint condition especially after many intellectuals expressed an affinity and nostalgia for his era. He expresses the modernity narratives which propelled India to its current euphoria.

For a party driven by history, the BJP always felt short-changed by it. Its leaders from Deendayal Upadhayaya and Golwalkar to Veer Savarkar appeared provincial or dated. Semiotically, the BJP realized it had to poach on the Congress pantheon, wean away part of its past into its own closet of memories. Gandhi was appealing but not modernist enough. Nehru could be hijacked as a style that fitted Vajpayee. The rest of the collection – the Rajajis, the Prasads, the Ghaffar Khans, the Hussains, the Azads – felt like forgotten commemorative stamps, lacking any emotional trigger.

Only one man had the symbolic chutzpah, the smell of history, the correctness of iconicity – Sardar Patel. Taste the name. The prefix Bismarck of India, makes one stand to attention. The textbooks say he prevented the disintegration of India in the aftermath of Partition. He was decisive without being sentimental, ascetic without being sensuous.

Clear-cut and precise. The Sardar. The original. An original who resonates with the public. Therefore an icon. An icon close to that other icon, Gandhi. Close to him and therefore sharing his sanctity without being sanctimonious. Patel fits the technocratic, managerial mentality of today. Clear about justice but without a socialist hangover. Patel was picture perfect as a foil to Nehru, a complement to Gandhi and a contrast to Jinnah. Both Jinnah and Patel were outstanding lawyers, but while Jinnah was a wog, Patel had indigenized himself. He was local, grounded and competent. Best of all, there was a feeling that Congress had ignored him and the virtues he stood for. Patel was hijackable. The political mindset of the Congress was so self-preoccupied it did not notice the appropriation.

The first to try on the Sardar's costume was L.K. Advani. He wanted to be Sardar because he often behaved like one. He also enacted this role around the Ramjanmabhoomi episode but it did not stick. His rhetoric echoed a different world, his body language evoked a softer idiom. The Spartanness of the Sardar was alien. His strike rate as a politician was also mixed. Being deputy to Gandhi added to Patel's mystique. Being deputy to Vajpayee created a perpetual secondariness for L.K. Advani.

Losing the elections and goofing up on Jinnah already conveyed a sense that history had bypassed Advani no matter how much he invoked it as muse and political ready reckoner.

The Patel legacy was up for grabs. Two great events added to the possibility. One was systematic and predictable, the other contingent. The first was the fact that the BJP with 'hints' from the RSS was spring-cleaning its house after its election defeat with Rajnath Singh as party warden. The process was both traumatic and ham-handed. A coterie of leaders in the BJP looked both restless and unemployed. Among them was Jaswant Singh. (He was one of the few people who had come out in support of Advani's views on Jinnah.)

He had been working on a book on Partition, tempted by the possibilities of revisionism. Viewed through the lens of the present, Jinnah looked neither hard nor hard-headed. It was tempting to consider Patel as a more plausible candidate for the guilty man of Partition. Singh waited till the elections were over to release his book. It exploded into a soap opera but as a soap opera it was read differently in Gujarat and Delhi.

Nationally, the BJP dismissed him, leaving him to play his afterthoughts on TV. For the BJP it was an act of political correctness. But someone more astute saw a different symbolic opportunity. For wiliness, it is difficult to upstage Modi. He realized that the issue was not Jinnah the relic but Patel.

Modi banned the book saying it hurt the sentiments of Gujarat by maligning a great leader. It was a decisive hijacking of Patel, which also showed who the decisive BJP leader was. While Advani chews on memories and nostalgia, Modi has already won round one of the next election. He has appropriated the Sardar. A brilliant symbolic poker has been played out. While Congress waxed ecstatic at the BJP embarrassment, a wily politician has upstaged it again. Politics offers fables to those who know how to read it.

The Economic Times
10 September 2009

Austerity Does Count

Years ago a politician asked whether one could work out an idea of sustainable corruption. On recounting the story, we laughed at the request and then realized that the question was an astute one. The politician was asking about the carrying capacity of a society to tolerate corruption.

The recent reports on the S.M. Krishna–Shashi Tharoor story reflect the above problem. Theirs was a case of conspicuous consumption. Living in a five-star hotel for three months can be a symbolic statement of affluence. Legally, there was nothing dishonest about it. One must recognize that both the ministers claimed it was their money. But it was not the money that made these two politicians the humpty-dumpties of the cabinet. It was their illiteracy of the politics of the symbol.

Both Krishna and Tharoor looked surprised and pained when reprimanded. Dressed immaculately, they suddenly appeared like ironic characters in a surreal drama. Once immaculate as brands, they suddenly looked like yesterday's graffiti. The press went to town with many enacting the spectacle of moral science classes. Both ministers gave replies that were literal. Tharoor responded by saying that it was not feasible to stay in Kerala House because it lacked privacy and a gym. In his blog, he added that the entire bill was paid from his personal savings accumulated during years of international work.

Politicians might make money but their real currency is the symbol. They have to present themselves in a certain way. Austerity is a symbol. For some, it is a way of life and those who live austerely accumulate symbolic capital. For instance, Mamata Banerjee might be intolerable, yet she has symbolic credit for living austerely, for displaying that she does not live off the state. She is authentic in her simplicity and yet shrewd enough to realize that she gets kudos for being that way. Oddly, austerity as a virtue is a bit like virginity. As a cynic put it, you have to be a virgin and seen to be one. It is a claim to a double authenticity.

One must clarify that commentators on the event didn't behave like accountants. They realized that the sum spent as payment could range from thirty to fifty lakh rupees, but were clear that the politicians had sinned in a different way. In fact they were clear it was 'a sin', not a crime. And sin they reiterated was a more complex affair.

A crime has a legal touchstone. Sins can be a violation of the ethical, even the aesthetic. Tharoor and Krishna had violated a code of austerity central to the myth of the Congress. The Congress realizes that conspicuous austerity may not be possible for all its members but it knows that conspicuous consumption might make it lose the symbolic war that politics has become. One needs to create an emotional resonance. One can't be a five-star junkie when one's party is talking of fighting drought or unemployment. It is not an ideological uniformity that the party was demanding but a symbolic consistency. All it demanded after the happy years of shining India was that politicians stay within the Plimsoll line of affluence. All one needed was some middle-class efforts at budgeting, of tightening the belt.

At these moments, affluence becomes unaesthetic. A display of an affluent lifestyle seems insensitive and demands immediate downsizing in a literal and symbolic sense. But Krishna and his deputy behaved like rich Rip Van Winkles, unaware that drought and recession had struck the land. It was a sense of arrogance and individualism that made them indifferent to the dialects of protest and pain in the bazaar of politics.

They were 'punished' for political illiteracy. Their prolixity was a symptom of political indifference. They were also soft targets for a Congress desperately looking for austere exemplars. Unable to find many, it opted for setting an example. The impact was devastating. The panchayat of righteousness felt good about this symbolic kangaroo court. Prolixity earned its symbolic lashes on TV and the print media.

At one level, there is a delectable touch of hypocrisy to the event. At another, one can call it the moral road rage of Congress politics. One can't talk of cutting corporate salaries when politicians reek of affluence. On a third level, one can cluck sympathetically and say that the duo ran out of moral luck. It is not the politicians that are interesting; it is the grammar of our politics that intrigues the observer.

One thing is clear. It is the Congress more than any other party that is struggling with the idea of austerity. To the Gandhians or the RSS it would be too obvious to mention. The Congress is talking to its past self, asking whether it should invoke the past to recharge itself or invent a more secular idea of efficiency and management. It is struggling between conspicuous consumption and conspicuous corruption, and falling between the two stools. It produces the tragicomedy of conspicuous austerity, a spectacle which fools no one. Questions turn theological. Instead of how many angels can dance on a pin, the Congress asks how many party men can fit in the economy seat or fly cargo.

Yet there is something redemptive about the episode. It allows excess, even greed but it can suddenly demand a sense of proportion. It demands a statement of caring. A symbolic indifference to the poor is not acceptable. Gandhi, Vinoba and Mother Teresa serve as symbols of this ritual game. The ideologies of socialism and nationalism helped sustain it. Memories of famine and drought served as mnemonics and a legitimization for austerity. Our polity recognizes that lifestyle is a part of politics, that the way you live communicates messages about your inner self. It helps create a tacit world where even affluence needs discreetness and table manners. It is recognition that while you can fool most of the people most of the time, you cannot fool all the people all the time. As a result, when symbolic justice strikes out of the blue, it is painful and ruthless. Yet it is a recognition that amnesia and indifference have their limits. Indian politics is hypocritical and contradictory but sometimes it gets its performance right. What one saw was cameo politics, with just the right flavour of concern, care, comedy and correctness. It is time to recognize it and move on.

New Indian Express
20 September 2009

The Red Fort Ritual Symbolizes State Sovereignty

Childhood memories of politics had two markers in terms of the state. The first was Republic Day, which was a carnival of the state, a day when the state created a sense of itself as spectacle. As a child, one did not see it as there was no television then. All one heard was the commentary on radio. It was slow, tedious, pompous, impressive; a verbal articulation of the dreams of a nation and a republic. It was the costume ball of the nation like a great fancy dress, each tableau articulating a social contract between people, security, sovereignty and development.

The second event was much more sombre. It had a different dignity to it, a different ritual quality. If Republic Day was staged in Lutyens's Delhi, Independence Day was at the Red Fort. Both events were staged representations of the state. But the backdrops provided different variants of symbolism. One imitated the pomp and carnival of colonial rule, the other the monumentality of the Mughal regimes.

The Red Fort or Lal Qila as a backdrop provided the magic and monumentality of the state.

Independence day was the province of the PM. If Republic Day was replete with the sights of jets, horses and tanks, Independence Day articulated itself as memory, as trusteeship. Between the two events, one's loyalty to the state as nation and the nation state was complete.

The colonial regime had found forts cumbersome. They used them as barracks. The fort as a symbol had shrunk. After Independence, the ceremonial of 15 August reclaimed the Red Fort for the state. It became symbolic of the state, visualized as large, capacious and monumental, a symbol of bounded security and sovereignty. It evoked permanence.

It was hard not to love the pomp and splendour of the state. Over the years the backdrop acquired a different meaning. During the Emergency, the Red Fort became a torture cell, used for interrogation. One suddenly felt that the state itself was a cordon sanitaire that kept civil society apart. The Red Fort was the formal state, Chandni Chowk (as the bazaar) was civil society.

Independence Day as an event was quicker, more political. Soon the prospect of a terror attack loomed around it and the VIPs came to appear even more distant. It was as if the state and its symbols were changing. A stray dog running across the Republic Day parade seemed more symbolic of freedom than all the panoply of tanks and soldiers.

One began to wonder if one was acquiring a sense of remoteness and distance. Was the living historicity, the gigantic monumentality of the Red Fort, evocative of the tangibility of the state, turning into a cardboard backdrop? Was scepticism about the state being reflected in the shrinking symbolism of history?

One had to ask oneself if the state itself was necessary. Did these bits of media drama add magic to the emptiness of the state? Did the ritual at the Red Fort renew the nation as a social contract?

It is important to realize the power of ritual. The performers might be weak, the leader might be effete; even someone you would not vote for. Yet, on that day, he appears larger than life. The Red Fort gave a sense of tangibility, or permanence that the politician as an ephemeral creature could not provide. The performance of the prime minister might be weak but the ritual drama goes on. The state renews itself in cyclical time.

The Red Fort, opened out as a canvas, becomes a reworked state. This reciprocity is expressed in the relationship of Lal Qila to Chandni Chowk, as equivalent of state to civil society. The canvas gets reinterpreted as text and context gets woven into a new interpretation of the state. The text of the speech seemed irrelevant. All one needed were words as a primordial bond, evoking a promissory note between state and society. The symbolism of Independence Day was reworked every time. In a Durkheimian sense, ritual replayed the 1947 contract, the re-enactment of the tryst with destiny. The Red Fort is a symbolism that regimes might change, but the monumentality of the state as a Leviathan stays. The ritual overpowers any act of politics.

By evoking a regime, the power of rule, the security of sovereignty, the Red Fort becomes the symbolic state. A minor politician can climb to its ramparts and still be leader, PM, emperor. The symbol works, so the state works. As a symbolic machine, the rituals at the Red Fort keep the state alive in its muscularity and monumentality. It is as if every citizen in a sacramental, almost Eucharistic, act says 'Give me red' and the state is reborn again. Jai Hind.

The Times of India
15 August 2010

Ramdev vs Hazare

The Politics of Saffron and White

There is something comic about the political circus unfolding in Delhi. Suddenly the huge political machine and pentagon of bureaucracies is playing court to two people it cannot understand. Two characters, who would have earlier been bundled out like village idiots from the capital, suddenly rule the roost, turning the government into a slapstick act.

Both Anna Hazare and Baba Ramdev seem puzzling to political cynics who have seen the Tikaits, the Naxals and countless anti-dam activists come and go. These two seem to belong to a different tribe, indulge in different rituals, and speak a different idiom. They seem naive, indigenous, and yet seem to threaten the polity in strange ways.

The pair demand allopathic treatment for corruption that our government prefers to treat with small, homeopathic doses. Both Hazare and Ramdev are obsessive, each in his own way. For one the Lokpal Bill is a panacea to all ills, for the other the end of black money is the beginning of a new Ramrajya. Two parallel battles, each seeking to fight two faces of corruption, one battling the cynicism of high places and the other targeting black money.

Their very names – Hazare and Ramdev – sound like characters out of *Amar Chitra Katha*. There is a comic book familiarity about them, and they attract in the same way. They appear normal but in action – speaking up on the stage or on television – they become caricatures of the characters that are deeply familiar to us. There is a touch of the Katha and the satsang about each; their protest is more like a festival rather than a movement.

Each appeals to a different collective unconscious.

Hazare is the Gandhian high priest of alternative development. He won the Magsaysay Award for developing his village, creating a sense of community self-reliance, a village proud of its own competence in technologies like drip irrigation.

Unlike his political rival, his emphasis is swadeshi simplicity. Life is simple, and simplicity is health. Hazare is the Gandhian ascetic who limits his needs. He is symbolized by white: the white kurta and cap of a Swadeshi Congress.

Ethics too are simple. Hazare is entirely matter of fact, literally as-is-where-is. For him corruption is obvious and we have to face up to it. Weeding out corruption is like spring cleaning. A community has to come together to work on it, just as a village comes together to work on drip irrigation.

Ramdev smacks of the indigenous, the native, the smell of soil, of Ayurveda, but Ayurveda reduced to yoga as theory and practice. Ramdev speaks of politics as health. Black money is an Ayurvedic problem. He lists its symptoms and treats it as a rich man's disease, demanding an instant purgative, a cleansing of the system. It is a doctor's prescription and if a collective emetic has to be delivered, so be it. There is little room for negotiation here.

Ethics are the sign of health for Hazare, while for Ramdev, the ethical act is a means towards the end of achieving health. Health itself is the culmination of physical and spiritual fulfilment for Ramdev. His keyword is not simplicity but adulteration, be it of materials, the body or the spirit. They each employ a different language of morality: Ramdev treats corruption as a sin, Hazare as a crime, which creates the illness of body politic.

Performatively what we are seeing is a double enactment of renouncer and ascetic, of saffron and white united against corruption as illegitimate excess.

Where the ascetic simplifies his needs, Ramdev the yogi gives them up altogether. The ascetic lives modestly even as a householder while the renouncer gives up the world to participate more keenly in it. Both command respect, but there is a different power about the renouncer.

Ramdev is the prophet of yoga: every word is a spiritual law. Hazare, in comparison, is a priest, and priests are ready for negotiation, ready to delegate decision making to their followers.

Hazare's ethics are more reasoned. He proceeds through a chorus of debate which is why he sounds both firm and hesitant. He is as effective as his chorus of negotiators. There are no ready-made communities that spread the Hazare message. Hundreds of individuals, NGOs work in solidarity with him. His following is amorphous, a collage of people who respect and believe him.

The prophetic Ramdev has more powerful forces at his command: the satsangs and now the BJP cadres who see him as a new kind of VHP (Vishwa Hindu Parishad) force, canning civilization into easily consumable parts. Ramdev conveys the crowd as a horde of numbers. Power in a democracy is built around numbers. Therefore the government fears him more.

The Centre is also sharp enough to realize that while Anna Hazare represents civil society, Ramdev is community as in samaj. He locates the roots of the social in the traditional forces, in idioms of folklore, a sense of *desh* rather than *rashtra*, capturing nuances and possibilities that elude formal English constructions.

The codes are different. Where civil society is more modest and associational, *samaj* can be hegemonic as a way of life, dictating to domains that a secular constitution might be protective about.

Yet there is a sense that both seek exemplary punishment. Both are targeting men at the top. There is no sense of bureaucracies and institutions or the rituals of clerks. Both are masters of the ultimatum. Together, they create a T-20 politics around corruption which takes years, decades to unravel.

I said the capital is a comic place. Comedy has its twists and turns. That great expert on theatre, Karl Marx, claimed that history repeats itself twice, first as a tragedy, second as a farce. But comedy is more lethal. It can invert history as theatre, to repeat itself twice; only this time, first as a farce and the second time as a tragedy.

Firstpost

4 July 2010

Corruption and the Spirit of the New Anna Hazare Movement

The Anna Hazare movement is new. The only thing classical about the movement is Hazare himself. He is an old-style, old-fashioned Gandhian committed to Swadeshi, character building and fighting alcohol and other predictable vices. The movement he has inspired is new, new in its approach, new in its tactics. This is why it has made so many of the older pundits and sceptics look silly.

The newness begins with the very attitude to protest. Protest was a dirty word for the middle class. Protest was what the old trade union movement practised, delaying work, holding up traffic, freezing the city. The old protest was a search for justice cast in a socialist costume. The new form of protest seems more like a happening, a spectacle. The articulation is different. This is a protest against corruption, and corruption is seen as an obstruction to mobility.

Corruption delays speed. Corruption is inefficient. This is a protest movement tailored to the neo-liberal era, speaking new dialects and evoking a different psychology. The idiom is totally middle class. The complaints are about birth certificates or traffic fines or a delay in ordering consumer goods. This protest articulates the world of the Information Revolution confronting the bureaucracy as a dinosaur. Corruption is the lag between the speed of information and the delay created by conventional or traditional bureaucracies. The new is however tied by nostalgia. The youth or what is called the 'Youngistan' of today needs a framework of time. Two historical myths, which also serve as positive and negative poles, act as chronotopes.

First is the national movement and the second is the Emergency. Between the two they create the new Manichean world. Nationalism was full of Gandhi and idealism. The Emergency represented Sanjay Gandhi and evil. The Congress represents both old and new as its current canvas is stretched between these frames.

Labelling, almost as branding, is crucial for the protesting groups. Their need for the anchor of nationalism as a value frame is clear. Branding the movement as the second national movement is predictable. It carries the legacy of history without the burden of it. Anna provides the vintage quality, the classic inspiration for the new. The slogan the Second Independence Movement (SIM) sounds like the Second Industrial Revolution and promises to be the harbinger of the future. For all its statements of certainty, the movement began tentatively like actors playing out a skit whose script was incomplete and whose props were improvised. The candle – large, white and standardized – provided the sacramental ritual. The T-shirt and Gandhi topi completed the complementarity of the old and the new. The digital media provided the medium, the humus for both gossip and the new agendas of action.

It was also clear, that no new movement would be complete without its spiritual annexe. Instead of the old ideologies of a Marxist or Gandhian kind, the rhetoric of authenticity stems from the new-age gurus like Baba Ramdev and Sri Sri Ravi Shankar. They provide a new idiom of authenticity, a rhetoric of legitimacy which makes protest part of the new middle-class search for spirituality. Protest becomes a kind of catharsis conducted like a new-age spectacle in youth camps. The sense of solidarity is expressed in new idioms. Spirituality and its complementarities of technique and ethics provide the answer the rigidities of old ideology.

The modernity of these movements as drama requires a sense of the spectacle. The media provides the memoir and the instant mnemonic for these movements. Television is the new mirror for the self. Television commentators like new-age gurus provide an affirmation for this new self. The narratives of the new are tailor-made by the media, editorializing while history is being made. It captures every move and thought and allows for an open confessional, an act of mirroring, which the movement found assuring. History becomes instant history in this act of spectacle making.

The Hazare movement is only Act I of a new drama of politicization. New metaphors are still embryonic to it. But one thing is clear. It is a revolution of rising expectations where relative deprivation becomes the key for protest.

Corruption is evil not because it violates morals but because it insults the great God of Speed. Evil is delay. Therefore corruption is the 'Slow death of the modern era' which has to be fought. An old Gandhian helps create the new vectors of modern politics.

The Economic Times
18 August 2011

The Narendra Modi Fast

All Hail India's New Caesar!

The Narendra Modi fast was held at the Gujarat University Convention Centre, Ahmedabad. It is part of what has been called the new Shamiana State. Earlier, kings camped at different places and wherever they camped, a world of tents came into being. This is where the monarch held forth, made decisions and this was where court politics played itself out. The Convention Centre looks like a huge shamiana, the festival site for the new monarch in power.

The ethnography of the fast is a part of the new ethnography of power.

The day begins impeccably. Narendra Modi visits his mother and she gives him a copy of the *Ramcharitmanas*. That morning, his second letter is already making news with a full-page proclamation in the newspaper. The first letter was about solidarity and harmony and titled 'Sadbhavana mission', evoking the technology missions of Sam Pitroda. The second is more personal.

He does not express regret, but asks forgiveness for his mistakes. Even that seems a lot from Modi. But he is quick to emphasize that his government has acted correctly during the 2002 riots. Any acknowledgement of guilt, responsibility, forgiveness disappear like a snowflake in summertime. He proclaims that he feels the pain of every victim and then claims communal violence helps no one. The letter is seen as historically significant since it occasionally exudes a sense of warmth, with doubt acting as a surrogate for ethics.

One enters the premises of the fast, and is immediately impressed with the logistics, the efficiency of arrangements. Security is tight but instrumentally efficient. The right ID assures you immediate entry. What stuns you first is the army of sweepers, ruthlessly cleaning up every bit of dirt. Arrangements for water are brilliantly done. An assembly line of purified water casks is arranged in neat rows. There is a sense of hygiene and sanitation. It adds to the sense of the sanitization of power.

Modi is a political enigma wrapped in a popularity chart. He sits grandly and stiffly on a sofa, as if he already belongs at Tussauds. His attire is impeccable, the collection of *angavastrams* ritually correct. There is a touch of Alice in Wonderland in the scene.

The crowds are representational. They represent ethnic power, religious power and the purifying power of uninformed school children. Within the first hour, a parade emerges of turbanized Sikhs, three huge battalions of Bohra Muslims walking with dignity. The sants follow, more confident of their power, dressed in various shades from dull turmeric to deep saffron. They are soon followed by Lions International. The effect is like a magnified Noah's ark; instead of two of each species, we have a few thousand of each category.

The trouble with the show is that it is too organized. This is not a crowd, it is a tableau and he is the director. He is in charge and in immaculate control of himself. One quickly realizes logistics is the microcosm of Modi's dream of power.

They come to seek his blessing, and bless him with power. The logistics of the assembly, the long parade acknowledging his power is presented as a microcosm of Gujarat. As a wag put it: he is the only politician who can go on a fast and look like a fat cat who has swallowed every ethnic canary. Each group that arrives is photographed with him. It is organized sycophancy passing itself off as acclamation.

The pathetic Congress party fast by Waghela at Sabarmati Ashram looks like a B-grade company hired for comic effect.

Modi is clear: what Gujarat does today, India will follow tomorrow. The keywords of achievement – Development, Governance, Growth – are all there. Gujarat becomes the ideal state and BJP, the ideal party. The power of BJP, he says, comes from two leaders: Advani and Vajpayee; their complementarity and partnership are unique in history, a partnership begun in 1952. One realizes he has come to demand consensus, not admit to guilt. Gujarat's display of solidarity is the birthday present he demands. The naysayers look moth-eaten and petty while people in their Sunday best greet him with acclaim.

His interviews are tactical. The Congress is a genealogy of hypocrisy and waste. Any audit will prove he delivers money's worth, whether it is in the choice of the site for his celebration, or the quality of investments for Gujarat. He is clear he is History and that the future is on his side.

What is missing is the smell of democracy, the power of dissent, the raucous debates of difference. The dissent of the Naroda Patia victims is quickly contained. This show is like a Cecil B. de Mille film on India's new Caesar. What he is offering is Caesarism – the possibility of a popularly elected autocrat who can provide stability, efficiency and growth.

Yet, despite his grand performance, Modi leaves two questions wide open: Has he achieved closure after the riots? Has he healed society and offered it reconciliation, promised it justice? He has not. Development is no substitute for justice. Reconciliation demands adjustment, not a unilateral politics. Acclamation is not plurality.

Second, does this spectacle set the stage for a national leader? The answer is ambivalent. Modi might be good for the BJP. He is immaculate in attacking Congress and its hypocrisy, but does not realize that it adds little to his claims that he will be equally good for the nation. The shows of solidarity – stage managed – do not work at the national level. He speaks a standardized language when a nation has to see as a plethora of dialects, allowing for difference.

The wonderful thing about tyrants is they are self-defeating. Modi has created a language, an idiom, a style, an early warning system for the future. The nation knows what it will have to avoid. A collection of growth indicators do not add up to a moral vision for the future.

Firstpost
19 September 2011

The Power of Mayawati's Park

Colossal, but Not a Waste

The political pundits have dismissed Mayawati's Rs 684 crore Noida park as a colossal waste. It is colossal but it is not wasted. Her idea of monumentality demands excess and exaggeration. Power has to symbolize conspicuous waste. Narendra Modi does it one way, the Congress does it another way. All Mayawati is effectively saying is, I can do it bigger and better.

Mayawati's search for monumentality is interesting. The Indian democratic state hardly builds monuments except as PWD structures. Our great monuments are either Mughal or colonial, as witnessed by the Taj, Red Fort or Lutyens's Delhi. Our idea of memory does not extend to monuments.

The great Gates of Mumbai and Delhi are odes to war and empire. Our tragedies like Bhopal or even the Partition have no monuments. Their memory is still etched in the hearts of the survivors. The statues that the Congress, CPI(M) or BJP build are forgettable affairs. Sculpture was never the style of these parties. But Mayawati is different.

She is shrewd enough to realize that there will be no archives for her, no equivalent of the Nehru Museum. She has created no future dynasty but she has a sense that she belongs to a genealogy of power. Her sense of political ancestry is more important than her sense of dynasty. She realizes that both the Dalits and she need to create an alternative idea of history monumentalized into public space in a way that cannot be easily erased.

She is sensible enough to realize that her following is mostly illiterate. But she has a sense of popular culture of what I call Dalit Bollywood in politics. She realizes that it was filmland which brought egotism to politics. It was MGR and NTR who through the film hoardings or their samadhis created a sense of power.

Mayawati knows hoardings are temporary and that electoral defeat might make their memory short lived. She knows her monument cannot be a ghat or a samadhi to be evoked or visited only on ritual calendar-marked occasions. She realizes it must be a public reminder which is publicly accessible. Her tribute to her Dalit self must have both monumentality and everydayness.

The answer logically becomes a park, a sound and light spectacle in concrete, where instead of trees and lakes, we have a gallery of icons – the Dalit Valhalla. A crowd moving through the park recites the names and it becomes a veritable roll call of history.

Try it yourself. Ambedkar, Kanshi Ram, Mayawati, Phule – and suddenly a new trajectory of history is born. The rhetoric of a new ideology with Dalit on its letterhead. The symbolic power of this public space, presented as a public good (a park) is enormously effective.

Of course it is a tribute to the egotism of power. But so is the Colossus of Rhodes or the Hanging Gardens of Babylon or the Taj Mahal.

History as expressed in power is excessive, but at least it is insurance against forgetting. A few years down the line some journal of popular culture will provide an ethnography of Dalit monumentality. Mayawati understands the necessity for a Dalit mnemonic because NCERT books and Nehru archives will give her icons little place in a history of the nation. Our middle class has its own biases and one of them is its silences about marginality.

True, it is not the most beautiful of monuments. It is not quite Taj and nor is it the Parthenon. It is a park. But it costs less than a dam, about half the cost of the Kudankulam reactor. It has not displaced people or destroyed livelihoods. It has destroyed a few thousand trees but its history in concrete shows the Dalits that where there is a Dalit will, there can be a Dalit way.

But it also comes as an important lesson. It shows, as one studies reactions to its monstrousness, that the elite, whatever the party, moves between snobbery and political correctness. Critics claim the money could have been given to the poor. Others would claim it is not a public good but a private act of waste presented as a part of the public will.

Actually these monuments tell you the Dalits are right when they call the Congress hypocritical. It names everything after the Nehru-Gandhi dynasty. You can travel from Connaught Place to the University in Delhi following roads named after the Nehru family. How many Dalits can you invoke when you travel through the excess of Nehruvian names as you move from one end of Delhi to another?

But there is a deeper truth. It is that power both corrupts and distorts Dalit, OBC and Brahmin. The park is a reminder of that lesson. It is not just a lesson in history, as Mayawati thinks. It is a lesson about history and politics. Power corrupts and electoral power corrupts through monumentality. It does not make a difference whether you are Indira, Mayawati or Modi.

Maybe some Dalit poet should render a version of Percy Shelley's sonnet, *Ozymandias* (1818). It is about the evanescence of power and the erosion of all monumentality.

I met a traveller from an antique land
Who said: 'Two vast and trunkless legs of stone
Stand in the desert ... Near them, on the sand,
Half sunk, a shattered visage lies, whose frown,
And wrinkled lip, and sneer of cold command,
Tell that its sculptor well those passions read
Which yet survive, stamped on these lifeless things,
The hand that mocked them, and the heart that fed:
And on the pedestal these words appear:
"My name is Ozymandias, king of kings:
Look on my works, ye Mighty, and despair!"
Nothing beside remains. Round the decay
Of that colossal wreck, boundless and bare
The lone and level sands stretch far away.'

Firstpost
11 October 2011

The Ambedkar Cartoon Row

An Act of Cowardly Populism

Babasaheb Ambedkar is one of the most fascinating figures in Indian politics. In hagiographic terms, if Gandhi is the father of the nation, Ambedkar is father of the Indian Constitution. Both have a legendary status which inspires hagiolatry. Any critique of them is seen as iconoclastic.

Gandhians tend to put Gandhi in moth balls in their ashrams. Dalits similarly tend to freeze Ambedkar, disallowing the slightest controversy. Strangely Hindu gods are allowed more leeway of behaviour and more plural narratives, but not our political heroes.

The Lelyveld controversy over Gandhi's relationship with Herman Kallenbach aroused the ire of Gandhians. Similarly, a 1949 cartoon of Ambedkar and the Constitution in a NCERT textbook has prompted a protest in parliament and an immediate withdrawal of the cartoon.

Two advisors to the NCERT resigned arguing that the cartoon as a text was not read within the entirety of the context. Two immaculate professionals were abandoned by the minister of human resource development (HRD) in another knee-jerk display of populist politics. The event needs to be analysed in detail.

First, as records go, neither Ambedkar nor Nehru had any objection to the cartoon. Shankar's cartoon is an affectionate one, cheeky at most. For a cartoonist to show irreverence is natural, but there is never anything insulting about a Shankar cartoon. It is usually presented in the form of a gentle chiding. Even the outlines are gentle, a cartoon without being a caricature. Shankar had a softness, which later political cartoonists like Ranga or Unny avoided.

The first objection to the cartoon is based on the assumption that what was good for 1949 may not be appropriate for 2012. The argument is as follows. The Constituent Assembly as a ritual process is over. It is now a contract, even a sacrament. Second, Ambedkar is now an iconic figure and to subject an icon to the irreverence of a cartoon is to insult him.

Third, Dalits are a greater power now and will not allow their icons to be insulted. The argument suggests that the memory of Ambedkar is as sacred to the Dalits as Mrs Gandhi is to the Congress or MGR to AIADMK. Icons are items of faith, not to be subjected to critical scrutiny.

It's sad the way our politicians responded to the cartoon. Pranab Mukherjee used all his wily scholarship to praise Ambedkar's role and decried the cartoon as inappropriate. Sibal jumped on the bandwagon by assuring parliament that a review of NCERT books had been ordered.

Others agreed with it, arguing that the cartoon was out of fashion in the age of political assertion. The sadness is that such a reading leaves two things unexamined. First, the cartoon itself and second, the imagination of the scholars who used the cartoon to enliven history and make it more understandable.

A look at the cartoon, not a great one anyway, shows it to be an innocuous piece. No ego is threatened, no status questioned. In fact, the constitutional process as a dialogue between Nehru and Ambedkar comes out clearly. As a pedagogic device, the cartoon works. As a piece of history, it is sufficiently memorable.

Contrast this gentle piece of work by Shankar with the Danish cartoons in *Jyllands-Posten.* These were twelve editorial cartoons, which reviled a prophet and insulted a faith. Kurt Westergaard's cartoons were insulting while Shankar Pillai's cartoons were an act of faith in the constitutional process, a tribute to its main architects. It is a piece of history, an accompaniment to the Constitution.

Instead of treating it as an act of pride, our politicians, in an act of cowardly populism, read it as something shameful. It is a misreading of politics, an act of bad faith, made doubly ridiculous by the fact that an HRD minister lets down a responsible group of academics.

Yogendra Yadav and Suhas Palshikar should not have resigned as advisers to the NCERT. Kapil Sibal should have stood his ground. He should have claimed Ambedkar as the nation's legacy and not just as a Dalit icon.

As a responsible HRD minister, Sibal should have stuck to reason and not played to the political gallery. The messages to the world of education whether through the A.K. Ramanujan controversy on the many Ramayanas, or the Ambedkar cartoon, are clear. Scholarship is something to be devalued before populism and democracy is to be respected as a text, but not in real life. There is a warning here that academics will not fail to read.

Finally, there is the question of democracy as a way of life. Our parliament of late seems to be redefining it in an Orwellian way. On Anna Hazare, our parliament acts as if civil society should be disciplined and punished for contempt of parliament. On Ambedkar, it ignores years of scholarship and the culture of cartooning as an intrinsic part of constitutional democracy.

By behaving the way it did, it was parliament that insulted the spirit of the Constitution. The sadness was that even Pranab Mukherjee, dreaming of becoming president of the nation, did not see the irony. Why should a search for justice or fairness get eroded by token acts of respect? Populism that we witness actually devalues the work of Ambedkar.

I think the great Indian disease is political correctness as a new strain of hypocrisy. It goes well with sycophancy. Power corrupts itself, the memory of a great politician and the world of the academic. To think Ambedkar belongs only to the Dalits is a travesty of history. To embalm him in political hypocrisy insults the courage of man. To deny him laughter, self-reflexivity, is the bigger crime. This much our academics understood, but our politicians did not.

The Economic Times
15 May 2012

Sordid Tales of Those Dark Days

The Emergency, a historical scar in the minds of one generation, is treated as a curiosity today. It is hardly remembered by younger generations and few of them can relate the trauma and torture stories of that era. In fact, attitudes to the Emergency remind one of a story political scientist Alex Cairncross used to recount about Hungary in the decades after communism.

Cairncross found graffiti scrawled on a wall that read 'Down with Communism'. Someone had crossed it out. Below there was a message: 'What is this communism tell us so that' (*sic*). Similarly, one might have to imagine someone saying, 'What is this Emergency that we may know it?'

One sensed that same tone of curiosity after Lal Krishna Advani's interview, where he warned that India lacked the structures to resist a second Emergency. Advani's statement was greeted with surprise and scorn but few read the concern in it. Many saw it as the complaint of a man abandoned by power. Advani, like Atal Bihari Vajpayee, was one of the heroes of the Emergency. It, unlike the Babri Masjid demolition, was his finest hour. It was also the lowest point of Indian democracy and one has to understand why.

The Emergency had few great chroniclers. One can think of Kuldip Nayar, Romesh Thapar, Ashis Nandy and the indomitable Arun Shourie, but even these passionate narratives fade before the sheer detail and ethnographic intensity of the Shah Commission Report. Indira Gandhi, on her return to power, tried to destroy as many copies of it as possible. A copy today is a collector's item and, even more, an analysis of the dismal banality of tyranny in India.

Tyrannies, as Justice Shah pointed out, run on hypocrisy and sycophancy. Talking about the attitude of intellectuals, L.K. Advani, the minister for information and broadcasting in the Janata Party government, claimed that when they were asked to bow they preferred to crawl. And crawl most Congress politicians, intellectuals and bureaucrats did. Worse, people, especially the middle class, loved the Emergency, its sense of apparent stability and punctuality – 'where clerks attended office and the trains ran on time'.

The Shah Commission narratives are a remarkable collage of sycophancy, cowardice, opportunism, ambition and evil. One encounters Jagmohan the town planner, B.R. Tamta the clerk as commissioner, D.K. Barua, whose one line 'Indira is India and India is Indira' immortalized him in the annals of sycophancy. There was Dhirendra Brahmachari who believed he could levitate and played the Rasputin of the Emergency, demonstrating the easy mix between spirituality and tyranny setting the stage for the epidemics of Asarams and Nityanandas. There were ministers like D.K. Chattopadhyaya, a professional philosopher who had no problem finding rationales for tyranny. But beyond this potpourri of vice one man stood out and became emblematic of evil. He was a completely mediocre man who anticipated the future mediocrity of the Congress, a man called Sanjay Gandhi, Indira Gandhi's spoilt son, who felt he had to discipline India.

The illiteracy of the Emergency, especially about democracy, is embodied in the man whose staccato messages, like 'work more, talk less', were seen as slokas of wisdom. Sanjay hated constitutional democracy because it slowed down politics. The Emergency was a literal suspension of parliamentary democracy, a speeding up of politics that anticipated the later pace of globalized politics. He came down on petty crime and small-time dissent, arresting shopkeepers who did not display ration prices or student leaders who objected to difficult examination papers. Sanjay reminded one of Fascism in Italy, where the Fascists cracked down on crime only to become its sole agents. Sanjay was mediocre as a mechanical engineer who became an apprentice at Rolls-Royce. Predictable, his ambitions grew as he left courses incomplete. He came back to India to create Maruti. The original was a ramshackle affair and the true index of his competence. When the defence laboratory tested the stereotype, it ran a marathon 42 miles before its doors dropped out. The later Maruti was a Japanese creation and had little to do with the original inspiration.

This failed mechanic's assistant dreamt of creating a new India where poverty was eliminated. Thanks to Indira and the circle of sycophants his every whim became an act of policy. Sanjay sought to eliminate poverty but ended up in eliminating or displacing the poor. In the face of failure, he scapegoated people and not the idiocy of policy. His alleged claim to expertise, backed by alleged planners like Jagmohan, had a deep streak of intolerance and righteous piety.

The French philosopher Jacques Derrida once said evil creates an anticipation of itself, as a warning signal for the future. Sanjay in the combination of mediocrity, banality and piety searching for speed was that warning sign for India.

His two modes of planning – urban and family – were anticipations of the pathology of development. His urban planning programme, acts of arbitrary city demolition, began when a stray dog rushed past his car and immediately a whole set of buildings came down. His demolition of areas around

Jama Masjid was an attempt to displace the visibility of poverty by throwing the poor across the bridge. Poverty, Sanjay felt, should not be seen near the centres of power.

His family planning programme was more lethal, especially as it focused on minority groups. Men going to movies found themselves surrounded and subjected to vasectomies. The Shah Commission reports the case of an old man who claimed he was too old to have children. However, the bureaucrat insisted he undergo a vasectomy as quotas had to be met. The quota raj of the Emergency acquired a more sinister tone as bureaucrats exceeded quotas to express their loyalty to the regime.

Indira Gandhi called for an election based on inaccurate intelligence reports and was soundly defeated. It was the poor, and not the supine middle class, who voted her out.

The Shah Commission's records have to be read like a novel. One must follow the obsessions of Bansi Lal as he spent the whole Emergency harassing a naval officer so that his milkman could obtain an alcohol licence. One must pause to reflect on Dhirendra Brahmachari using the Emergency to evade customs duty. The banality of tyranny unfolds in this everyday opportunism.

There was resistance but in pockets. A few bureaucrats dissented; parts of the press, particularly Goenka's *Indian Express*, defied the Emergency with acts of sheer courage. Stalwarts like George Fernandes and Subramanian Swamy became legends for their courage, but state power was acute. The Lal Qila today represents not just Mughal history, but one of the major scenes of torture during the Emergency.

In a way India has not learnt the lessons of the Emergency. The Janata regime that came to power was anarchist and narcissistic and collapsed soon. The Emergency deinstitutionalized India, destroying the autonomy and integrity of courts, insurance companies, trade unions, universities, and the bureaucracy in general. Few institutions recovered their normative power, their foundation as rule making agencies. Sadly, the Congress never apologized for its role in the Emergency, remaining pompously indifferent to its sins of tyranny.

One wishes the Shah Commission Report is republished so that the Emergency becomes subject to acts of storytelling. Analysts have never captured its logic or its psychology content with metaphors from the Nazi period and the work of the Frankfurt school. One wishes there is a return to analysing the Emergency and understanding how states of exceptional violence and tyranny become part of the normalcy of the later years. The Emergency reveals how ordinary people can accept the normalcy of evil and tyranny. I think this is what Advani was trying to convey in an ineffective way. It is time for the media and social scientists to retell the Emergency story and recreate in their telling the fables of democracy and tyranny it left behind as an untold legacy.

The Asian Age
25 June 2015

Part 3

Global Angles

The Dance of Democracies

The dance of democracy among Tunisians has broken not just the power of dictatorship but the power of Western stereotypes about them. The wonder of democracy is not just that people return to it but that they return to it in surprising ways. The eruption of democracies has caught the governments of the world by surprise.

Look at the way states and governments respond. People march in the streets and die protesting and idiot spokesmen say they are viewing it with concern. Our antiseptic commentators in India even pose the illiterate question, 'Does democracy in Egypt threaten the global order?' Thank God it does because today the global order is an iniquitous one. At one level, we have the Government of the USA that dreads any expansion of democracy as a threat, an epidemic. One of the paradoxes of the twentieth and the twenty-first centuries will always remain the paradox of America, of a great democratic nation that sustained the most tyrannical dictatorships outside it.

Yes, democracy threatens the dictators. It also dissolves the Western stereotypes of the Arab world. Suddenly the Arab was not just the fundamentalist, but hungry for democracy in a way that one's heart went out to him. Let us face it. The Arab

Spring threatens the global order. They threaten the tyrannies of Jordan and Saudi Arabia, the puppet Arab regimes which will fall like skittles as democracy breathes again. They expose the inanity of the Indian government which sees democracy in Nepal, Myanmar, Pakistan and Egypt as too alien and disturbing to sustain. Our foreign policy in its search for realism practices a desiccated ethics which would make Nasser or Nehru wonder what they fought for.

Lest I be considered premature in my celebration, let me state what I am proud of as an Indian and an Egyptian. People born in the 1950s are honorary Egyptians who understood the dreams of Nasser and the Non-Aligned Movement. We were countries united by dreams, seduced by the same imagination. Memory binds us in a way no twenty-five-year-old will understand. We were tied by the dreams of rationalism and freedom before the dreams went sour. The breaking of stereotypes allows for a recovery of memory.

The dance of democracy one witnesses breaks more than the textbook stereotypes imposed by the West. It breaks the assumption that leadership provides the magic of democracies. It challenges the idea that a people without a leader are only a crowd. One has to understand the power of acephalous groups, grasp the irony that we appreciate the intelligence of birds but not a group of protesting people. One has to understand the idiocy of the old question: 'Who is in charge here?' The answer is everyone and no one, everyone because while no one is in charge, everyone is responsible. Every man is there, feet first to represent himself.

A people protesting can be tremendously responsible. They know they have to walk the way of peace even as the police shoot them down. They realize that protest is not something you delegate, that politics is not something you outsource. It is what you stand for literally. It is presence in the ultimate sense, where every man speaks for his ethical self and stands in solidarity with another million. History has reached such a moment that a people realize they can no longer wait. It is a plea to fast-forward democracy but with a determination to stand up as long as it takes.

There is a poignancy to the drama and the performance. The body language speaks. The body claims democracy as a space for itself. The body refuses to be cowed down by the tortures of a police state. The body acts in spontaneity and discipline. This is not a lynch mob. This is not a mindless crowd. This is history moving on thinking feet, choreographing every moment. This is democracy enacting the ballet of 'We' as in 'We the people'. There is drama and everydayness to it. This is a people saying thirty years are too long and too much and we want democracy everyday and today.

Let us push the idea of the performative act. The movement is not a mere act of protest. It wants other promissory notes. It wants rights. It wants free elections. It wants a full theatre of freedom which asks not just for the spontaneities of democracy but the institutions that guarantee that Mubarak will not return.

Look at the symbolism of the response. Watch Hillary Clinton behaving as if the USA must grant permission to the possibility of democracies elsewhere. Look at Israel, shaky that democracy in Egypt might further lobotomize its already numbed democratic imagination. Democracy in Egypt does not threaten Israel and the USA's barbed-wire-prone security systems. It threatens the tyrannies of the Arab world itself and the artificiality of Saudi Arabia. But before we condemn them let us face the Indian regime's autistic reaction to the enactment of history, pretending it can see no democracy, hear no democracy, touch no democracy. We use the word 'concern' as a synonym for indifference.

The cautious might say that silence is a sign of maturity. But caution is a failure of the moral imagination. We let down democracy in Myanmar, treated electoral democracy in Nepal with contempt. A Gandhi or a Jayaprakash Narayan would have spoken out but our eyes are too focused on a United Nations Security Council seat where we will exchange ethics for table manners.

The sceptical might say wait, Mubarak might return. Historians might add that democracy in its moment of effervescence can never last. One realizes that the dreams of democracy might curdle after the first fortnight. But who can forget the ferment of the moment, the dance of hope we see in the streets of the cities of Egypt and Tunisia? One is moved by the hospitality of people sustaining a people, bringing water and food to those keeping the long vigil. For once, let us forget the security analyst and the foreign policy expert. Their illiteracy is obvious. They predict history only in retrospect but freeze when they see it happening. This is a moment of grace. The million people walking in protest in Cairo walk for all of us. Democracy in Egypt adds to democracy everywhere. That is the beauty of the movement and that is the power of its politics. If it dies, something dies in each of us. If it lives, we can tell our grandchildren we were witness to a grand moment of humanity. That much we can be sure of.

New Indian Express
9 February 2011

Waging War, Cooking Peace

His Holiness the Dalai Lama once commented on George Bush by saying, 'He brings out the Muslim in me.' Put with all the delicacy and humour of the Tibetan monk, it was still a devastating observation. Beyond empathy for Islam, what the Dalai Lama was claiming was that Bush's behaviour, his treatment of Islam and the Muslim was unfair, untrue and almost barbaric.

Watching the recent plight of Pakistan, a country corroded by the Americans and devastated by its own military, I am tempted to say, the trouble in Pakistan brings out the Pakistani in me. For an Indian to say it, sounds at first sight, discordant and disloyal. But on reflection, I think only an Indian can, should, will and must say it.

Our media has been shrill and silly about Pakistan. I can understand its angst against a rogue state, a military regime which was always in cahoots with militarism and fundamentalism. The Pakistani regime has always encouraged crime and terror in India, often making us feel that the Pakistani army and the ISI are merely a continuation of war and terror by other means. Yet think of this: Pakistan as a society has suffered more from terror than India. Pakistan suffers from continuous attacks of terror as

India suffers from prolonged drought. In both, the casualties run to thousands. If we go beyond anger and hurt, we will realize we can be one of the trustees of democracy as a future prospect in Pakistan. Let us be clear, the Americans and the Chinese will strip-mine the country till it has almost no possibilities left.

The irritated reader can ask: Why India? Our hawks might treat it as unpatriotic, our pragmatists as ethically silly. So let me state my position and invite a conversation.

The Partition of India was a trauma and memory we have never quite confronted. The murder, the holocaust of 2.3 million people dead and twenty-six million people displaced, is an event we have not analyzed. Partition has to be seen as more than one event. It created a flow of people swinging desperately back and forth between 1947 and 1955. Our historians and, in fact, we as a people have never confronted it as an event that needs exorcism, therapy, a mutuality of storytelling, a Partition Katha for instance.

Second, despite the Partition, there are more Muslims in India than in Pakistan. Islam is a part of our syncretic identity and Islamic theology has always been fertile in India. It is time to reclaim our role in Islamic thought, show the diversity of Islam and challenge the mullahs of Saudi Arabia to a theological battle. The time is ripe as Arab people themselves are fighting for democracy, tired of fundamentalism but proud of Islam.

Thirdly, there has always been the powerful possibility of a South Asian imagination. One thinks of Saadat Hasan Manto while invoking this. Let us not forget that Manto was not just a great storyteller of the region, that his work was and is part of our legacy. Manto belongs to us, just as we would be proud to claim more contemporary intellectuals like Asma Jahangir, Ziauddin Sardar, the late Iqbal Ahmed or more recently Daniyal Mueenuddin.

We have a SAARC university but an object created by administrative fiat is born half dead. We need to re-dream it as

South Asian University to create alternative metaphors, new attitudes to peace, ecology and civilization. To abandon such an idea is to accept the mediocrity of our current foreign policy, both Indian and Pakistani.

Let us face it. India has been strong in defence but poor on peace. When Americans devastated the entire area from Pakistan to Afghanistan, we were timid about it. We needed a civilizational policy which stands up to China or the USA on these issues. We have to make the Pakistani people see that we can share our common dreams without being patronizing or pompous.

Democracy cannot stop at the borders. Our democracy has to be open-ended, open enough to meet the Pakistani dreams and their dialects of democracy. We need to create new structures of law for South Asia. To nibble or be parasitic on Chinese ambitions or American hegemony is to be timid. We have to create a new vision of South Asian cities, an alternative idea of knowledge, of the creative role of religions in our society.

Finally, we have to think of peace as more than the absence of war. Peace begins with the everyday, with work, family, livelihoods, with our common trusteeship of rivers, our shared commons of the Himalayas, our religions and our medicines, dialoguing with each other, even when our politicians are talking past each other, in fact, past everyone.

To play big brother to Pakistan is to only invite bigger protectors and more formidable bullies into our region. India needs a theory of lived peace if this is to be a South Asian century. An Indian century without a sense of South Asia is an abomination. We have reached a stupidity where combating areas in a riot dub themselves 'India' and 'Pakistan'. That is genocidal. To wage a war is silly but to wage peace demands wisdom, a confidence and a humility beyond our current categories and our current leadership. We have to begin with what we have, a democracy which needs a different vision of the region, which refuses to accept terror as a way of life, and which refuses to be terrorized into any other way of life which fears peace.

I think our civil society has leaders who can make the first move. I think it is time that we as a polity need to create a different sense of the future. We need Indian ideas, Pakistani ideas, Nepali and Bangladeshi ideas, projects to make sure that we can escape the future as mediocrity which the great powers of today are nudging us towards.

Think of dual citizenship, common academic platforms; open trade collaborative projects, porous boundaries for our people to float across. They are open possibilities beyond the dullness of security and the black box of sovereignty.

The democratization of democracy begins with India-Pakistan. That much I can feel as true. That much Bollywood, our sportsmen, our civilizations, our folklore, our cultures will accept and understand. That much we must promise our children and our ancestors. As a great Jesuit poet said, 'A piecemeal peace is a poor peace.'

IBN Live
20 May 2011

The Tibet Question

What Kind of India Are We?

The BRICS summit in Delhi on 29 March has been touted as a big event. It is a coming of age of a new coalition of powers, each of whom can alter the world stage on its own. The mind boggles to see what they can do as a united force.

As the history of BRICS as a new muscular power is being written, there will be one strange footnote, a tiny piece of protest that acts as a question mark. Ahead of Premier Hu Jintao's visit to Delhi, the local police cracked down on protesting Tibetans in the name of security, especially after a Tibetan protester set himself on fire. Delhi is doing all it can to prevent any embarrassment to the mighty Chinese premier.

In an age of superpowers, when armies and economics spell success, Tibet is an anomaly. Years ago, Stalin, referring to the Pope in the Vatican asked, 'How many battalions does the Pope have?' Watching the Dalai Lama however the same question sounds silly. The Dalai Lama, like Mother Teresa, does not need an army. He is a moral force who has added to the spiritual power of India. The harshness of nation states is such that no one except Tibet can say the meek shall inherit the earth.

The general attitude to Tibet reinforces the cynicism we feel about power. A society without battalions is seen as a society outside history. But the Dalai Lama is a reminder that India is a civilization and not just a nation state expressed as a brute fact of territory, sovereignty and citizenship. The way we define Tibet and treat Tibetans will be one of the tuning forks of our civilization. To abandon Tibet is to abandon ourselves to the Chinese way.

Tibet is a strange mnemonic. Its activists, especially its youth immolating themselves, raise the symbolism of the vulnerable body against the might of the body politic. A body immolating itself is a frightening spectacle. It cannot be banalized by referring to other acts of self-immolation. Each act is unique, each is a message to an indifferent world.

There is an irritation about Tibet as its very presence is an embarrassment. The Dalai Lama is refused invitations by nations who do not wish to incur China's disapproval. Even South Africa after apartheid is forced to turn him down. Hollywood might swoon over him but the US regime prefers China.

Demographically, Tibet is a minuscule society while China is a billion-plus market. China has veto at the UN and Tibet lacks a presence, let alone membership. Yet China finds Tibet the most irritating counter to its search for success. It choreographs a stunning Olympics and finds itself confronting the Tibetan ballet of suffering. It knows it can win the Olympic medals of war but because of Tibet, it cannot aspire to medals of peace.

Despite all this there is a sense that Tibet is doomed, that its freedom is a small price to pay for Chinese alliances and Chinese hegemony. Sadly, India is dying to be a superpower like China. The two great moral moments of India as a nation state were when it gave refuge to the Tibetan refugees after the Lhoka uprising (1959) and to a million Bengalis after the genocide in Bangladesh, a hospitality that does not usually go with the pragmatism of a nation state.

The Indian government today is on shaky moral ground. It sees China as a more powerful entity and Tibet as a handicap. It seeks a globalization of power rather than a globalization of ethics. India sees its goodness as a deficiency. When it does that, security dominates human rights, power shrugs off decency and protesting Tibetans become a law and order problem. Tibetan areas like Majnu Ka Tila get cordoned off and Tibetan students going to college are escorted by policemen.

But India cannot abandon Tibet because Tibet spells the Indian difference in the way Mohandas Gandhi and Mother Teresa did. By offering it refuge and hospitality, India stands up to China and therefore stands up for itself.

If India abandons Tibet, it abandons itself.

Firstpost

30 March 2012

The Cowardice of Salman Khurshid

Betraying Snowden, Nehru and India

India is a peculiar nation. The more efficient we get and the more productive we become, the less confident we seem to be. As a Third World, non-aligned, developing, just independent nation, we had the confidence to stand up to superpowers. The cold war did not faze our confidence. Krishna Menon and Nehru could speak their minds in the UN. Indira Gandhi could look Kissinger and Nixon in the eye and liberate Bangladesh.

Times have changed. Today we are a BRICS nation, a great market economy with a spineless regime. Our government has become an embarrassment to our people. The values we hold as a civilization, as a national movement and as a great democracy are being eroded by the idiocy of statecraft. Watching Salman Khurshid is embarrassing. He acts as if he is still conducting an Oxbridge tutorial while he excuses US spying tactics and refuses asylum to Snowden. We refused asylum to Julian Assange, but in his case, Wikileaks was at least embarrassing to our government. Snowden, on the other hand, did us the favour of showing us that our sovereignty was being invaded.

So why did the foreign policy establishment behave so

autistically on Snowden? Was it a feeling that freedom and dissent were local commodities without global value? Was it fear of the UK and the USA which can freely offer asylum to dictators and hoodlums while we slink away to be labelled as the only regime to approve of Obama? Did we think we were going to get brownie points for our Boy Scout apathy?

And what if we had given Snowden asylum? If the US had objected, we would have cited similar acts of the US itself. If Ecuador, Venezuela or Somalia can stand up to US pressure, why does India look so supine?

Or did our government submit because it too is assembling equivalent systems of surveillance to watch our own people? It does not need a John Le Carré to tell us that such systems corrupt an intelligence establishment and a regime, tempting it to use security objectives to corrode a democracy. As regimes lose confidence, they turn against their own people. National security and surveillance are the real refuge of scoundrels in an Internet era.

In the twenty-first century, India needs a new kind of confidence, a confidence which is reflective, thoughtful and strategic. Its foreign policy has to possess a knowledge which plans for the future, much as the Chinese who strategize in long blocs of time. Khurshid instead behaves like an inept babu hastily hiding documents to cover his tracks. It is little wonder that the US treats China with respect while it repeatedly brushes our government aside.

India ought to have embraced Snowden as an exile without a country but with a conscience, but for the spinelessness of the Congress regime that is now almost legendary. It makes one wonder whether this current regime would have given refuge to the Dalai Lama and the Tibetans or stood up for the Bangladeshi fight for independence?

The Supreme Court may have the strength to stand up for the citizens of the country and reprimand a multinational like Novartis – firms like Cipla can defiantly produce life-giving medicines – but the current Congress has become an amnesiac, forgetful of its own history. No wonder it is easy for the opposition to appropriate Vivekananda, Sardar Patel and even Nehru, stripping the Congress of its own legacy.

Politicians across the political spectrum, in their speeches and interviews, be it a Sitaram Yechury, Advani, Nitish or Lalu, reflect our nationalist legacy, displaying a pride in autonomy that we can no longer associate Manmohan, Rahul, Sonia and their ilk with. The Congress regime may be dynastic in continuity but represents a betrayal of the Nehruvian imagination, reduced to a scam-tainted regime with an alphabet of corruption proceeding from 2G to 3G.

Firstpost
4 July 2013

Our Chinese Complex

Prime Minister Narendra Modi's trip to China has raised a whole array of anticipations and anxieties. As metaphor and presence, China for the last few decades has been problematic for India and, some would add, the idea of India. The subject has been reduced to a foreign policy problem and is analysed by security experts and foreign policy analysts; rarely do ordinary citizens respond to the issue. Can an ordinary citizen bring a different perspective to it?

Let us begin with the current folklore. We are two large nations, two large land masses, two of the oldest civilizations confronting each other. Today we are seen as the two largest markets in the world and futurists claim that this century belongs to India and China.

Our elite is less confident. It feels the world respects China more because it is more decisive, more demanding and more masculine. Every time we confront eye to eye, it is India that seems to blink and then go hysterical. The last time we felt superior was when Jawaharlal Nehru pretended to be the head of the non-aligned world, and the Chinese watched him with amusement.

For China, India was always mentally colonized. The Chinese do not forget that Indian troops, especially Sikhs, were used by Britain to suppress Chinese rebellions. Deep down, the Chinese leadership had a bit of contempt for our subservience to England. Even their attitude to leaders like Mahatma Gandhi and Rabindranath Tagore was ambivalent. Tagore's Santiniketan did not produce an active dialogue between the two civilizations. Worse, the Chinese attack in 1962 broke India's confidence as a nation and left Nehru's reputation in tatters. The Henderson-Brooks report on the Indian Army is still treated as a secret, as if it is a report of India's lost virginity. For decades our relations have been asymmetrical. China's one gift to India is the Maoist idea of revolution promoted through Naxalbari and it still haunts our security forces. India's attitude to the Chinese living in India after 1962 is a clear violation of human rights.

As an ordinary citizen with a bit of social science training, I wonder why we feel inferior to China. Our recent fixation on smart cities is in many ways a Chinese idea. Someone has to tell the Modi government that imitation-Shanghai cities are the last thing we need.

Sadly, one realizes also that the West, for all its trumpeting of freedom, rights and democracy, prefers to do business with the Chinese. In turn, the Chinese elite sees in the American universities the one thing China's future needs, a reservoir of ideas, and has created an epidemic of scholarships for its citizens.

Ties between overseas Chinese and the regime are much more systematic, especially in terms of investment and networks. China seems to have infiltrated Sri Lanka, Nepal and Pakistan and has set itself as a rival of Indian efforts in Africa. So what we have is an opponent, a possible enemy either indifferent, contemptuous or keen to browbeat us. Yet, how can India as a society, as a civilization, as a nation and a civil society, respond to China?

The challenge is simple yet profound. China looks formidable and does raise security issues, but as an Indian with a sense of

India, I am not impressed. I know our elite today wants to be more masculine and technocratic and suffers from China envy as India does not have a permanent seat in the UN Security Council.

As a nation we are looking for physical and economic parity and hypothecating our future to technology and totalitarianism. Playfully, I think we can out-think China and the West by exploring alternatives, creating diversities, inventing new margins in a way the Chinese and American elite cannot dream of. These countries are caught in their own image as empires, as 'continuities' of the Roman imperium as an idea. India as an also-ran has the freedom to invent, to redefine the rules of the game, to even preserve what was best in Chinese and American ideals. Our model is the original goal of our national movement, which was to rescue England from the travails of modernity.

It is time to rescue the Indian reading of China from defence analysts, security experts and technocrats. Let us make Chinese society and civilization part of our curriculum. India was always a criss-cross of religions – Jainism, Sikhism, Christianity, Islam, Buddhism. Let us now create a civilization encounter. Let us 'by heart' the Chinese in the way we read the West. China need not be the alien other.

Our media goes gaga over Chinese scholars singing Raj Kapoor's '*Awara Hoon*'. Let us stop orientalizing each other and look at Chinese architecture, philosophy, science, and compare notes. If China is a neighbour, it is time to create a neighbourhood, break the grimness of China watchers and celebrate China. It is every Indian's neighbour from today. This demands that we stop sequestering China into trade, security, technology, and look at it holistically, explore common philosophies, the logic of difference and the need for alternative pathways.

By watching China, we understand India's options clearly. Let us do a comparative sociology not as a zero-sum game but as a jugalbandi and ask how Indian and Chinese films, cities and education differ. This will make our elite both less hysterical and provincial and make India more cosmopolitan. The novelist U.R. Ananthamurthy once noted that an illiterate Indian speaks five languages and a convent-educated student speaks one. It was he who suggested that Indians should look at things in terms of front yard and backyard, not centre and periphery. The front yard is official, ideological and formal, the backyard is about gossip, storytelling. Let us create conviviality about China. It will make us more Indian and confidently Indian.

I am suggesting just one exercise as an illustrative example. Let us propose a Himalayan project. Himalayas is a subject of trusteeship which Nepal, Bhutan, India, China and others share. Let us study it together rather than measure the length of border roads. A conversation like this goes further than any contract and memorandum of understanding. It will add to the power of our universities. (In fact, why not make Nalanda the new centre for Chinese and Buddhist thought?) It will give us an opportunity to say in Chinese what the Chinese may not be able to articulate themselves.

All this shows that security kills the imagination, and democracy and diversity open it up. It is time to invite every Indian to be Chinese so that he can be more Indian.

Deccan Chronicle
14 May 2015

PART 4

It Is Not Always a Party

What's That Musty Smell? Oh, It's the CPI(M)

The recent two-day politburo meeting of the CPI(M) in Delhi was a damp squib. Every time I watch the CPI(M) in action, I remember *TIME*'s reaction to Charlie Chaplin's comeback movie, *The Countess from Hong Kong*. *TIME* magazine panned it, observing it was 'pickled in the formaldehyde of the thirties'. There is a smell of preservatives about the CPI(M). The sadness is that if the CPI(M) did not exist, it would have to be invented. The challenge is: How does one reinvent the CPI(M) beyond the tutorial-college Marxism of its ideologues.

Oddly the CPI(M) needs the very thing it would condemn as a bourgeois weapon. It needs psychoanalysis to exorcise it of its Stalinism. Stalin might exist as a folklore icon in India. While children are still christened Stalin, the ideologies and ideas of the man were literally genocidal. The CPI(M) needs an ojha to exorcise it of the last vestiges of the man. I am saying this not out of any love for the more romantic Trotsky but because one feels the Left and the party Left need to be anchored in a new vision of justice and struggle. What prevents this?

Firstly, the CPI(M) is a party of babus. Behind the epidermis of ideology, there is the sin of the clerical. Ambedkar's dismissal of them as 'a bunch of old Brahmin boys' still rings true. Yet this very bunch of Macaulayite Marxists literally criminalized a state. The criminalization of politics was not just in UP and Bihar. The CPI(M) acquired a patent on it, brutalizing a society by turning the party into a collection of low-level Mafiosi. The crime of the CPI(M) was its destruction of hope in Bengal. Not that Mamata is the answer. But a society desperate to get out of the CPI(M) stranglehold was desperate for any answer.

Secondly, the CPI(M)'s own definition of competence has created a set of blinkers that makes the party indifferent to marginals. The plight of the tribal in the development process, the fate of Dalits, the question of ecology, found it indifferent. The CPI(M) needs to consolidate its sense of parliamentary skill and trade union competence. It needs to relook at the informal economy, and the commons to create new imaginaries for itself. Hiring JNU professors who sound like clones of Joan Robinson, the much-touted English Marxist, will only put it in cold storage.

Thirdly, one needs a more playful sense which takes the keywords of modern democracy like secularism, rights, governance and minority, and rework them more creatively. The non-party Left in India is still a playful one. If the party were to interact more, the process could get interesting. It must allow for dissent. Karat and Yechury sound like joint secretaries in the ministry of ideology. The CPI(M) needs an input from social science, a sense of new imaginations. It has to realize that its idea of Marxism as common sense is neither common nor sense.

Such changes need an intellectual and moral courage which combines ethics and politics into a vision of history and democracy. This the leadership lacks. The politburo functions as an octogenarian club. Karat himself realized this when he said that the politburo for the first time had members under eighty!

The party has to go radically beyond seniority and senility and create an imagination for a younger generation.

The CPI(M) used to be an imaginative thinker on foreign policy. Its sense of solidarity with the Third World, as it was originally called, added to a sense of justice internationally. Today that sense needs to be reworked.

But there is something more critical. The CPI(M) needs a framework of radical pluralism which includes critiques of the ecological, feminist imaginations. Brinda Karat's fight with Dr Sabu George against female feticide is important. But the CPI(M) has to go beyond its scientism. Its fetishization of science and secularism has blinded it to the creative role of religion. By treating religion as a pathology and fetishizing fundamentalism, the CPI(M) has emptied religion of possibilities.

A few decades ago Joseph Needham, the Marxist Sinologist remarked that Marxism was too German and should be translated into English and articulated in local dialects. He was referring to the English Marxists. We too need Marxism of local imaginations instead of the standardized homogeneity of party Marxism and its lethal response to dissent.

Marxism does not need new commissars or death by committee. It needs a new commons, a new network of debate which transforms it from a piece of intellectual property to a people's imagination. That time is now and the future will watch the new jugalbandi between Marxism and democracy with fascination. The mind boggles at the sheer hopefulness of the process.

Firstpost

16 April 2012

An Obituary for Ten Years of the UPA

I hate watching institutions and regimes die. To me, the Congress and the United Progressive Alliance were legendary. The alliance was a microcosm of Indian society and reflected the interests of all minorities, marginal groups and castes. It was like a giant family, and absorbed all the strains and stresses of political life. But today it's like a crumbling haveli emptying out, with only a few members tenaciously hanging on.

The UPA was like a fairy tale which had its beginnings in the early 1990s with the masterstroke of liberalization and the rise of Manmohan Singh. By introducing economic reforms, Singh created new expectations, and exorcised ideas like class warfare that had dominated the mindset of a generation. Young people now read about the virtues of Indian nationalism – patriotism, non-violence, nation building – in official textbooks, but were never asked to live them out as previous generations had been. Nationalism became an act of nostalgia. The city became pre-eminent, and a new sense of the body developed that did not belong to the age of scarcity and the ration card, but to the age of consumerism and a more open sexuality. All this was aided by the artefacts and ideals of technology – including the mobile phone and social media – and by a growing diaspora that played out new possibilities of efficiency, mobility, meritocracy and a certain vision of the good life. When the first UPA government took office in 2004, it represented not just a political regime, but a circus of new world views.

The regime began to create from this circus a unified social imagination. Initially, the UPA's policy approach was broadly twofold. It had an economic dimension championed by Singh (who seemed like the cartoonist R.K. Laxman's Common Man, but with a PhD) and Montek Singh Ahluwalia, and a social dimension shaped by the National Advisory Council, which comprised some of civil society's best and brightest, including Aruna Roy and Jean Drèze. In 2005, Roy, along with Harsh Mander (who joined the NAC in 2010) and others, helped conceive and pilot the Right to Information Bill, which became one of the greatest civic acts of recent decades. That same year, together with Drèze, they created the National Rural Employment Guarantee Act (NREGA), which expanded the idea of rights to include a right to employment. Rather than remaining abstract, rights now extended to the everyday survival of marginal groups. The poorest, the landless, the widowed and the orphaned knew that employment was now almost an everyday affair. The Ministry of Rural Development's 2014 annual report on the NREGA claimed that it provided employment to an average of fifty million households per year since 2008. That is roughly one-fourth of all rural households in this country.

The early years of the UPA thus fused political economy and democratic rights into a coherent vision for a decent society. The pity is that they were unable to sustain it. The NAC had the right hunches but was not backed by the political will to follow them through. Instead, India was presided over by a triptych of figures – Singh and Sonia and Rahul Gandhi – that reminded one of the business theorist Peter Drucker's distinction between a leader and a manager: a manager does things right, but a leader does the right things. If Singh was a manager, Sonia, as head of the Congress, was supposed to be the leader; Rahul was the leader in waiting, but was learning to be a manager. Each was affected by his or her own form of aphasia: Sonia Gandhi appeared like a vacant mask, with her alien, disjointed Hindi; Singh had a tight-lipped indifference, though it masqueraded as immaculate innocence; and Rahul read Shakespeare as if it were a Noddy drama. This turned out to be critical, even fatal, because the UPA's failure was one not only of achievement, but also of storytelling.

The debate which emerged about NREGA at the beginning of the UPA's second term, in 2009, revealed the weakness of the regime's social and narrative imagination. In a battle between efficiency and justice, the market eventually won, and was embraced by the government as if it were the best guarantor of the commonweal. As Drèze suggested in *Frontline* in 2009, the complaints of a few economists were judged to be more important than those of millions of workers. The government evaluated NREGA as if it were the sort of development project that an institution like the World Bank would create, criticizing it for a lack of accountability, delays in payments, leakage of funds, and the manipulation of muster rolls – that is to say, for the standard inefficiencies of babudom – instead of understanding its ethical and political implications. The Act was seen as damaging the farming sector, because the labour of farm hands became more expensive. It should have been seen instead as an experiment in reviving local economies through local projects, a form of employment opportunity and a potential source of empowerment.

The RTI Act too was eventually criticized for its misuse, and lost its halo. What the UPA failed to grasp was the political space its own Act had opened up; the RTI was a weapon of the vulnerable against displacement, a figurative *aangan* where the poor could discuss political strategies and obtain some sense of dignity in the battle for survival. But the regime failed to communicate the power of both the RTI Act and the NREGA, because its own understanding of justice and social security was flawed.

In short, the UPA drifted from a rights-based approach to a more technocratic one. In 2009, the government discovered that the idea of cash transfers and a unique identification scheme would be far more attractive and attention-grabbing than the NREGA. The country moved from the sensitivity of Drèze and Roy to the managerialism of the former Infosys executive Nandan Nilekani. If the former emphasized survival and coping, Nilekani made poverty a governance issue.

Straying from its original Gandhian commitment to the poor had devastating consequences for the regime. Roy, Drèze and others resigned from the NAC during the UPA's second term, claiming that the government was hypocritical about inclusive growth. In an interview with the Press Trust of India last March, Drèze noted, with his meticulous numeracy, 'Our social sector programme base is hardly six per cent of the GDP. Even in developing countries, such social programmes amount to twenty-five per cent.' He hoped that workers would organize themselves to fight the destruction of such critical experiments.

After that, the decline of the moral imagination of the UPA was easily discernible. The Planning Commission's redefinition of poverty was the next embarrassment. It drew the poverty line at a daily consumption level of Rs 29 per person per day, without being able to define the lived world surrounding that amount. In this, it went too far in the direction of a technocratic approach to poverty that has existed since Independence. Statistics, as the Hungarian writer Arthur Koestler warned, do not bleed. Poverty suddenly seemed to decline to unrealistic levels, which required an explanation. The country faced rising costs of health care, utilities and food, as well as declining nutritional levels, but the Commission seemed impervious to the impossibility of a human being surviving on the paltry sum it used to demarcate the poverty line. Skirmishes over the poverty line's implications for fiscal discipline overflowed into a wider battle over the social construction of poverty and its interpretation. It was as if the various sides of the debate lived in different worlds; the failure of dialogue was damning.

In many ways, the corruption scandals that later dogged the government – the 2G, 3G, Commonwealth Games, coal and Posco scams, among others – emerged from the UPA's failure of social imagination. Even as the UPA shrank the notion of poverty, it allowed corruption to swell into a monster. Consider the coal-block allocation and Commonwealth Games scams. In the former, the government did not follow a process of competitive bidding; according to the Comptroller and Auditor General, coal blocks worth Rs 1.86 lakh crore, or roughly $30 billion, were handed over, without clear criteria, to private mining firms. The former coal secretary P.C. Parakh has written that Manmohan Singh originally wanted to hold open auctions, but allowed himself to be overruled by a gang of politicians running the coal ministry. The Commonwealth Games scam displayed a different texture of indifference. Beginning in 2004, nearly 400,000 people from three large areas of Delhi were displaced, in a series of indiscriminate evictions reminiscent of the last days of the Emergency, to make way for new construction connected to the Games. The tournament infrastructure was built with rampant violations of protections like the Minimum Wages Act, and with the widespread use of child labour. The litany of moral failings could go on. The production of the Games was like a monstrous urban inversion of NREGA; it was as if the UPA's left hand gestured at battling poverty while its right hand sought to eliminate the poor.

Corruption turned the state into an inverted commons where coal, forests, cellular spectrums and human labour were strip-mined for private benefit. Singh, despite his ostensible goodness, lacked the will, the courage, the imagination to fight this rot; instead, his reputation for probity glued together the varieties of corruption in his regime. Vital experiments in problem solving were stifled. The Congress politician Jairam Ramesh, for example, attempted to open up biotechnology from a shareholder club to a stakeholder democracy by creating an independent regulator for genetically modified crops and initiating a national consultative process that would debate their impacts from an agricultural as well as scientific perspective. So far, his attempts have gone nowhere. Even more daring in its simplicity was the ecologist Madhav Gadgil's classification of forest land in the Western Ghats into 'go' and 'no-go' zones in order to protect ecologically sensitive areas from the consequences of development, such as corruption, pollution and displacement. Although this taxonomy was the product of a committee set up by the UPA, the regime, in its idolatry of growth and development, rejected Gadgil's recommendations and convened a second, more sympathetic committee. It was yet another ethical test that the government failed.

The decline of the UPA can be read as three concentric dramas. In the first, the UPA flattered as an act of social imagination, only to deceive as an act of politics. This failure was thickened by the drama of the second circle – serial waves of conspicuous corruption. The third circle was the UPA's manner of self-projection: its spinelessness, its failure to defend its social activists, and its inability to look allies in the eye and say no to corruption. Unable to project and sustain its better instincts, the regime became cynical about change and contemptuous of its own moral responsibilities – a sure formula for decadence and decline.

Caravan

May 2014

Why We Need AAP

One of the most difficult things to write about after the current elections is the fate of the Aam Aadmi Party. The AAP was many things to many people and yet to all of them it represented a sense of hope, the optimism of a new politics.

Yet as one sees AAP leaders reflect or react to the defeat, one misses this sense of reflexiveness. I want to contrast it with the many letters of concern one has been receiving from AAP supporters and activists. Unlike the leadership, they are not worried about the elections; they are worried about continuity, about community, about building on the many little hypotheses that flowered over the last few months. There is a wonderful sense of tenderness, caring and concern, a sense of perplexity about the future of the AAP. One senses, and I am not being unfair, that the rank and file, the anonymous enthusiasts want the AAP to continue, to invent according to their dreams. It is necessary that AAP is and continues to be what it originally promised. Such loyalty contrasts with the behaviour of more publicized leaders like Shazia Ilmi, Gopinath, or even Arvind Kejriwal, who are absorbed in tactics.

One incident that stunned most of the AAP enthusiasts was Mr Kejriwal's see-sawing announcements after the election.

Deprived of Varanasi, he was attracted to Delhi again. He rightly confessed that the AAP had let its followers down when he resigned from the job of chief minister. One respected the belated hindsight, but when the AAP followed up by evincing interest, even enthusiasm, for forming a regime with the Congress in Delhi, it left its followers incredulous. Even as a temporary fascination, there was something obscure about the wish. Saying we shall go to the people appears sanctimonious. There is something called ordinary ethics and Mr Kejriwal and Manish Sisodia do not have to go to the people for that. Such antics, even if they were attempts at thinking aloud, add little to the party.

The soap opera that followed around the Gadkari defamation case had a touch of the ridiculous. Mr Kejriwal refused a bail bond in what looked like an act of defiance. The moral of his protest was not clear and one realizes there is a difference between experimental and dogmatic politics. The AAP as a party seems confused or at cross-purposes. The AAP has to realize that as a trustee of new hope it cannot be indifferent to its followers.

Sometimes I feel the AAP is two things, two separate messages. To its leaders, it might be both a vehicle for ambition and a dream but for its followers it was, and hopefully will be, the incredible experiment which gave a new meaning to the everydayness of politics. The AAP's value stemmed from this huge collection of supporters, ready for a new democracy, a re-energized polity, ready to put new meaning into tired old words used by cynical old men. This almost children's crusade of old and young people was an efflorescence of naivety, creativity, courage, idealism, which changed the nature of Indian politics. It was a reservoir of support for an idealistic, reinventive politics not witnessed over the last few decades. It brought drama, meaning and excitement to ordinary lives. The results mattered but this group was ready for a long innings in politics feistier and more durable than some of the leaders of the AAP. It was a commons of politics any nation would envy. The AAP did two critical things. First, it refined the act of listening in politics. Secondly, it let people articulate their problems and the possible solutions. It went beyond participation to empowerment.

Yet, after the elections, the supporters watched the leadership behave like any bunch of politicians. Resignations were bandied around but there was little assumption of responsibility. True, electorally the AAP was not a success but the results in Punjab showed the little niches of hope and the imagination that creative politics could create. Kumar Vishwas's campaign was impressive and paradigmatic. It was he who undermined Rahul Gandhi's legitimacy in Amethi. Mr Kejriwal's battle was heroic and the AAP had a lot to be proud of. One sensed this among the followers who saw it as the first leg of the long race. They were ready to fight for the politics that they dreamt of.

Somehow the AAP leadership has not responded to this, or at least they have not communicated this to their constituencies with clarity and integrity. The beauty of the AAP is that its followers can pursue a decentred politics. So let me as a citizen and an AAP enthusiast state that the AAP is critical to Indian politics. Like the philosophers' rhizome, which often operates at right angles to conventional expectations, the AAP will reinvent itself. The reasons are many. First the language of current politics – whether it is the BJP or the Congress – is outdated. The AAP at least for all its vulnerabilities and mistakes pursues a new way of thinking. Secondly, as the Modi regime is sceptical of NGO politics, and magnifies the power of the state against that of civil society, the AAP remains one of the few bastions of alternative thought and action. Ideas like the sustainability of the ghats, the problems of Kudankulam, the fate of the informal economy, the drug problem that is corroding Punjab can only be kept alive by the AAP. Moreover, the AAP made promises during the election and these promises do not disappear with defeat. They have to be honoured in more inventive ways. There needs to be an AAP panchayat where all those who campaigned for it share their memories in a festival of politics. Such a commons of memory can be a source of critical insight. The AAP also has to go public on the nature of the internal debate on its own assessment of elections. That ritual of honesty is non-negotiable. Finally, many movements that kept a distance from the AAP – condemning them as new, naive – might see in this electoral baptism traces of authenticity which could set up new dialogues of politics. The AAP is a futuristic party with a history. But history cannot wait for long if the party were to play Hamlet. The script is ready, the actors are there. All it takes is an act of will to enter politics again. A nation waits watching in critical scrutiny.

The Asian Age

5 June 2014

Congress

Wake Up, Own Up, Take Charge

A party in the doldrums is always an invitation for analysis. The eerie aspect of the Congress's decline is the reaction to it. Its spokesmen tend to be echolalic, repeating 'Sonia Gandhi is our leader' like a mad litany. Sadly, those who have shown some individuality or even intelligence have been sidelined as spokesmen. It is almost impossible to get Congressmen to speak on TV. The silence of the Congress is part of its pathology – silence echoes either submission or sycophancy. Given this, it is the outsider who must take the role of analyst and strategist. One thing is clear: while its current leadership might be irrelevant, the Congress as a party must be revived. It has to play a critical role as opposition.

The Congress, or at least its leadership, seems to be suffering from abbreviation of memory. The Gandhis seem to think that the nation and party are hypothecated to them. What one needs is a basic reworking of memory, a revival of the myths and the wonderful folklore that kept the Congress alive as an institution.

Recently I was at a fascinating seminar on Maulana Abul Kalam Azad, which was followed by a play. It focused on

Azad's role in fighting the Partition, in working as an antidote to Muhammad Ali Jinnah, but what it showed, above all, is the inside of a Congress leadership – Nehru, Patel, Pattabhi Sitaramayya and others – discussing the question of freedom and the role of the Congress. There was an authenticity and sincerity to the discussion. This might sound like a utopia, but it is precisely such a conversation that the Congress needs to have.

I would like to suggest that if this is not possible at the national level because of the Procrustean hold of the family, it could begin at the regional levels. G.K. Vasan, while breaking away, suggested that the Congress in Tamil Nadu was a regional party with its own history of leadership. A Congress going back to Rajaji and Kamaraj echoes a pluralism, an alternative history to Rahul Gandhi's history of the Congress. It becomes an alternative way of looking at the party where national, regional and local combine in constructive ways.

In looking at the memory and history of the Congress, even the United Progressive Alliance deserves close scrutiny. It did have a more imaginative idea of civil society than the Modi regime. Its role in the making of Right to Information, Mahatma Gandhi National Rural Employment Guarantee Act and biotechnology debates are worthy of appreciation. Just think of the different attitudes to the biotechnology debates. The Bharatiya Janata Party stopped the introduction of Bt brinjal at the behest of the Rashtriya Swayamsevak Sangh (RSS). UPA's minister for environment, Jairam Ramesh, had declared a moratorium on it after summoning various reports and inviting stakeholders for a debate. A problem was examined from many angles and the debates were transparent. While I am against Bt brinjal, I feel the Modi regime should have allowed debate. There is a pedagogy to politics which the regime is missing. The Congress needs to exploit its civil society linkages and set the stage for more serious debates in politics. Of late, the voice of social movements seems to be on the decline, while Delhi is being deluged with think tanks. The Congress must be moved for more open policy debates.

A party which was in power for almost ten listless years should own up to its mistakes. It must recognize that there is a ritual dignity to owning up to a mistake. Admitting to corruption is one thing, but the need to apologize for its behaviour in 1984 and its aftermath is something more significant. What one needs is a sincere attempt not to foist the Tytlers, Bhagats and Sajjan Kumars on Delhi. This, in fact, should be an almost non-negotiable step where the Congress exorcises its own past. It is not the 150-year-old history that is problematic; it is the history of the last few decades that's the issue. As a party that confronts 1984, the Congress will ethically and politically be on a better footing than the BJP, which is too pious to apologize for the 2002 riots.

Policy-wise, the Congress should focus on two or three issues and build a societal consensus on it. First, it needs to redeem the damage it did to education, create the new equivalent of the Kothari Commission Report on education. Kapil Sibal did inaugurate such an idea, but then abbreviated it. It is time for the Congress to float an education report that looks at the future of knowledge and offers a credible alternative to the RSS's attempts to 'tinker' with education.

The other major issue is environment. Despite the Ganga project, the BJP's efforts on democratizing environmentalism are questionable. It has discarded the recommendations of the Gadgil report on the Western Ghats. The Congress, on the other hand, needs to go beyond the growth obsessions of its past and read environment as a part of livelihood and sustainability without which development in any serious way is not possible. The Congress has to quietly challenge development models, not out of spite because the Planning Commission was shut down but because the reciprocity between the needs of the environment and those of development must be worked out.

I am afraid this also demands a small change in attitude on TV. Some of the Congress spokespersons have been valiant. But a soldier dying meaninglessly for his party is not what we want. We want the Congress to tap into its availability of intelligence to take the conversation beyond Mr Gandhi into the institutional future of party and nation. The Congress needs a new cadre on TV the way the BJP marshalled its TV campaign before the elections. From Ravi Shankar Prasad to Nirmala Sitharaman, the BJP had all their stalwarts debating every day.

There are other issues one can emphasize. The Congress has to examine its complicity in corruption and violence and realize that history cannot be an antidote to current ailments. With a touch of modesty, a sense of its mistakes, the party can rework itself. It owes this much to the Indian people.

The Asian Age
14 November 2014

Part 5

Federal Episodes

Listening to Manipur

Last week, a friend of mine asked me, 'What do you think of the problem in the Northeast?'

Let us begin with the obvious. The 'Northeast' is a colonial construct. The very act of labelling distances it. The plurality of places, spaces, memories, ecologies we call Arunachal Pradesh, Nagaland, Mizoram, Bodoland, and Assam gets homogenized into a flatness of the Northeast.

We have increasingly orientalized ourselves after Independence. Once we homogenize, once we orientalize, we behave like colonizers. And the three together create what sociologists call the self-fulfilling prophecy. What is familiar through the People of India Survey is now behaviourally reproduced by attributing strangeness to such behaviour. Manipur is more distant than Madison. Do we even think of the difference between Hindu Manipur and Christian Mizoram?

An integral part of India is read as an item of foreign policy. And people from there respond in turn by saying, 'Go back, Indian army!' Of course there is insurgency there and the insidious fingers of the ISI. But is ISI the marker to a problem or are we as a democracy going to wrest the issue of Manipur from ISI and redefine it for ourselves? The youth of these societies are already part of the Indian and global mainstream. They are prominent in every educational institution both in their ability to be westernized and yet retain their separate individual identities. When the PM, sensitive though he is, says we have to retrain bureaucrats for the Northeast, he might be falling into the same stereotypical traps.

There is a second part of the story. My late colleague Giri Deshingkar was a defence expert with a heart. He knew that statistics could bleed. Deshingkar once talked to us about a problem of law and order and not, as he emphasized, a 'law and order' problem. For instance, the atrocity of Assam Rifles or the insurgent violence could be read as a problem of law and order.

The problem of law and order dealt with the paramilitarization of our society. Deshingkar observed that India as a society has over a million paramilitary forces outside the army. Many are equipped like army units and yet function for internal order and control. He talked of a decade when almost all the awards for gallantry the army got were for action against our own people. What then happens to the idea of civil rights and people's security? In that sense women's protests against the rape and murder of Manorama Devi by Assam Rifles is something that concerns us all. How do we stop the paramilitarization and brutalization of our society?

I am not ignoring the problem of terrorism and insurgency. It is common sense that terrorist groups, whatever their inaugural acts of liberation, gradually degenerate to fat-cat tax collection agencies. The monstrous jugalbandi between terrorism and paramilitarization literally asphyxiates democracy in a society. When atrocities like terrorism and rape are met with silence, protest must be genuinely creative to break through the crust of complicity and silence. That is what the nude protest in front of Kangla Fort achieved. It demanded a response beyond questions of rights, feminist propriety, security and the other cliches of the 'Northeast problem'.

What do we do as ordinary citizens and concerned Indians? Do we leave it to the experts – retired ministry officials, security denizens and exiled politicians desperate to make a comeback? How do we respond to the Manipur in each of us? There is in each Indian a part that wants to secede and another which desperately clings to the idea of India. Each of us wants to be separate and Indian – Tamil and Indian, Gujarati and Indian, Sikh and Indian. The term 'and' is crucial for Indian identity.

But there is more. Since media is so central, do we restrict it to the visual spectacle of protest of the women or do we demand to hear voices, discourses from Manipur and not from Delhi? Sometimes one feels it is Delhi that has seceded from the rest of India. Can we insist on a newspaper panchayat where citizens can demand the news, voices, views they want so that Manipur gets more space than the socialites on Page 3? A newspaper panchayat would allow conversations across states between people. Let Manipuris speak for themselves and let India don a hearing aid and listen to these voices. If protest is a scream of pain let us insist on hearing it without experts brokering the idea of Manipur. We have to decide whether Manipur is only an issue for the state or an idea for civil society.

A few years ago when earthquake struck Gujarat, people from every part of India rushed to help. They came with the little they had, but ready to share. An atrocity is like a social earthquake. When people protest atrocities in Manipur do we remain silent in the rest of India forgetting that every gift demands a return? Silence magnifies the terror and brutality of an atrocity. Worse, if the only way to discover some parts of India is through a tourist folder or an atrocity narrative. The first destroys the sacred geography of India and the second demeans our democratic imagination. Let us sustain the Manipur in all us. One hopes that the prime minister's visit inaugurates a small beginning in this reciprocity of decency and conversation.

The Times of India
24 December 2004

Delhi Cannot Hold

I think the message of the Information Technology (IT) revolution and the rise of the regional parties has been lost on us. We read IT as the dominance of private over public. We read the new success stories in cricket and Bollywood as the rise of small town, as a diffusion of the myth of mobility. But our politicians and bureaucrats still behave like satraps from the capital visiting remote domains when they drop in on Gujarat or Kerala. The message coming from all over India is that Delhi is irrelevant. It might still legislate but its laws make little sense outside.

The danger of Delhi is that it feels an idea is good only if it exists in Delhi. So every tribal academy, research institution, major university has to be in Delhi. Ask yourself a simple question: Why is national equal to Delhi when it is in reality an isolated city without even the vision of a cosmopolitan city state? Delhi legislates but it rarely invents, it controls but can hardly create. Every inmate sits with a committee gene in his soul. What Delhi does not realize is that India is seceding and the state does not even know it.

A nation state like India cannot remain intact without a collection of secessions. Secession is a hypothesis we must encourage. It need not be an act of treason, it could be a ritual of renewal. It should be as seasonal as migration.

Any imaginative democracy allows for secession, especially as temporary segmentation. Our notion of the Centre should not demand the fixity of Fevicol. The Centre should be a hypothesis reinvented constantly by the regions. Why should the idea of national be certified by Delhi? I am not denying the need for order, quality and standards. But why should order, control, hierarchy stem from a single source called the capital? Consider a set of simple anecdotes.

Imagine I want to start an institute for ecology. I begin the idea as institute for understanding pastoral and nomadic change or an attempt to look at the future of tribes. The standard notions of development, homogeneity, hierarchy would feel (a) that tribals should not have an idea of a tribal institute, and (b) to call it a national tribal or nomadic institute is an oxymoron.

If I am tribal, I am marginal; if I am nomadic, I am already decentred. Why do I need the capital's certification to be national? The vision of national, regional or state-level institutes is a hierarchized one. It makes no sense to a tribal in Jharkhand to create a national centre in Delhi. It is a form of detribalization. Anyway, most of the new national institutes are mere fiefdoms for IAS officers out on a limb or planning a leisurely retirement.

Push the issue deeper. Our notions of security are Delhi-centric. We respond to any model of tribal rights as secession. If marginal tribals and peasants protest they are all dubbed Naxal. What if I as a tribal were to say that forests belong to me? What if tribal areas were handed to local tribal councils? What if we were to say no forest land can be appropriated without a local referendum? Why can't national interests be decided locally? Why should the idea of locality be so parochial? In fact, nationalism today requires the cosmopolitanism of localities thinking in terms of size and scale.

A nation state is a poor notion of the complexities of a nation. Just ask yourself a simple question. Why should the diaspora, which has virtually seceded, be given dual citizenship while a nomad or a pastoral group is arrested for crossing a boundary line? What is so sacrosanct about a boundary that we have to censor any picture that distorts it? A lot of what we call border violation is merely an expression of old ways of life, old memories questioning the illiteracy of boundary, a memory-less empty line that destroys ways of life that are struggling to survive. What is it about identity that needs fixity?

Modify the problem a bit. Why should we have an ICSSR (Indian Council of Social Science Research) in Delhi? In fact, why an Indian Council? Why not let different regions invent their own social science? Why bureaucratize it? ICSSRs don't create social science any more than a Knowledge Commission creates knowledge. Knowledge Commissions only talk about science as certified statist knowledge.

What if we had a series of 'local' reports on tribal and craft knowledge, women's knowledge, marginal ideas of coping, reports on how slums and neighbourhoods create science and use it? We might arrive at more enlightened notions of waste or sensitive models of medical knowledge. A nation is a collection of absences. Secession is a reminder of the presences the nation treats as noise or silence. An aggregation of such reports would have at least given us a better idea of innovation that we currently have.

It is paradoxical that we talk of decentralizing the organization and not the nation. A few minor flexibilities, a few acts of delegation become canonized as decentralization. We need to invent alternative possibilities, temporary acts of secession which tell the Centre it actually does not hold.

Secession does not have to be seen as threatening. Secession is first a playful attempt to rethink the frame of Centre/state. The Congress was once a collection of secessions, that is why it held India together. Today the Congress is a centrist frame, a little club in Delhi pretending it understands the country. English viceroys had a better sense of India than our prince in waiting in the party.

The diversity of India to which democracy is tied demands we break away from the current idea of Delhi. We have to invent alternative worlds before Delhi destroys us. The challenge is simple. Find ways to secede such that Delhi does not know it. The old slogan 'Delhi door nahi' should now be 'Delhi door rahe'. Think of six ways to secede without the state knowing it.

Indian Express
28 March 2008

Fissiparous Federalism?

Federalism in India is seen in terms of the mistakenness of the concrete. One envisions the Centre–state situations as if they were tangible objects like a cake. One can almost visualize portions being moved from one side to another. This idea of cutting a cake or a sense of a visual balance creates a misleading sense of the idea of the federal.

Currently federalism is a whole created out of dualisms. Centre and state are constructed as opposites. Responsibility becomes a division of powers. The whole relationship is visualized like a social contract, a fixed-rule game, which privileges some forms of thought. Balance is crucial and any attempt to give more powers to the state is seen as fissiparous. Secession, segmentation, rebellion are seen as violations of the federal code. Similarly, over-centralization is seen as tyranny, except while thinking about sovereignty. In this sense, federalism becomes a mechanism for sustaining the nation state, especially the national security state. Since the nation state is seen as inviolable, anything that disturbs its sense of order and classification is regarded as taboo.

This essay would like to argue that the metaphors with which we like to think of the federal arrangement are outdated. Bad metaphors make for bad politics. Take geometry as geography. The idea of centre and periphery creates the sense of the marginality of the outer, instead of the diversity of the whole. Every centrifugal moment becomes a questioning of a centre that cannot hold. Politicians then follow the metaphors in their head and take police action accordingly.

Before we think of Telangana or Chhattisgarh can we think of alternative metaphors? This suggestion might seem remote and academic but I think the politics of the future will be determined by new ways of thinking. There is an inherent confusion in political theory between size and scale. Size invokes quantity, space, homogeneity and an idea of bigness. In the idea of size, critical thinking creates decentralization as a form of downsizing. Small is seen as empowerment, and also beautiful. It is the entertaining world of Gulliver where we alternate satirically between the Lilliput and the Brobdingnag. One often forgets Swift's narratives were a critique of the Royal Society as a mode of scientific thought.

But both science and politics have grown today and have realized the wisdom of savants like D'arcy Thompson and Leopold Kohr. For the latter, it is the genius of scale we must understand.

Scale is about the politics and biology of levels, and levels are not homogeneous. Here notions of dualism and hierarchy lead to the diversity of polyarchy. Such ecological systems think of size but through the diversity of qualitative levels. Unlike decentralization which divides power, polyarchy does not replicate the same anarchic solution. Each level represents a separate universe that dovetails into the next. Diversity in decision making is essential for problem solving. Once we redefine the problem, the demands on problem solving are different. When the Centre refuses to respond, the predictable answers were secession, separatism and the epidemic of fissiparous tendencies that came in the wake of Nagaland,

Kashmir, Khalistan or the demand for small states from Chhattisgarh, Jharkhand and Telangana. But in the moment of victory, these states merely replicate the same mentality of conventional statehood. The rhetoric of small is beautiful eventually becomes a need for alternative bigness. Everyone wants a capital like Hyderabad. Soon we replicate the same bureaucratic mentalities and the battle of tweedledum and tweedledee continues elsewhere.

One witnesses this in two ways. One is the sons-of-the-soil syndrome, where nativism insists on priority for 'natives'. It packs a bully-boy rhetoric which creates a politics of the outsider as a perpetual scapegoat. The Thackerays in Mumbai and the Shiv Sena exemplify it. The other is Jharkhand, where a new state only means a transfer of rapacity. Patna yields to Ranchi as the new site of corruption. One separates in order to mimic the corruption one should have fought. The question we have to ask is: Can democracy make the grids of federalism more supple and muscular?

If democracy defines federalism as a social contract, then federalism becomes a rigid rule game. If democracy is read as populism, we get a situation like Telangana. One hunger strike blackmails an entire system of politics. Let us be clear, fasting and hunger strike are two separate systems. A hunger strike is a threat, an instrumental way of achieving a politics. It is a refusal of dialogue. The body is a mere tool for a political function. Fasting seeks harmony. It is accompanied by prayer not threat, conversation and not a refusal of dialogue. Between the fast and the hunger strike stands a world the French philosopher, Jacques Derrida, called 'negotiations'.

Negotiation, for Derrida, implies 'the impossibility of stopping, of settling into one position'. It is the mobility between several positions, places, between which a shuttle is needed. Federalism has to be a negotiation and not a social contract, a to and fro between positions, places and choices. Negotiation does not freeze choices except when the language of time enters the text of federalism along with space. The territory then becomes ecology. Power can be seasonal. It is the politics of diversity rather than homogeneity. Unfortunately, a search for the small that mimics the uniform offers little. Substituting politicians does not change the dismal logic of current politics. If the various parts of Andhra Pradesh – Telangana, Rayalaseema and the coastal districts were to federate in a different way around agriculture, watershed management, education or even the future of craft technologies, a different variety of experiments rather than an atlas of neglect would have been created. We need different geometries for understanding. The current politics can create an indifferent or empty Centre, enacting a form of federalism where the whole is less than the sum of the parts. It is time for a different form of thinking to invent a way out of trouble. A politics of populism is stale. Unless we relive our keywords, violence and intolerance are the only predictable answers to any request for difference.

New Indian Express
2 January 2010

Part 6

Elections as Soap Opera

Politics as Soap

The Emptiness of India's Elections

Democracy, like Hinduism, is a way of life. In both, festivals are heralded as celebrations that weave together belief and ritual. Nothing emphasizes our commitment to democracy more than our faith in elections. Yet, elections today seem an empty exercise. Politics in India has divorced elections from questions of citizenship, democracy, justice and corruption.

Ironically, it was the Congress party that began the fragmentation of the political. The finest skill of the old Congress was its ability to link Dalits and Muslims, minority rights and development issues. This was a complex and skillful act and it formed the warp and woof of the democratic imagination for decades. Today, the Congress seems to have outsourced itself from politics by handing over this task to political parties that cannot play at it. The complexity, the organized confusion, even the hypocrisy of the Congress is a fine art that the other parties could not match. Unfortunately, in terms of political grammar, the party today perceives itself as a noun, when it should be performing like a verb. Worse, the BJP treats it like an adjective creating a portfolio of insults rather than a repertoire of issues. The Congress has to return to the active voice and realize that technology and back-room boys are no substitute for politics.

Such a recovery of politics is exacerbated by the semiotic finesse of the BJP. Be it myth or advertising, the BJP, like Ekta Kapoor, has a tremendous sense of the symbolic. It has emptied the political domain of issues and convinced the media and a vocal section of the middle class that politics is only the fine art of selling Dalda. The question is no longer one of leadership but of brand positioning. Vajpayee as a product has positioned himself more carefully than his rivals. He is Horlicks to Sonia's Complan. He apparently tastes better, and has endeared himself to more people. So what if Sonia is medicinally better. Should we merely see them as products in a supermarket or a multimedia shelf?

There is a chutzpah to the BJP manoeuvres that one must acknowledge. It is almost as if Pramod Mahajan appropriated the Infosys annual graph and presented it as a reflection of the BJP politics. Such was the sleight of hand called the 'India Shining' campaign. The pity was that the Congress instead of claiming that it was the TCS (Tata Consultancy Services) of Indian politics, behaved as if it was a fresh start-up with Rahul and Priyanka as the new venture capitalists.

There is a second set of frames that have vitiated the political. On 1 April 2004, Finance Minister Jaswant Singh claimed in an interview, 'This is the first election since 1957 where development issues like planning, progress and economic growth are returning to the campaign area.' It is not the statement but its silences that are worrying. Is the Shining India of Jaswant Singh only a collaboration of the Pratap Reddys, the Narayana Murthys and the Piramals? Or is there also a place in it for U.R. Ananthamurthy and Mahasweta Devi, Aruna Roy and Medha Patkar?

I am not validating one over the other. I am merely asking how these two creative constituencies can talk to and surprise each other at election time.

To the failure of the political parties, we must add the emptiness of discourse and narrative. One is not invoking the predictability of media narratives but the failure of political theory itself. As a result, questions of poverty, justice, redistribution, somehow lost their nerve in the public domain.

Simultaneously, we diminished the richness of political debate to concentrate on the techniques of election strategy. Politics became a pseudo-technocratic domain bubbling with coefficients and percentages when the theoretical basis of election studies ranked a bit below matka or horse racing. What began as a well-intentioned exercise in empiricism became a commercialized display of scientism.

At one level, the problem of election narratives is a bit like a cricket match. The commentaries cannot merely be a ball-by-ball account of the game. They need value addition. One uses statistics to create folklore, explore connections and achievements. Election studies fail to create that interpretative strategy for a democratic imagination.

What we have instead is the spectacle of film stars being showered like confetti on the voter. This is not to be confused with the earlier phenomenon in the south, where film provided the symbolic grammar and impetus for political movements. A Chiranjeevi or a Rajinikanth still understands and responds to that language. But a Govinda steps into politics the way he steps into a B-grade movie. If he represents one form of political correctness, the academic represents the other.

Since standard intellectuals have little to offer, let me paraphrase Aishwarya Rai at a recent conference. She said, 'I have come to talk not about the idea of India but an India of ideas.' Perfect timing. What our election needs is an India of ideas, ideas like justice, innovation, diversity, rights, citizenships and consumerism, ideas that need to be aired. Otherwise, our society will become a huge collection of middle class clichés.

The Times of India
1 May 2004

Election Riddles

The Search for a New Political Paradigm

Three scenes dominated the post-election drama. First, the picture of Bahadur Shah Vajpayee, disconsolate over the loss of his empire, seeking consolation in poetry for losses in politics. Second, Sonia Gandhi's use of the idiom of renunciation to stymie the National Democratic Alliance (NDA). Third, the simultaneous presence of a Sikh prime minister and a Muslim president – a national celebration of pluralism.

We need three sets of visual metaphors to interpret these different frames. First, we need the cultural mirror to see the images of our broader self. In this mirror one celebrates the renunciation of Sonia and the rise of Manmohan Singh. Secondly, we enter the hall of mirrors to see our distortions and our caricatures. Finally, we employ the lens. The lens is more analytic in that it unravels the logic of the system.

What did the election results reveal as a set of messages?

What one senses first is the 'missingness' of socialism. There was no nostalgia of recall, yet one sensed the need for a new vocabulary to talk of hunger, water, suicides and the many varieties of development. The shorthand of bijli, paani, sadak was too glib. This is not an electorate that has voted liberalization out. It is debating, instead, the kind of democracy that accompanies liberalization. Since we see events in terms of personalities, let us read each structural problem eponymously.

The first icon centres on Chandrababu Naidu. His scale of defeat is only matched by the poignancy of the rejection. It was not a defeat inflicted by an angry countryside, but by the city, and the youth. Announcing his victory, Rajasekhara Reddy declared free power for the peasantry while condemning Naidu's indifference to the suicides by farmers. Naidu's politics might have been a trifle pre-emptive but the paradigm he created cannot be wished away. Naxalite ambushes and farmers' suicides cannot eliminate the challenges that biotechnology and modernized agriculture are confronting us with. Naidu understood what governance meant. He knew the cost of removing sewage, and realized, unlike Reddy, that it can't be a free lunch. Like Digvijaya Singh's idea of social development, Naidu's idea of cyber development pluralized development beyond the linear bureaucratic imagination. He raised questions about the future of smallholdings, about investment in agriculture, about where the locus of innovation and employment lay. Naidu has been voted out, but Naidu as a conundrum remains to be tackled.

The second presence is Murli Manohar Joshi. Joshi did not have a new imagination to offer but his very obduracy reminded us that this election had little to do with India as a knowledge society. Even the IIM controversy was misread widely. What the IIM offers is the vision of a meritocracy with the assurance of mobility, while what Joshi talked about was a sense of justice. Mobility is guaranteed through bank loans, justice through some form of affirmative action. The discussion did not raise broader issues because IIM was seen as a club rather than a school. Issues about autonomy led to a closure of the debate rather than a widening of the issues of social responsibility. Joshi left behind a precipitate of crucial issues on education, which our society has not answered beyond the provincialism of Left and Right. The third iconic figure after the election is Sitaram Yechury. The electorate has a way of keeping constituencies alive, of sustaining Marxism at a time when it is disappearing across the world. Is the substitution of secularism for class, enough to create a new paradigm for the Left? Arun Shourie exposed the hypocrisy of public sector socialism as a form of parasitism. Today, the Left threatens the house that Shourie unbuilt but what alternative can it propose in terms of innovation, efficiency and responsibility? This election is the last chance given by a sensitive electorate to the Left to redeem itself as an imagination.

Stalking the scene more cockily is Lalu Yadav. His rhetorical amalgam combines caste interests, terror and populism. Is Bihar offering us a model of populist democracy without development? Are the railways going to be subject to Mandalist politics without modernization? Does the chemistry of being secular dissolve the other constituents of the imagination? Or is the electorate insisting that even rhetorical or populist democracy is superior to any promise of development? How do the constituencies of the UPA – Left, populist, casteist – react to each other in remaking the democratic imagination during the era of economic liberalization?

Looming over all of them is Sonia, identified with the Congress and embodying a sense of charisma and normativeness in politics. The electorate redeemed the Congress in its moment of decline. The question is: Can the party become more internally democratic, less sycophantic, more oriented to normative social change?

Finally, the figure of Manmohan Singh, representing the goodness of professionalism in politics. Can goodness survive in politics or will it disappear before the interval as often happens in a Hindi movie, where the good cop, teacher, father, politician, bureaucrat is eliminated by the forces of corruption?

Development and democracy raise mythic riddles just as the gods of Greek and Hindu pantheons did. This is an electorate that has not voted liberalization out but is assembling the politics to modify and democratize it. It is persuading politicians to enter history, not abandon it.

The Times of India
22 June 2004

A Vote for Decency and Development

Everyone loves a winner. But the winner of this election is not the Congress, but the people. What came up clearly was the wisdom of the polity. While every pollster was discussing tactics, especially the instrumentality of alliances, the people of India gave a clear signal for strategy. The voter as a collective entity had two realistic options before him. He could have created a hung parliament, leaving every party foraging for votes. This would have brought down the politicians a peg or two.

Secondly, the voter could have given a clear message. What we received was a vote for decency and development but the message came at several levels. Firstly, the Communist Party of India (Marxist) (CPI[M]) has been decimated in Kerala and Bengal. At a national level, the CPI(M) had played the dog in the manger and has been voted out for its negativism. At the regional level, it has been responsible for murder and rape. Anyway, it was a walking anachronism and deserved to be dumped.

Yet one hopes that while the Left as a party has been voted out, the Left as an imagination will survive. This in fact is going to be one of the great challenges before the Congress. It will be called upon to create a new vocabulary of rights and justice, especially around the informal economy. This election has been a middle-class lesson, a vote for decency and development. The decency comes from the fact that the Bharatiya Janata Party (BJP) is out of Orissa. No party responsible for carnage deserves to survive and alarm bells rang at the right time for Naveen Patnaik to respond.

The message is clearer in Lucknow where the electorate expects Page 3 to stay out of Page 1. The electorate has expressed its impatience with the Amar Singh kind of interventions whether around Jaya Prada or Sanjay Dutt. The same relief operated in West Bengal where the electorate, tired of rape and murder, has unloosened the self-imposed grip of the boa constrictor called the CPI(M). It is not that the BJP has done badly. It merely fell prey to its favourite virus, complacency. This is an election that will say goodbye to a whole generation. One feels a touch of loss for L.K. Advani. But one accepts the logic of time. One must emphasize that the youth voted not for youth but for the party that struck the best balance between youth and experience. The Congress between Rahul Gandhi and Dr Manmohan Singh created that effect. In that sense, it was a vote for governance and not dynasty. It is not soft support but a reminder to the Congress that the millstone of CPI(M) politics is no longer there. It is a nudge to remind it about the reforms it has been lackadaisical about. The Left and BJP have to rework their image. The BJP has to realize that Hinduism has rejected Hindutva. The Left has to create a more innovative idea of justice.

Justice is not an egg hatched by the commissars of the party. In this context, Nitish Kumar's victory is impressive. His victory shows how an *ism* can still create a model of governance. Nitish Kumar has created a time machine which has moved Bihar into modernity. In fact, Mamata Banerjee and Nitish Kumar have created history, one negatively and the other positively. To expect Banerjee to expand on her victory may be looking a gift horse in the mouth. The real question is around the BJP. The era of Atal Bihari Vajpayee and L.K. Advani is over and what it has left is a Narendra Modi attempting to bridge communalism and development. Can Modi's model of development be even more dangerous than his model of communal politics? The Bahujan Samaj Party (BSP) has been told something simple. As long as its politics follows a vision of inclusion, it will survive. It will succeed as long as it gives pride and dignity to the marginalized. But it must realize that narcissism is no substitute for human dignity and that monuments show little understanding of the politics of sacrifice.

One must be clear that this election is a transitional one. It has emphasized decency because no grand vision was available. It has rejected archaisms especially if they were cantankerous, pompous or dogmatic. It is a gentle hint that the Congress must go back to retain the mentality of a coalition. But to say a new middle-class imagination is emerging is to jump the gun. We still need new theories of justice, sustainability and plurality. No party has attempted to create them. The electorate has only created a space of clarity. It is also asking the Congress to complete the experiments it began. Can the Congress do for India what Nitish Kumar did for Bihar? There is a rider. It is also asking the Congress to create a model of development without the traumas that Modi promises to attach to it.

This is the vote which rejects marginal opportunism, while asking for diversity. It is clear that it wants security but not one based on machismo. This election has no finality. It is more like an interval within a movie. The action will soon begin. Yet one should never see politics only in terms of the events that happen. There are players backstage. One of them is nature. Nature has been kind to India, to the Congress over the last few years. It is the moral luck of nature, expressed in the absence of major droughts that shaped the Congress victory. Secondly, the Congress can claim a stable economy undamaged by major recession. This too is actually an achievement of the past, of a conservative economy, which is really a socialist hangover. Nature, history and the electorate have given a provisional 'yes' to the Congress.

Deccan Chronicle
17 May 2009

Why Battleground Varanasi Is Different?

Election time is a strange period for working out the relation between the stated and the unstated. The language of realism helps articulate the obvious. Realism claims to be pragmatic, obvious, palpable and predictable. The real is what you are sure of and can even invest in. One feels confident of the real. Consider Varanasi. People feel Modi's victory is obvious. Modi, they claim, is larger than life. He seems inevitable. When Arvind Kejriwal challenges Modi in Varanasi, experts appear dismissive. They argue that Kejriwal's challenge sounds futile and unreal, a children's crusade no one is bothered about. It is the Modi juggernaut that sounds real. Even the media sounds definitive about it, claiming it to be a no-contest. The miracle man of the Delhi elections appears naive and less magical. But the real has a way of dissolving as categories change, as definitions alter, as debates shuffle patterns. One is tempted to ask what Kejriwal is trying to do. Is it to defeat Modi in the election or is it to delegitimize him? Is it an electoral battle or a symbolic crusade? Can Kejriwal's quest be read differently? One can understand this better when one contrasts the battle of Vadodara with the struggle in Varanasi.

When one watches the old Congressman Madhusudan Mistry contesting as the Congress candidate from Vadodara, one sympathizes with him but there is little response. Mistry's battle is pure electoralism. The Congress has to set up a candidate and it does so. There is no challenge to the current debates, no sense of a new politics. The Modi–Mistry tussle looks like a simple equation of forces. The pluses and minuses are clear. The Congress has maintained a semblance of dignity by setting up a gentle warhorse against the Modi machine.

The battle for Varanasi is different. As Kejriwal announces his candidature and embarks on a train, Modi recites a Prasoon Joshi poem. It is nationalistic enough but one worries more for Prasoon than Modi. An advertisement confused as a poem, recited in an old-fashioned way is a harangue. The poetry of a nation drains out in what reads like a predictable catechism. Maybe someone more tentative and playful than Modi could have read it better. It sounded more like a loyalty oath to be forced on reluctant citizens than an invitation to fight against forces destroying the country. A poet like Subramania Bharati could have done a better job. Sadly, poetry is often a more difficult task to master than patriotism.

Watch Kejriwal as he folds hands on the train. His appearance is normal, he appears a bit tentative. He is confident, yet behaves shyly as if he is waiting for Varanasi to invite him to contest. Modi seems to claim Varanasi as a right. Kejriwal understands the rules of hospitality and representation. He moves in more coyly and tentatively. There is a second tacit contrast. Modi sees the Varanasi of Hindutva. Kejriwal claims a more relaxed but lived Hinduism. He signals a holiness, which allows for difference, which generates the secular. He hints at the Varanasi of amity, of many faiths. For Kejriwal, the colours of Varanasi go beyond saffron and he is not ready to yield the symbolism of saffron to the Sangh Parivar. There is a quiet contest about what it means to be Hindu without invoking the opposition of Hindu versus Muslim.

Varanasi thus becomes a definition for a different political battle. The recent Delhi election was about defeating a decadent Congress. Varanasi is about inventing and invoking a new era in politics. Varanasi breaks the Bharat–India, Muslim–Hindu divide that Modi seeks to enforce. Varanasi is about the empowerment of categories and people. Sadly, the chaiwala has now become the agent of corporations. When the chaiwala is an Ambani man, Kejriwal asks, who then is the common man we seek to empower? Modi seems to present himself like a collection of dogmas, a God-given diktat; Kejriwal is experimental but is clear that Modi is the one to be defeated and in Varanasi.

One quietly senses Modi as a political text being reworked from the centrality of Gujarat to the cosmos that is Varanasi. In a cosmic space, a development agenda as a petty form of clock time seems secondary. Justice makes more sense, empowerment sounds more relevant to the Gujarat of Modi. The development model shrinks before Varanasi. The notions of development and nation state have to confront bigger civilizational questions, even go beyond the standard polarities of secular/communal, development/non-development. Kejriwal is suggesting the battle is different, that he and even Modi are irrelevant. The choice and challenge before India as a civilization, a nation, a democracy and a community is to decide what kind of a decent society we want to be.

It is in this context that we have to read the symbolism of the two campaigns. The Bharatiya Janata Party (BJP) seems to place a savage wager on Modi, even if it cannibalizes a party. One feels a twinge of pity to see the old guard cast away because as old soldiers they refuse to die or fade away. Watching Jaswant Singh cry was, I think, demeaning for the party because he felt what was insulted was the discipline of old loyalists. One wondered whether the Rashtriya Swayamsevak Sangh (RSS) was so desperate for victory that it was ready to fragment the party. Yet, one wonders if Modi really trusts the party as his cadre of enthusiasts seems to operate parallel to it.

Secondly, Modi seems to appeal to Bharat, yet is confounding it with saffron waves. The point Kejriwal is tacitly and quietly asking people to open themselves to is that it is precisely Varanasi as a way of life that is a challenge to Modi's politics. Varanasi as a holy city allows for the other without treating secularism as the other. It seems to suggest that some forms of the holy, instead of becoming intensely theocratic, create their own thresholds of the secular and the syncretic like a persona called Bismillah Khan.

What Kejriwal is asking is that Varanasi become more reflective and, therefore, initiate a more dramatic investigation of Modi and his politics. He is asking India whether the Congress and the BJP as parties are the limits of the dream. Is Indian politics to be a little Punch and Judy show between the decadent and the conventional? What Kejriwal is saying is that he is only a trigger. It is India that has to decide what kind of a polity it wants. The issue is no longer about Modi but about the eternal question of empowerment. In fact, he is presenting himself as a comic clown against Modi as king and asking what Vajpayee asked of Modi: What is Rajdharma? Do the emperor's new clothes, which he calls development, tell us something about the middle class? Who then talks of the marginal? Is power always frozen at the top or can it melt and coat an entire system? In asking these questions, Kejriwal is inviting India to the new possibilities of democracy.

Let us not be naive. Kejriwal's trip is like a pilgrimage. Modi's organization is like an invading army that is camping outside the city. Kejriwal's attempts in terms of political scale would be modest. His message is like a conversation – homely, humble, even self-deprecating. Modi has the persona of a loudspeaker, amplifying his own repetitions. Kejriwal has place for the small and marginal, for the gossip of the nukkad. He is a listener. Modi's persona comes out better as a dictaphone. The contrasting styles are a signal to the contrasting messages of the two opponents. Kejriwal is content to be the quiet catalyst who changes not just electoral democracy but the drama of citizenship. Kejriwal is leveraging Varanasi to challenge the Gujarat that Modi presents. It is a battle of texts, discourses, messages which will be deciphered again and again. In this lie the value and drama of Indian Democracy.

The Hindu
28 March 2014

Aggression of the Ascetic

Deconstructing Modi's Semiotic War

I come from a family of scientists who are as Nehruvian as you can imagine. For them, Nehru was a metaphor, a way of life, an intellectual style that was both cosmopolitan and aesthetic. Over the past two decades, one saw attempts to revive and re-articulate the Nehruvian model. These efforts remained elitist and cosmetic. In reviving Nehru, they did not reinvent him. They created a nostalgia, at most a set of table manners as a form of political correctness. But the real death blow to the Nehruvian vision came in Amethi this election as Modi stormed the Congress fiefdom to campaign for Smriti Irani. Nehruvianism died a natural death as his epigone oozed mediocrity, confused family and nation, and forgot the axiomatic principles of the founders. But that was the self-inflicted part of it. India has also seen a symbolic war that has destroyed the Nehruvian imagination and regime. And this we need to understand.

In writing history, it is the taken-for-granted we often forget. Modi's semiotic war does not begin with Modi, it begins with the RSS. There is a tendency to be paranoid about the Sangh but deny it as anachronistic or tragicomic. The RSS is a powerful machine, and to achieve its aims, it realized the BJP had to achieve power at the Centre. For this, it was even prepared to spring-clean the BJP of its old stalwarts. It also needed a man with the mindset of a pracharak who would magnify the RSS view to shape the nation's imagination. This required not the logic of size, which could be inflationary, but the logic of scale. One had to rebuild the imagination layer by layer and word by word.

Think of Narendra Modi. A dour, ascetic, almost colourless man, a chaiwala dressed in dull white. He is the Eliza Doolittle of the RSS. Modi of thirty years ago reminds me of the little drawings and cut-out dolls my sisters used to have. There were bare outlines to which one could add any costume; colour it, build on it, transform it. The rules were simple but the possibilities infinite.

Think of the first image of the man. He exudes aggression. He is a nukkad hero, angry with history and Delhi. He feels history, official history, has been unfair to Gujarat, and that Delhi is merely a secret code of exclusion that makes Central power the preserve of the Nehru-Gandhis. Modi is a colourless soul who needs a touch of colour, of style. He has to be rescued from drabness. His kurta blossoms as peach, light green; his gamchha is now an angavastram, crafted for the symbols of style and leadership. His bare head holds a turban, dyed red, spectacular and ritually deep, with a touch of the primordial. Now, one must manicure the man. The beard is trimmed, the receding hair fights a valiant and victorious battle. A set of waistcoats and Murari Bapu sleeves completes our designer doll. Till now it is a silent movie. Everyone knows a bully is a temporary cameo. Bullying works only in some contexts, and one then realizes a leader transcends a bully. Leadership allows for a bigger canvas. This leader internalizes every step. The bluster leads to silence, to a habit of listening. Silence sustained becomes an act of patience, a virtue. He still needs a new vocabulary, something that goes beyond the repetitiveness of riots, of accusation, denial and counter-accusation. The contentious history of the 2002 riots and the redundancy around it has to yield to a different narrative, one that opens out to India's middle class like a new promissory note, yet signals a new social contract for minorities.

Development becomes the new ritual of proactive citizenship. It was a secular, technocratic concept but could also be used as a politically playful dialectic. Thus, one could have the Gujarat or Kerala model of development. On an optimistic day, even the Bihar model. Modi used the halo of the disciplinary technocratic term, 'development', and then hijacked it politically. Development was now a politician's game, which economists could join as knight errants or consultants, secondary characters in the development battle. It was desperately seductive, and the Bhagwatis, Panagariyas, Sens, Nick Sterns and our local pack of social scientists joined in, splitting indices in a ritual reminiscent of the battle over the poverty line after the Green Revolution. Development was now a video game, an object of a fixation like PlayStation or X-Box.

You corner a word and create a turf, a set of rituals, and then outsource it. It is now your game. You could create a new civics out of it. Add a variant called Governance, and you elicit a Pavlovian drool. With two words, you have grabbed the high moral ground; you have created a new discourse that all the volumes of the *Economic and Political Weekly* cannot drown.

Modi is now Mr Development. It is a conceptual coup that combines a word and a world with brilliance.

Development also performs a few other magical functions. It erases the past and makes one forward-looking; demand for development is a demand for a better future. It erases memory, whether it is a tribal's past or a Muslim's view of a city caught in the agony of genocide. Now his past is seen as hypochondria. It is the Muslim's past and therefore parochial. In a bid to escape the past, Modi invites Muslims to the fair land of development.

This is the new civics of citizenship and erasure, its rite of initiation. This suggestion works not so much on minorities but on his constituency – the new middle class.

Modi and the RSS were shrewd enough to grasp that to create Modi as a leader, he had to be co-produced; that is, mutually recreated along with his constituency – the new middle class. This class was not confined to the old bureaucratic class of socialists with a mentality as wide as a ration card. It stemmed from consumerism, desire and entrepreneurship, and its origin owed more to Ambani than Nehru. It was a class proud of money making and ownership of shares as an intrinsic part of citizenship. Aspirational and mobile, it thought beyond caste and sought to create an urbane image of success. While embedded in tradition, it clutched at certain symbols on the way to modernity, like Linus and his blanket. It adored technology and doted on the nation state. It loved Indian culture as a spectacle and was unapologetic about religion. It was tired of being laughed at by secular intellectuals. And Modi became the champion of this new middle class. He embraced this majoritarian Hinduism by giving it a consumerist veneer. By linking it to the nation state, he literally created a new political project. Three key terms – 'middle class', 'nation state' and 'development' – would provide the nodes of his politics. Ready with costumes and a new vocabulary, our actor now had to initiate the new costume ball.

The target: Delhi. The object: the Nehru-Gandhi dynasty. The project: the delegitimization of the UPA regime.

One begins tentatively with five-finger exercises. Little forays. Little acts of sniping. One adds to the adrenalin as the audience watches. Gujarat has to be built as the New Paradise. The Congress cannot invoke UPA I, but UPA II has to challenge the promise of Gujarat. A developmental contest begins, and Modi inaugurates its Olympics, each indicator prized like a gold medal. It was a brilliant move. Gujarat's entrepreneurial successes, its urbanization experience, its spectacular recovery from the Bhuj earthquake were all highlighted, with Modi orchestrating the show. It was a symbolic battle of numbers, and Modi could piously add that not a single riot had taken place since 2002. Gujarat, the new cornucopia, was contrasted to Delhi. Now Delhi as a construct had to fall symbolically.

For Modi, Delhi was always the Delhi of the Mughals and the Nehru-Gandhis, of outsiders who had appropriated history and built a false iconography. Delhi had undermined democracy by undermining federalism. Many states could create alternative societies if Delhi let them; some had already seceded without the Centre knowing it. Supine, Delhi had also failed as a guarantor of security. It had little vision of India as a global power.

Vertebral Modi, ready to take charge of an absentee state called Delhi, would tie the ignored nationalist history of Sardar Patel, Vivekananda and Ambedkar to an India of the future. To achieve this, India had to exorcise Delhi of the dynasty.

Exorcisms and openings were to follow. It was, however, a waiting game, full of middle moves, each creating a grid of expectations. India had to be trained to think across a semiotic grid. Modi realized that positioning 'Gujarat versus Delhi' was not enough. He had to shrink criticism, reduce the role of opponents. Criticism was read on the insider–outsider grid, as informal sedition stemming from Delhi intellectuals, the outsiders, the old English-speaking elite. Gujaratis knew better. Second, he had to create a new mentality as a confidence-building measure. Gujarat could receive justice from history only if it asserted itself and narrated its achievements. From its *asmita* (pride) to its economics, it became the antithesis of Delhi.

Yet, symbolism, to be complete, needed characters. Delhi was populated by puppets like Manmohan Singh and Rahul Gandhi. Their denigration was Modi's next act of semiotic destruction.

It was an act of baiting and bludgeoning that rendered the Congress and its leaders effete. Of course, Modi had moral luck as his opponents stumbled from scam to scam – their handling of which hurt them more than the scandals themselves. With 'governance' becoming a hallowed term, the moral emptiness of the Congress was not difficult to demonstrate. What had to be fastened to its sticking place was Manmohan's powerlessness.

Let us look at Manmohan symbolically. The UPA I was legend and he was seen by many as the economist hero, literally a philosopher king, a man who put his money where his mouth was. India was proud of its academic prime minister. Brahminic India waved him like a flag. One had to deflate this, do what a wag called 'a Churchill' on him, portraying him, as Britain's PM had described Attlee, as 'a modest man with a lot to be modest about'. By UPA II, Manmohan was literally that. His was a goodness that was correct, functional and clerical. Where square pegs had to fit square holes, the Manmohan regime had everything in place. Yet, when things turned erratic, his goodness and style of acquiescence proved inadequate. It could not cope with epic corruption under the regime's watch. Manmohan's goodness became autistic, regressing to a silence that suited Modi, who treated him with contempt.

Manmohan the functionary was easy to neutralize. But the real target was the Prince Charming of the regime, the modernist as Boy Scout – Rahul Gandhi.

By UPA II, India had a new generation with no memory of either the freedom movement or the Emergency. It was an aspirational generation, globalized and upwardly mobile, open to a new symbolic India of the Information Revolution. To a generation that had microchips as genes, Rahul lacked cybercool. Worse, he treated politics as an avocation, projected an absent-mindedness that was disconcerting. He was a successor who acted as third in command. He was almost echolalic in speech, talking of his 'mummy' and 'nani' when a nation expected assertiveness. For the semiotically hungry Modi, he was a perfect target.

The play of opposites was fascinating. Modi was focused aggression, while Rahul was quiet reticence. Modi was aspirational, while Rahul held up his family genealogy like a BA certificate. Modi gloated over performance, while Rahul signalled empty promise. Modi offered speed, while Rahul signified delay. Modi was inventive, Rahul correct. Modi was responsive, even as Rahul's learning curve stayed flat. Modi screamed for attention, Rahul was absence personified. Modi summoned Patel, Vivekananda, Savarkar, Ambedkar and Vajpayee as if he had a full-fledged pantheon of nationalist heroes working for him, while Rahul's language was simplistic, his invocations limited to family names. One suggested an epic, or at least a soap opera full of myth, the other barely survived as a limerick, too relaxed to convey even a Haiku-like tension.

The drama of contrasts became an exaggeration of opposites. Modi may have been an acquired taste, but Middle India was making him a habit, like tea. He had the right flavour, the right intensity, a local Wagh Bakri ready to be an orange pekoe – the right brew ready for the politics of the time.

But, Modi was not ready as yet. He had to pass the institutional test, obtain clearances from the Nanavati Commission and SIT (Special Investigation Team). Time slowed symbolically for Modi, but his tactics worked. He realized that dissent was entropic and critique tended to burn out quickly. It was a waiting game, but wait he could, like a crafty Odysseus, while secular battalions exhausted their script. The SIT report sanitized him further. With civil society in disarray, Modi was ready for the final battle.

The battlefield had to change. The 'Gujarat versus Delhi' story was too parochial. The war had to be grander. Now it was an idea of India, not just an India of ideas. A new, aggressive idea of India – a match for China, proud to be at Davos – had to be articulated. This needed a mix of symbols both traditional and modern, Swadeshi and technocratic. Problem solving had to have a touch of machismo. And our boundaries, like our integrity, had to be immaculately clear. By then Brookings and the World Bank had hailed him as the prophet of governance. The Congress, in contrast, sounded dysfunctional.

One needed that last touch of ruthlessness, a clearing out of the stables only the RSS could achieve. This regime was not to be a gathering of yesterday's heroes. The RSS knew this was its sole chance. This would not be the regime of a Vajpayee who needed a stabilizing double in Advani. Unlike Vajpayee's inclusive method, this was science, a semiotic war to put a new regime in place for the next few decades. This was not a battle for popularity, but for survival. If the future was a scythe, it had to behead people from both sides. The future was Modi, the RSS and India. No other force was relevant. The semiotic machine had to strike clean. Modi was to be campaign manager and party supremo. The rest did not count. It was clear-cut, this RSS decision. The election war had an economy to it.

If a week is a long time in politics, ten years can feel like compressed time. In his capture of symbols, Modi has been ruthless. He has captured history, development and a middle-class imagination in these years. As a spectacle, he is impressive. Television's idolatry of him is awesome. He is seen as the exemplar of his own paradigm. Replaying Patel, squashing Nehru's epigone, and creating a new chapter of history – but as part of the subconscious. The dramas, though, are of a different order. As Nehruvians shrink, Patel arises as a grand archetypal statue, the legend of Indian politics. Remember, small victories will not do. One must pulverize the Congress. Numbers must speak, reciting the epic victory of Modi.

As the Modi juggernaut reaches Lutyens's Delhi, one is still left with many questions. How much of India will be Nehruvian, how much Modiesque? What kind of role will civil society have? Will the state crush dissent? Will the marginalized have to accept a majoritarian consensus? What is swadeshism in a 'Modified' society? Will it be a form of technocratic fundamentalism? These are not easy questions to answer, and as one who belongs to the opposition, one must ensure that Modi does not answer them in a facile manner. Democracy as trusteeship cannot be left to Modi alone. This much an opposition should gracefully and forcefully promise to uphold.

OPEN Magazine
16 May 2014

Part 7

The Necessity of Dissent

A Plea for a Peace Movement

Loren Eiseley in his *The Firmament of Time* has a lovely anecdote about an atomic scientist. The latter, an old man, had spent his youth at Los Alamos. He is walking through a forest and sees a little tortoise and says, 'It will make a lovely present for my grandchildren.' He walks a few more yards and stops and puts the animal down saying, 'I have interfered enough with nature for a lifetime.'

It is this sense of living in a moral universe that one missed since India exploded its series of bombs. Both in the coffee house of conversations and the epidemic of phone calls, there was a disquiet, but little moral anguish. But it is growing gradually. There is a sadness. A slow anger. Something has happened to us. A dream of India was turning into a slow-motion nightmare. One man said it was like a child's drawing. Beginning in happy colours, green and blue, it darkened, becoming full of greys and strange browns as it lost its innocence.

Added to this sense of loss was anger at the nature of protest. The jingoism of the state was meeting with knee-jerk protest. It could have been a rape, a riot, a dam displacement. Even signatories to letters behaved in a stencilled way. Almost as if there was a standardized form. A sense of being on a tired assembly line where differences between rights, ecology, gender, anti-development had blurred. Also the same names signing the same letters added to the tiredness.

One realized what was missing was the presence of a peace movement.

We claim a heritage of peace but where is that heritage today? Groups like the Gandhians sit silent while Shankaracharya and Dalai Lama write references for the atomic establishment. This is as obscene as Vinoba Bhave approving the Emergency. Where are our moral philosophers? Why do we feel morally weak-kneed over technical issues? Why was the peace movement missing? There are some immediate answers.

Firstly, the radicalism of the Left, of ecology, human rights, even feminism had shied away from national security. The latter was a tacit zone of taboo for all protest movements. Question the bomb and you become anti-scientific, anti-national. These are charges most groups want to avoid.

What made it worse was the troubled legacy of Gandhism. Gandhi today belongs to the taxidermists or to Tussauds. Whatever revival of Gandhi there is owes more to Amte, Bahuguna or Patkar than to any of the official custodians of Gandhi. The best of Gandhi has already moved abroad. Think of the great Gandhians today and they are all foreigners: Lanzo Vasto, Martin Luther King, Steve Biko, Bayard Rustin, Danielo Dolci or Vaclav Havel.

We are also masters at deceiving ourselves. We invent panchsheel, non-alignment and satyagraha and never confess that all this ceased after 1962. After the China encounter, we have sought the killer instinct and the culture of machismo. We want to be a superpower. But our notion of a superpower is more a bully in a slum rather than a modern state.

Worse, our notion of peace is parochial. We are the new NIMBYs (Not In My Backyard). We don't care about peace as long as our neighbourhood is safe. So we were silent about Afghanistan. Quiet about Indonesia. Iffy about Tibet. Even on Sri Lanka we had no peaceniks forming human chains protesting Rajiv's idiocy. Who protests about Kashmir or the paramilitarization of our society or even bothers that most of the awards for gallantry our army received recently were for action against our own people?

Ironically, while peace as a vision shrinks, security has become fashionable. The metaphors of war are catwalking happily through our society. So we talk of food security and the war against poverty as military problems. No wonder the real casualties are the poor. We need to recapture both our sense of the nation and of peace. Not as entrepreneurship for milking foundations or shedding tears in the *Ecologist* and *Resurgence*. We have to rethink it civilizationally as a preferred vision of society. This needs a sense of life style, the courage of satyagraha and scholarship. Few peaceniks today can match the Brahminical legacy of K. Subrahmanyam. Finally, we must have the courage to see technical issues as challenges to citizenship. In sustaining such a vision we must remember three things. Firstly, we have to recapture the nation state from its current monopolizers. We must remember that peace is not only the absence of war. Converting guns into development is not enough. Development may be as war-like in its casualties. Secondly, peace as a vision must interact and encompass rights, livelihood and ecology. Finally, it cannot be subject to fashion. This is a danger, as radicalism and newspapers have attention spans of a fortnight. Watch the nuclear issue disappear as the budget becomes the flavour of the week. It is these amnesiacal landscapes we must evade to keep the peace movement alive. We must remember what Teodor Shanin once movingly put, 'I shall be studying peasantry when it is out of fashion, when it is in fashion and when it is out of fashion again.' We must stick to peace to the last.

From the author's files

Publication details unavailable

Reinventing the 2001 Quake

Disasters are sites for reflection and not just news events. The 2001 earthquake in Gujarat was a momentous event in many ways. First, the timing. On 26 January, when the state was enacting a spectacle of order and development, preening itself before its citizens, nature provided a mirror inversion, as a collapse. The vulnerability of the state was brought home in the collapse of cities as Bhuj and Anjar looked like Dresden after the carpet bombing. A fancy dress ball looked in the mirror to discover a mass funeral.

Reports on disaster emphasize the drama of disruption but recovery has its own special fascination in Gujarat. Three aspects were particularly memorable. The Gujarat earthquake signalled the competence of the Indian middle class to orchestrate a process of recovery. The quake triggered a social movement across India, where civil society at home and abroad rushed to help. The middle class proved it could move into action without waiting for the 'mai-baap' state. Another point of equal interest was the facility with which caste groups came to the aid of their community evincing a particularity of care. It was an affirmation of traditional affinities. Thirdly, Gujarat affirmed a new trend in disaster relief. Challenging the competence of secular NGOs and international relief agencies came cultural, religious and fundamentalist groups who emphasized disaster management as a part of their core competence.

The role of the RSS, Anand Marg, and VHP is significant in this context. The VHP leader, Pravin Togadia, as a professional doctor (his lesser-known incarnation) provided one of the clearest critiques of the logistics of disaster management covering everything from rituals of mourning, psychiatric aid to the need for a new Rapid Action Force for disaster relief. Equally impressive was the logistics of the Swaminarayan sect, their distribution of food which could provide a classic management case study. These groups also altered the idiom of relief by talking the language of food and hospitality instead of aid and philanthropy. A different philosophy was inspiring a different style of relief work.

As an event the Gujarat earthquake provides many fables and parables of disaster management. In fact, if disaster were sites of paradigm change, the breakthrough came from civil society groups. Civil society's response can never be sustained and long-lived. One eventually has to relook at the state, and at issues of law, organization and governance. We have to explore questions of what happened as society returns to normalcy. What mnemonics carry over and are reflected in the routines of law and management. The evidence appears mixed here. An Ahmedabad that was hostile to a high-rise urbanism realizes that market forces are making alternatives impossible or beyond the reach of the average people. Many people have returned to the very buildings they abandoned, forced to acknowledge that a threatened house can still be a home.

The sense of injustice, of a flawed normalcy, stems from two key events. Almost all the builders who flouted building codes are out of jail and back to their work. In fact, there is oddly a sense that the national building codes are too imperious and strict. What has also been suggested is that such building codes do not work because clients cannot afford the cost. It is odd to sense an argument that safety is unaffordable. The pragmatic overwhelms the ethical in contending that we cannot maximize or optimize on building safety. A lowering of standards is often openly argued as a pragmatic response to market requirements. There are major issues here which need open debate. There is a danger of a pre-emptive foreclosure, a forced return to normalcy which we must challenge. The question is not just of building codes but of new responses to disasters. It reminds us of one of the Kafka stories, probably the only one he wrote on India. I am providing my version of it.

A village at the end of the forest decides to perform a sacrifice. One full moon night, the villagers gather, assembling a whole array of flowers and fruit. The village priest arrives and just then a tiger kills him. There is pandemonium in the air but undaunted the villagers decide to hold the sacrifice again. The full moon comes, the priest arrives and the tiger finds another victim. This occurs several times. The villagers are desperate. Just then the village idiot comes up with a brilliant idea. He suggests: Why not make the tiger attacking the priest a part of the ritual? The idiot later became a UN consultant.

Just as the tiger became part of the ritual, disasters have become part of the normalcy of the state. We have transferred routine to respond to disasters. Our indifference to building codes is a mere example. Kafka rules in Gujarat. The earthquake of 2001 attests to this.

DNA
25 January 2008

The Value of Rave and Rant

The recent strictures passed by the Supreme Court on the lawyer Teesta Setalvad raise a whole gamut of questions. Setalvad had raised the issue that the delay in courts' handling of cases relating to the Gujarat riots mounted to an act of indifference and injustice. The Court in response noted a case of impropriety marked with impatience and condemned her for it.

There was a great sense of relief, even euphoria, at the Supreme Court's response. The Right felt Setalvad had no right to speak for the victims as she was not representative of them. It saw Setalvad's protest as an act of arrogation. Better-behaved activists also exuded an 'I told you so feeling' about one of their more visible contemporaries.

Today activism is a career; a style that prefers negotiation to the scream. Many activists and journalists find Setalvad 'screechy, loud, hysterical', the kind of symptoms which one associated with the ammonia-snuffing hysteric on whom the Charcots and Freuds built their discipline. When activism is a form of consultancy, one does not want to take it to the streets. Today you don't want to deal with the obsessive behaviour of someone in the perpetual act of washing his hands. It is like a tic that is forever distracting.

Yes, Teesta Setalvad is a difficult person. I remember when Professor J.S. Bandukwala talked of forgiveness, she let loose the Madame Defarge act. She screams, screams on behalf of the victims, because the scream is the only answer to the silence of Gujarat. The communication theorist Colin Cherry once described noise as unwelcome music. Setalvad's scream is doubly unwelcome as it is an act of witness.

No one could contend that a Teesta Setalvad is easy in public. She often sounds like an official mourner, reminding one of the grief we should have felt. She does not sound like a 'finishing school' product. She stuns, she appals, she rants, she raves and she repeats it all over again. Listening to her, one realizes whistle-blowing is not a symphony.

Societies like ours that are routinely conformist or banally indifferent to the violence around us should thank these obsessives. When you want to discuss the latest film, they intrude to remind you about human rights. When you talk of Ekta Kapoor, she repeats the litany of Gujarat. It is a form of bad behaviour that society needs. Setalvad has to work overtime to remind us of the ideals we have forgotten.

Let us be clear that dissent is not easy. A letter to the editor hardly causes a ripple. A procession is seen by the middle class as a mere brake on traffic. Trade unions are passé. Civil rights reports don't have a Page 3 rating.

When Setalvad or Cedric Prakash protests, lesser motives add tend to be attributed to them. There is a malicious hint that such behaviour is a search for a Magsaysay or some European human rights award. More banally, it is seen as attention-seeking.

Protest about anything around you and sense the loneliness and ostracism you feel. People will drop in to inquire about your distress as if it is a personal ailment. Then they will imply that you are not mature enough, not strategic enough. If you persist, advice becomes threat, threat becomes ostracism and ostracism graduates into other forms of social deterrence. Idealism is seen as a disease you should have lost years ago like acne or measles. Only then does one realize how tiring it is. Dissent is not one scream. It demands an epic chain of protests. The stamina for it demands that you understand the loneliness of political long-distance runners.

The Teestas, the Medha Patkars keep our society alive, vibrant. They are tuning forks telling us we have not lost our sense of music.

Protest has its quirkiness. There is the one-point person, who will talk about Bhopal in every seminar about disasters. Such figures remind one of the radicals of the earlier decades who asked 'What about class?' in every seminar regardless of whether it was about Beethoven, Gandhi or globalization. I admit they do distract and irritate in demanding their pound of flesh. But we need them; in fact we have to invent them.

There is also the jumper. For them, last week it was Narmada, this week it is farmer suicides. You realize there is a trail of fashion in disasters as in dress. Yet the jumper is a reminder that we fail to connect. Try talking about the disaster in Bhopal today. People feel you are recommending a quaint tourist destination or merely respond by asking you to read Dominique Lapierre on Bhopal.

Dissent is doubly difficult today. Every act of protest is questioned as to its authenticity. It is argued that each voice needs the right form of representation. No one asks why one citizen can't represent the other. As citizens, we share a common membership and humanity.

There is a political correctness here we must challenge. Protest too demands civility but it does not have to be the civility of the drawing room. A scream is not just a cry of pain but an act of witness. It does not have to follow the codes of the drawing room. Being correct and being true are two different registers. Setalvad's protest shows that correctness might hide an evasion of truth. One must keep the dignity of the court but a society must allow the protests of Setalvad. More, it must respect and sustain people like her as precious forms of life.

Indian Express
7 March 2008

A Fable Called Singur

Democracy can sometimes have a plurality of viewpoints but little conversation or negotiation between them.

The Singur plant has produced its quota of violence and hysteria but as this phase wraps up, what one feels is a sense of the unsaid. Today we realize that democracy has to be a shareholder and a stakeholder game. I believe it is the slippage between the two that reveals one of the deep problems of Singur as a democratic drama.

Let us treat Singur as a fable of modernization. Singur is not a history-less struggle. Behind it stands the experiences of Baliapal, Narmada, Singrauli. These struggles over industrialization and modernization have had a history which is not often found in textbooks of development.

In fact voice, memory and world view become crucial parts of any Singur-like fable. It needs the literary power and the sociological imagination of a Mahasweta Devi to understand why Singur happened. All too often industrialization which comes in the guise of an ACC cement plant or a Birla factory, has meant the rape of the countryside. The tribals and peasants who own the land find their way of life marginalized.

The standard terms 'compensation' and 'participation' don't

do adequate justice to the situation. Compensation as money or as a substitute piece of land does not provide a measure for a way of life. When you lose control of land, you lose control of a way of life.

The decisions that are crucial may be made miles away with little possibility of appeal. Participation is a strange word because what participation invites you to do is to engage in a new and different world. The frames are already different.

Time and again in the history of struggles around displacements created by dams and factories, the defeated and marginalized have been forgotten. It is almost as if any appeal to rights or alternative development falls on deaf ears.

Singur as a struggle claims as members many of the leaders and NGOs who have participated in such struggles. Many sound screechy and fundamentalist but modernization and progress are also terms which carry their own bag of intolerance. Politics carried out in these names often hide their genocidal quotient.

Now consider the other side of the story. There is India's most respected firm, the Tatas, led by a dynamic chairman, Mr Ratan Tata. For those who grew up in Jamshedpur, it was the ideal welfare society, India's Sweden in microcosm.

If you talk to the employees and their children, Jamshedpur comes close to being a living utopia. But if one asked tribals in the Dalma Hills and around the Tata mines at Jadugada, the sense of exploitation was explicit. Yet Tatas for many were the ideal employer: efficient, considerate, innovative and caring.

During the Singur debate, Ratan Tata made some outstanding arguments. He claimed that the Tata investment in Singur was not a 'hypocritical investment'. He added that Tatas were suspending activities because their employees were being intimidated. Safety was always a Tata priority.

At the very beginning of the controversy, Ratan Tata made a profounder point. In a TV interview, he said, 'There is a choice the locals and we as a society must face.' He asked whether we wanted to stay at the level of subsistence. He tacitly recognized subsistence as an option but then added that humane, responsible development might be a better prospect. Tata added that change was already visible and that as society around Singur changes and industrializes, subsistence as a way of life may no longer be available.

Let us widen this argument. Tata appears to realize that there are two modes of development, the first, sequential and the other, simultaneous. In one, a tribal or peasant society can change into an industrial society. In the second, the tribal and the peasant pursue their alternative paths parallel to industrial development. In the first, the tribal is our ancestor; in the second, our contemporary.

For many of the activists and intellectuals associated with the farmers' struggles, a sequential development is genocidal. It displaces and deculturates the population. This would be the position of a Medha Patkar or a Mahasweta Devi. Mamata Banerjee emphasizes another dimension of this by claiming that land cannot be compensated for. She wants agriculture and industry to coexist as ways of life. The above positions are not Luddite arguments but press for plurality.

The CPI(M) argument is less profound and more pragmatic. It is a party that believes in progress and modernization. For it, the Tata plant is a symbol of progress. The Nano would do for Singur what the railways, according to Marx, did for colonial India: modernize it. The rhetoric is simple, the poetics simpler. Singur is good for industrial development. The Tatas were far-sighted enough to realize that the Marxists were being more open-minded about industrialism. They read Buddhadeb Bhattacharjee right but misread Mamata Banerjee's intransigence. What made the debate murky was violence. Singur became the meeting ground for two of India's great dissenting imaginations – the anti-development movement and the Naxalite, both confronting a pair of easy bedfellows, the CPI(M) and the Tatas.

Two facts marred the controversy. The first was the violence, the terror and intimidation that CPI(M) and Naxal groups engaged in. But what made Singur a tragedy in the long run is the absence of mediators, translators, negotiators. It was almost as if each position was a recitation rather than an argument. Singur was a traumatic gathering of fundamentalisms, unyielding positions on industry, progress, modernization, development and their social, economic and cultural costs.

The West Bengal governor's intervention was welcome. It bought time and has brought to the national stage a welcome figure. Such a mediation, however, was a band-aid one because it still had to differentiate between shareholder and stakeholder loyalty. Secondly, it fails to address the question of violence and how violence, especially of Naxals and CPI(M), contravenes the rules of controversy. Thirdly, while it focuses on the land issue, it does not create the social audit of development projects many intellectuals and movements which came in support of the Singur protestors demanded. One has to realize Singur embodies more than Singur. It represents the wider debates of democracy and development. It is an open challenge to party, corporation and the movements to develop new rituals for democratic debate and its resolution.

The Economic Times
23 September 2008

The Fate of Idealism

I teach at an institute for information technology. Many of my students see news announcers as larger-than-life journalists, often telling me that is who they would like to be. They see Barkha Dutt and, to a lesser extent, Vir Sanghvi as stars almost like our cricketers, faces we see every day, who enter our lives in a meaningful way providing drama, competence and excitement. They create a framework of ideals, a sense that there is a sense of integrity to be admired and looked up to. The track records of these journalists were immaculate. Their understanding of violence seemed intense and immediate, their empathy with people seemed almost pervasive. When the Radia tapes were printed, there was a hush, a sense of astonishment. My students could not believe it. It was almost as if Sachin, Dravid or Kumble were accused of match fixing. Something dies out in you. The world shrinks and something shrinks in you.

The reader might ask: when everyone is talking of power politics, why are you worried about what students think? I think the maximum damage of the Radia tapes was its destruction of ideals and idealism. One of my friends asked why they don't come on 'We, the People' and explain themselves. There was a sense that these TV programmes went beyond voyeurism to provide a sense of understanding of power.

Let me explain. The feeling among the students is one of disappointment. It is not kangaroo court at least among the young. They only want to know what happened, whether telling the truth would continue. It is a simple, almost wordless, request. It won't go public but there will be a sense of loss like when a fairy dies. I began wondering whether the Radia tapes were a fable for our times. I keep asking why people one looks up to let us down. I always ask why heroes shrink into ordinariness, why few legends survive a lifetime.

I was thinking of the political radicals of my time. The Left produced a whole generation of idealistic people. They lived ascetic lives and quoted Marx as if he were a collection of proverbs. They believed and many of them gave up a lot of their belief. Even when communism died, in Russia, my friends would say, 'So what, the revolution is still alive in our hearts'. It might sound romantic but it was real for them. Many of them went out, left college, joined the Naxal movement and suffered. They were arrested, tortured, beaten up and many never recovered.

Yet, when one sees the same Left today, it looks fat and pompous. The revolutionaries are now UN consultants or diasporic scholars with a complete amnesia of their adolescent years. Some were even more cynical and saw ideology as an avenue for mobility. One sees many of them on committees today, utterly cynical about power and position. One wonders once again what happened to such outstanding people. Sometimes when I visit my generation in Delhi they seem a cacophony of committees. They nod as if I was an unsuccessful nomad too insignificant to be invited for a drink at the India International Centre bar.

When revolution faded and NGO politics became fashionable, one saw the same trend again. I have known many who showed courage during the Emergency look indifferently at debates later. They were too busy consolidating grants. It was a strange division of labour where funders came looking for idealism, they found these con men waiting for them. It was a commodification of idealism of an unprecedented kind.

In fact people looked for a cause as a source of investment. I know one NGO office that had a ready letter which began with 'We, the following organizations condemn…', and had blank space to be filled appropriately. The Xerox machine was a great aid to NGO politics.

This is one reason I admire the Narmada movement. It fought the dam, fought it at a great sacrifice. It lost but not before it kindled the imagination of the world. It made mistakes, tactical and political but it never failed to capture the idealism of a generation. One is grateful that a generation showed its spunk in some way and did not disappear wordlessly.

I guess there is a difference over the decades. The earlier battles had some sense of a search for justice. It was the litmus test of all the movements from Naxalbari to Chipko to the Narmada struggle. Today's battle seems to emphasize a search for individual mobility, identity and dignity. The iconic idols change from radicals to corporate figures, from social workers to executives and bankers. But the question of integrity haunts and hovers over all of them. I keep wondering why so few survive.

One of my friends who is a consulting editor to a major magazine told me about how the texture of life changes. He said, 'We lived life in a sequence. We lived poorly for years. Today's group wants it now. We worried about livelihood issues. The new gang worries about lifestyle.' Sacrifice has become a project in philanthropy.

Following this idea with others, I realized idealism is a focused goodness. It needs little advertisement. Almost everyone remembered a schoolteacher who sustained ideals despite the muck and despair about him. I make my own list of idealistic virtues. For me the first is the ability to stand alone, to stick to your point and live it out without being fundamentalist.

It needs grace under pressure. It needs the ability to live on less when everyone is striving for more. It needs the ability to pursue ideas and a way of life without getting distracted. Eventually integrity is courage, grace, honesty and generosity. So few make it.

The reasons for not making it seem clear. The ones who give up seem tired. They talk as if their ideals were a poor investment. For others co-option is so seductive. Power seems so capacious. A committee can be such a seductively friendly thing. For some, idealism ends with bachelorhood as marriage becomes the reality principle. For many, a life of threadbare asceticism appears like a punishment. They act as if they conned themselves.

Looking back, I can recollect only four figures of my generation who survived the integrity test. I feel a sadness about it and wonder why integrity and goodness seem so helpless today. Is it because there are no large movements like nationalism or Marxism shaping a generation? Is it because of the lack of dissent and eccentricity where every successful man seems like another? But this much I believe. We need to honour the idealistic and the eccentric, the dissenters and the whistle-blowers. We need to salute those who turn honesty into an art form.

New Indian Express
21 October 2012

Nuclear Energy

No Longer a Sacred Cow

An anti-nuclear activist in India is a marginal creature, frowned upon as anti-national and anti-scientific. I have been a part of the anti-nuclear movement for years, watching and debating with outstanding scientists. The nuclear energy establishment was almost sacrosanct, the technology a passport to modernity. Those who challenged it were therefore seen as dinosaurs in the age of twenty-first century technology.

But sometimes things change.

The other day I was watching TV and listening to a whole generation of scientists defend a nuclear project. These were the legends of the time, but now just looked cantankerous. And I realized that every activist must turn spectator. It is not just a switch in perspective, but it also allows one to obtain a deeper sense of drama.

The Indian nuclear establishment has been full of Brahmins, especially Tamil Brahmin hawks. Displaced in their own state, they have become custodians of the atom state. They have been the most eloquent defenders of the relation between atomic energy and the state. No bunch of Jesuits was more loyal to the cause than the Indian nuclear technocracy. The Brahmin hawks of the nuclear establishment were either dismissive or ferociously arrogant about dissent. When questioned, they bristled, often acting as if their science, their patriotism or even their integrity was being questioned.

Dissenters, even outstanding scientists like C.V. Seshadri or Amulya Reddy, were brushed aside as if they were unnecessary viruses. The latter two offered a whole dream of alternative energy, linking it to the socialist and democratic imaginations. The only other exception was Satish Dhawan, director of the Indian Institute of Science and one of the brains behind space research. He encouraged the debate on the Kaiga nuclear project in Karnataka. But scientists like Raja Ramanna, who was head of the Bhabha Atomic Research Centre, behaved like fascist bullies when confronted with questions. Ramanna would dub journalists critical of atomic energy as anti-national.

This problem was compounded by the Nehru regime. The Bhabha–Nehru friendship added a sense of grace to the nuclear project. Stories that the Pugwash movement almost began in India added nuances of sensibility to it. The Congress under Nehru and Indira Gandhi created an almost incestuous link between state and nuclear science. It embodied a combination of science as expertise and atomic energy as security, to create an establishment that operated for decades outside the political domain. For years, questioning atomic energy was taboo in India.

Things have changed. There were several reasons for this. People in their ordinary lives found scientific evidence unconvincing. Secondly, human rights movements were surprised to discover crucial issues being brushed under the carpet of security. Thirdly, the Science of Science movement had emerged, providing a critical frame to look at nuclear energy. It was a process that took time and it was aided by a few journalists and social scientists like Praful Bidwai, Ashis Nandy, Dhiren Sharma and Jit Uberoi. These individuals showed courage, scholarship, stamina to survive the assaults of the establishment providing dignity and transparency to the debate.

As scholars, they were impeccable and as dissenters, extremely durable.

But in a broader sense, it was democracy that brought nuclear energy into question. I must emphasize it was not the political party. The political party was always subservient to the social contract between science and the state. Prime Minister Manmohan Singh was ready to resign rather than weaken the will to nuclear power. The CPI(M) did open up issues about the Indo-US nuclear treaty, and expose the fairness of nuclear contracts to scrutiny. Of course it was questioning the American connection rather than the fact of nuclear energy. But it was civil society, particularly social movements in ecology, rights and science that opened up the debate on nuclear energy.

The movements at Rawatbhata, the Jaitapur plant, the struggle at Kudankulam, slowly challenged the nuclear officialdom. What also helped was the devastation of the Japanese nuclear plants after the tsunami. At that moment, the sanctimonious certainty of our scientists was irritating. It felt out of place. While the world was debating nuclear safety, our scientists were insisting they were above debate.

Another fact that added to it was TV. Television as a media has always loved scientific experts. They are summoned whenever the people need to be reassured, and TV summoned many of the best. Just as it exposed the frailties of Nixon's temperament during the US elections, TV revealed that scientists, many of them now retired, were irascible. One realized that they had little idea of democracy or debate and seemed to think they could legislate with impunity about it.

One of the most fascinating parts of the nuclear debate was the scientist's discovery that people can think and even question them on science. It was sad watching scientists from the Nehruvian era turning apoplectic about democracy. One respected their nationalism, their commitment to an old paradigm, but one realized that their words and their worlds no longer carried conviction. They appeared mothballed. They seemed to have forgotten that both science and society have changed in the last two decades.

The intellectual climate has changed and new generations are being asked about energy in terms of democracy, participation, plurality and lifestyle. Words and concepts get interesting in this context. The conflation between people and population was fascinating. The scientists preferred the word 'population'. Population was abstract; it could be reduced to number. The 'people' was a vague term. It refused representation. Like the subaltern, it wanted to speak for itself in a variety of dialects, and talk about livelihood, rights, survival. For the scientists, the people became the crowd – irrational and unscientific, like mobs in history. Every nuclear scientist behaved like a harassed Galileo without the redemption.

The nuclear debate thus becomes a fable. We always looked upon science as an act of invention and then discovered democracy has to be more inventive than science. The scientific establishment has to have the humility to realize its arrogance bordered on illiteracy. One needs a new imagination where science no longer behaves like a sacred cow and opens itself to a more playful imagination, where science can accept its mistakes and engage openly with the people without treating them as illiterates.

The citizen as scientist demands that the scientist also be a citizen. It is only such a reciprocity that can guarantee the democratization of democracy.

Firstpost
20 October 2011

The Meaning of Kudankulam

Kudankulam is a play, a drama that nullifies old historic scripts and stereotypes. Firstly, it is not just about nuclear energy. By forcing it into one domain, the broader ethics of the struggle is lost. Kudankulam is about communities struggling with the nation state. A community as a local entity seeks its own interpretation of the future. It seeks to script its own voice. Kudankulam is not just about free speech but about the right to retain one's livelihood. A livelihood is more than a job. Jobs might be substitutable in an economic calculus. A livelihood demands a sense of place; it is a way of life and a world view. Kudankulam argues around the world view of fishermen.

Cognitively, fishing is an amphibian exercise. It thinks from land to sea and sea to land. A sea is a mode of thought, not just a body of water, a dump for waste. It reminds one of what the representative of Tahiti said when arguing against French nuclear testing in the Pacific. John Doom claimed that the sea and the Tahitian islanders need to be represented and understood. Most experts, he said, think from land to sea but the Tahitians think from sea to land. Water was their way of life, their ecology for thought. The Kudankulam argument has shades of this world view. It is interesting that the protesters have carried the struggle to the sea.

Kudankulam argues that livelihood and the ecology of the beach as an intermediate commons of sea and land offers a perspective beyond mere security. The concept of security summons the blinders of the nation state. It is a summons to uniform when a diversity of thinking is essential. Yet, Kudankulam, for all its noise, is a conversation. It debates that mysterious word, insists on opening up the black box of awe that we call 'national interest'.

The duo of the words 'security' and 'national interest' has often been used to suppress debate suggesting that these two words represent the greater good. What Kudankulam playfully and sometimes desperately asks is: 'Who decides?' Is it New Delhi representing the nation state as articulated by Prime Minister Manmohan Singh and scientists or J. Jayalalithaa as the chief minister of Tamil Nadu? Where does the subaltern voice enter the theories of the nation state? Kudankulam raises wider issues about development and democracy where nuclear energy only becomes a site of a bigger debate. In that sense, Kudankulam is metaphor for a deeper tragedy, both global and Indian.

One has to eliminate three canards that often besmirch the debate. The first was raised in its most obscene form by that wily Shakuni of Indian politics, Subramanian Swamy. Swamy claimed that the protest is led by Christian priests and nuns, seeking to point out that they are cultural spoilers. Christianity is as old as AD 52 in India. It is part of the syncretism of India. Christian groups have played a major role in politics. One cannot visualize the great fishing struggle without them. Let me also emphasize that the fishing struggle was led by dissenting priests who had to fight both the church and the party.

The second is that old spoiler, 'the foreign hand'. Indira Gandhi attributed the Emergency to it and the media showers the phrase like confetti. The foreign hand is opposed to the invisible hand, the wisdom of the market. One must recollect that the Indian national movement was full of foreigners from Annie Besant and Allan Octavian Hume to Gandhi's comrades, Madeleine Slade and Charles Andrews. If the second national movement began today, New Delhi would suppress it as a 'CIA plot'.

Thirdly, S.P. Udayakumar of the Kudankulam anti-nuclear movement and other activists are tarred as NGOs. Let us admit that there are numerous NGOs that have to get their accounts in order. But we need to be open-ended here and apply judgement from case to case. The idealism and commitment of Udayakumar is not in doubt. He is a satyagrahi in the true sense of the term.

Kudankulam is about the imagination of a local democracy where fishermen are asking whether words like safety, efficiency, cost are the preserve of state experts or are they terms to be debated in an open democracy. Does the fact that the technocratic saint, A.P.J. Abdul Kalam, declared nuclear energy to be safe anoint the term or do we need to unpack the term and debate it all over again? Our experts, especially our economists and our scientists, use technical words to beat down a people. Fortunately, there are enough dissenting scientists, especially at IISc, Bengaluru, including Madhav Gadgil and the IISc director, to continue the open scientific traditions of Satish Dhawan and Amulya Reddy.

I want to make one last point. Kudankulam is not just a battle for rights. It evokes rights when the state suppresses the movement but it summons a second imagination which is surfacing quietly in India. Kudankulam evokes the idea of the commons as a complementary imagination to rights. Rights focus on the individual but the commons works the ideas and ecologies of communities, the modes of survival of marginal groups. It claims that the sea and the coast are commons.

They belong to the people and the future. The state and the corporations cannot appropriate them. It argues that the dam, the mine, the reactor enact the true tragedy of the commons in India and people have to debate this. One cannot ask for more or demand less from these great struggles.

The Asian Age
24 September 2012

The Chronicle of a Struggle Retold

If you were to ask middle-class individuals today what the most significant act of history in the India of the last twenty years is, many might say the rise of Narendra Modi. But to me, the most important historical event of the last two decades has been the battle over the Narmada dam.

Symbolically, Modi and the dam stand as contending symbols. When the struggle against the dam began, he was the chief minister of Gujarat and an advocate for raising the height of the dam. Now, he is the prime minister who sees nuclear energy as the dawn of the second modernity. And he sees civil society and non-governmental organizations as potential agents of sedition. As an act of memory, of remembrance, as a battle against forgetting, the Narmada Bachao Andolan (NBA) needs to be analysed and celebrated.

Calendars are symbolic favourites of regimes. In fact, revolutions love to create new calendars to reset the time of history. Yet, occasionally, time produces inversions, and the defeated, unable to stand the silence of defeat, produce their own mnemonic of resilience. The Narmada Bachao calendar for 2015 is one such act and deserves to be talked about.

But first the background, in brief. The Narmada traverses

three of India's western states: Gujarat, Madhya Pradesh and Maharashtra. The Indian government's plan, with World Bank assistance, has been to build a complex of dams along the river as part of the 'Narmada Project'. It has been a project that has focused on the so-called collective good, without paying attention to environmental degradation. In due course, the project has faced mounting opposition from a variety of sources, but chief among them has been the one under the leadership of Medha Patkar, the principal figure associated with the movement and the NBA. Alongside Patkar, the social activist Baba Amte provided moral leadership to the cause.

The battle over the Narmada dam reflects a journey, a pilgrimage, and a recollection of thirty years of resistance. Numbers alone cannot make sense of it because it demands a different kind of storytelling. This struggle is about a collective history of a people challenging the official history of a nation state. It is symbolic of all the struggles of the displaced, the landless, and the marginal communities. The calendar becomes an invitation to this new citizenship of memory. Because of the new enthusiasm for development, which borders on fetishism, one forgets that the Narmada dam is an act of sacrilege across one of the most sacred of India's rivers. This calendar is about both a visual protest and a peoples' history created as footnotes to be inscribed over an official history. Protest notes mingle with dates of committee decisions to create a mix that reminds you that the dam is, was and will continue to be a site of contestation.

Merely citing the dates creates a particular poignancy. On 5 January 1961, Jawaharlal Nehru laid the foundation stone for the Sardar Sarovar Project (SSP). Yet, in three decades, a wave of protest met the dam, providing a litany against the standard chorus of development. Dates can be read like a crossword puzzle just as one reads the 'five across' and 'six down' of history. Saturday, 4 April 1993: 'An Adivasi woman of a village being submerged was stripped and gang-raped by the police'. Thursday, 16 January 1992: 'A 500-strong police force with bulldozers and guns enter Manibeli on the pretext of shifting eighteen houses. Police rape two Adivasi girls.' Suddenly one senses that in the mind of authorities, rape is a correlate of displacement and development. Sunday, 7 January 1990: Sharad Pawar visits the Narmada dam site and declares that not a single inch of land would be submerged without satisfactory rehabilitation, which makes one wonder what goes into the creation of such Teflon-coated political statements. May 1995 is a month that brought about a temporary respite when the Supreme Court restrained further construction of the dam. One must pause here for a moment to ponder over the philosophical and ethical role of the Supreme Court. At one level, the highest court of the land, with its National Green Tribunal and its trusteeship of human rights, is an institution to be proud of. Its judges, as its Krishna Iyers and its Hans Raj Khannas, have been stalwarts of freedom. But as the discourse shifts to development and science, the Supreme Court, because of its dependency on official expertise, gets into a problem area. It is strange that a confederation for development calls the dam an example of sustainable development. If that is an act of contempt of the court's judgment, so be it, because it violates the life-giving assumptions of justice.

Let me get back to the calendar. On 30 May 2003, a Friday, Patkar began a fast in Nashik demanding the immediate resettlement of 3,000 families who would have been affected by raising the dam height to 100 metres. The calendar, innocuously but subtly, reminds one of the Argentine writer, Julio Cortázar's classic work, *Hopscotch*, later made into a brilliant movie. The power of *Hopscotch*, as a novel about a murder, is that it defies linearity. The book can be read even by skipping chapters or by shuffling them. In this case, the Narmada calendar is not about murder but about ecocide, which is the destruction of the natural environment, especially when deliberate. The only similarity is that the shuffling of dates creates a similar effect. It is the same litany of committees, experts and promises condoning great acts of ecological/livelihood devastation and portraying them as great acts of development.

The Narmada story continues when a series of committees and judges visited the area, listening to tales of distress and corruption. On Friday, 11 June1993, the first house in the Bhubhai Tadvi in Vadgam, Gujarat, was submerged. Have those who are for development ever pondered over the fact that a house is a fact of memory, and that when a house submerges, a way of life disappears? Committee reports like those of Asia Watch (1992) and the Morse Commission sound like helpless footnotes being swept away by a new riverine history.

In the Narmada calendar, the days of protest are even more poignant and desperate when juxtaposed with committee reports and political promises. Who can forget some of the visuals that emerged during this period – of posters, superbly sketched, demanding 'Free Narmada, Stop the Dams'.

Let me move to the July page of the calendar. What happened then only adds to the roll-call of resistance. In this month, what was striking was a photograph that showed a defiant Medha Patkar rousing people to battle. On 15 July 2000, Admiral (Retd) L. Ramdas inaugurated the satyagraha in Domkhedi, Maharashtra. On 9 July 2001, Baba Amte invited President K.R. Narayanan to visit the Narmada Valley to understand the extent of displacement and submergence. On the same date, a satyagraha was launched. All this makes one wonder whether civil disobedience, reason and satyagraha, as weapons of struggle, are effective against the dogma of development. This sounds even more poignant today as the Modi government seems intent on erasing sustainability for security and dubs civil society's every critique of development as an act of sedition. In majoritarian India, suffering can only speak the language of sedition, which is the sad aspect of a democracy.

And now to the next month. On 17 August 2001, Sadhana Amte flagged off the 'Jeevan Yatra' as hundreds of displaced children marched from Kasaravad village to meet the president of India. 19 August 2001: 'Despite the non-availability of land, the NCA [Narmada Control Authority] decides to increase the height of the dam to 100 metres.' The scale of suffering increases almost exponentially with every metre of increase in the dam's height. 31 October 1997. There is a flicker of hope as oustees celebrate three years of stoppage of the SSP's construction. But in the Narmada story, hope is ephemeral as on 31 October 2000, there was a padayatra to Delhi to protest against the Supreme Court verdict to resume dam construction.

I come to the last month, December, which is almost like a scrapbook filled with examples of repression. On 25 December 1990, the Narmada Sangharsh Yatra, from Rajghat to the SSP dam site, is stopped at the border village of Ferkuva in Gujarat. On 12 December 1992, one witnesses a physical attack on NBA activists during a debate in Jamnagar, Gujarat. On Wednesday, 13 December 2000, more than 350 people are arrested during a dharna in front of the Supreme Court, while trying to present a memorandum to the Chief Justice of India.

Thus, this calendar chronicles a festival of resistance, of protest, a people's history of what they think development should mean. As one comes to the last page of the calendar, one feels both hopelessness and a sense of what can be called the poetry of resistance. Today, the movement faces defeat as the new India confronts it with indifference, silence and erasure. Why? Because development has become the new religion of the middle class. And yet the question of the dam – as a problem for science, ethics, history and democracy – stands as an act of defiance and, no matter how weak, resurrects its perpetual questions.

This calendar is a small statement – about memory and defiance. Yet, I wanted to celebrate it because it speaks memory to silence, conscience to indifference and truth to the centrality of power. Maybe it sounds quixotic, even romantic. Yet one hopes that every secretariat and every room in the Prime Minister's Office and his revitalized planning committees will carry this calendar. It will be a small reminder of what we have done to our own people. Also, this essay is a small 'thank you' to all the groups that created this act of memory as a reminder that conscience is not dead in India.

The Hindu
6 August 2015

PART 8

Taking Policy Seriously

Law and the Public Good

In the recent debate on the Ambani gas finds, the media raised the issue whether oil was a public good or an item of private property. What was floated as a question is actually a bundle of major controversies.

Let us list them out. Chhatrapati Singh, the philosopher, argued that Indian customary law distinguishes between stock and flow. Land is stock, it is immovable. Water is flow. Those who have water on the land can use it but cannot own it. Water belongs to the community.

The second issue concerns the nature of a public good. Firstly, a public good is not a public sector good. The latter is only a devious form of privatization, where even the state as a public good has been privatized. A public good is not a commodity because the form of its being resists commoditization. It is a matrix of being where welfare encompasses profit.

A good redefines the nature of any contract by positing the fiction of the third party. This third figure is the future as a community demanding perpetual representation. A good cannot be defined purely in terms of market efficiency. It demands sustainability over time. Renewability, diversity and justice are hallmarks of a good. A good is polyarchic in that it has to cater to a variety of problem-solving situations. Oil, water, air are 'public goods' where the juxtaposition of the two words resists both privatization and commoditization.

Unfortunately, the idea of the public good operates within a limited discourse. It lives within the gridlock of public and private, an opposition which does not exhaust the world of community. The public operates within the horizon of the commons. Yet Indian law has turned the word 'commons' obsolescent. The destruction of the idea of the common begins with the idea of the eminent domain in Anglo-Saxon law where the state owns the land, rendering the tribal homeless. All it required to displace a few thousand people was some diktat centring around 'development' or 'national purpose'.

The 'commons' came back as a specialized but limited term around the Internet community. But we need to go back to the original idea of the availability of resources, the access to them and the presence of skills and knowledge to utilize them. To make land minimally public, the community has to participate in decisions about its livelihood and food. Without that, nationalization merely becomes another form of appropriation. If land is a public good, the communities living on or near it need to have a say in what it is good for. Without the idea of the commons as a creative imaginary, the idea of the public good flattens out, becoming a fragment of a limited *Homo juridicus*. The environmental debates centring around nature and land as a public good have been both subtle and sustained. One of the classic debates revolved around whether trees should have a legal standing. But to comprehend this, the language of nature and the anthropomorphic nature of rights has to change.

Homo juridicus, the legal man like *Homo economicus*, the economic man, is a fiction that creates a framework of reality. Unfortunately, *Homo juridicus* is becoming subservient to the logic of *Homo economicus*, serving to create conditions for private property and legal contract. The juridical man is not yet an ecological man who is at home in the notions of complexity and uncertainty. Its pervasive scientism has little understanding of the precautionary principles or the idea of uncertainty that pervades regulation in biotechnology or nanotechnology. But more interestingly, what law does is to aid the economization of the world.

Take violence. Once one subjects it to a cost–benefit analysis, it obtains its own forms of legitimation. The economics of dams, which obtains its calculus of displacement, claims that the displacement of an entire people is a bearable cost of a dam. When a people or a culture becomes displaceable as a cost justified by law, *Homo juridicus* shrinks into a handmaiden of economics.

Death, particularly mass death, merely becomes a form of obsolescence regarded as necessary and inevitable in the idea of development. One can then read a riot or a disaster as a real estate operation, freeing land from old and cumbersome collectivities for innovation and entrepreneurship.

In fact, it is this particular notion of economization that creates a contradiction between first- and third-generation rights. In a generational sense, the 1947 Universal Declaration was a first-generation right, the socialist framework, a second-generation right, and the laws of innovation and intellectual property a third-generation right. Third-generation rights are property rights that seek to redefine life as property by creating the idea of intellectual capital. When you patent 'life', you alter its very axiomatics. In that sense, life is secondary to property, creating an obscene contradiction at the centre of the rights discourse.

Zygmunt Bauman, the sociologist, in a classic book on waste, points out that the economization of rights went through two phases. In the earlier phase, he shows, the idea of full employment at least humanized man as a resource. The right to work was part of the dignity of man, even if the work itself was exploitative. In the second phase, men are seen as global waste. The displaced, the unemployed, the refugee, the marginal, the obsolescent, are not even recyclable, only disposable. In economizing law, we have destroyed the power and claim of human rights. Genocide then becomes an extension of cost–benefit analysis, mass death an extension counter of development. All one is arguing for is a return to the fundamentals of law. The *Homo juridicus* we have created is a narrow pre-ecolate creature.

We need to examine our law and Western law as a set of fundamentalisms about science, the individual, contract and property. Otherwise the rule of law might be just a law of rules rather than the fluid that creates and seeds a more supple democratic imagination.

Deccan Chronicle
24 August 2009

Rethinking Education

The other day someone asked me what I thought were the three most important ministries. The standard answers would mention defence, home and finance. Some would hyphenate foreign and defence. I must admit these are important ministries, if law and order and security are the most important concerns of the state. But in a futuristic sense, as a vision for creativity, the three most important ministries are health, environment and education. These constitute the framework for the future. Today I want to focus on one of them: education. The reason is that we are being out-thought by the West.

Education in India is creating a mimic man, an imitative society content with being a fourth-rate America, glad if it has Donald Duck or Spiderman on the flag. It is turning us into a third-rate global regime. We are so pleased with our success abroad, from Spelling Bees to a two-inch column in the *New York Times*, that we don't recognize that we are being bypassed intellectually.

Competition is good in its own way but what are we competing about? Our leadership is quite happy to have reached the nineteenth-century of ideas in a society they still treat as a fourteenth-century one.

Our dynamism is misdirected because our language and theories of education are flawed. Look at how we approach education. It is through the language of productivity and numbers. Our HRD minister speaks as if he is talking about buildings rather than education. He sounds more like a housing minister. Building education is a totally different game. The numbers game sets up a sense of targets but an obsession with the latter forecloses the debate on quality, plurality and content. We play the multiplication game with slogans of more IITs, more IIMs, as if we have patented a way of cloning institutions. No one takes a critical look at these institutions beyond an occasional critique of their admissions policy. The IIMs and IITs have research ratings which would embarrass a modest, even provincial, US university.

Ironically, we are still children of Macaulay. His ghost overpowers the Gandhian vision. There is an irony to it because Macaulay made us middle class English speakers. It is our comparative advantage in English that powers our economy. Our model of education is still the tutorial college. More students have grown up reading K.K. Dewett and Ruddar Datt than the management expert C.K. Prahlad and the economist Amartya Sen.

What is the tutorial college? It is the ultimate fantasy of reduction and miniaturization. A society's inversion of Macaulay's perverse dream. Macaulay's arrogance proclaimed that all of Indian civilization is not worth a shelf of Western books. The irony was that we literally reduced Western civilization to a shelf of dull functional books. We then bowdlerized it, simplifying it to its crudest elements. The kunji or 'Cog Book' was born. We reduced Western civilization from a text to a textbook and religiously updated it. These books are the publisher's ultimate fantasy and run up to forty editions. We turned education into an instrument like a lathi or a screwdriver between the kunji and the tutorial college. The ultimate dream of the tutorial college is entry into IIT, and IIT pays back by imitating its pedagogy.

If imitation is a sign of flattery, India is the ultimate mimic civilization. Mimicry may be a form of temporary survival but it cannot be a substitute for creativity in a democratic society.

More crucially, India cannot create a history where education mimicked the violence of colonialism. Imperialism could, with the aid of homogenizing development models, museumize tribe and craft, or condemn them to assimilation. We need plural structures of knowledge and education where craft is reworked as a new hand-brain hyphen, and our linguistic wealth, both written and oral, is sustained.

We do not have a theory of the modern university. Our university is still the examination machine of the nineteenth-century, meant for turning out clerks and bureaucrats. Our mandarins still emerge from that system and exemplify it. We are masters of the exam system but mediocres in research. We are poor at knowledge creation and it is in the domain of knowledge creation and knowledge strategies that India is losing out.

We need a gradient of knowledge systems from the primary school to the centres of advanced study. We have to realize it is one chain of being, like a food chain, and violence to any part damages the whole. To a theory of integrated knowledge, we have to add a theory of knowledge itself.

We have to keep the varieties of knowledge in our society dynamic. We have to realize that the democratization of knowledge demands that the tribal, the peasant, the hawker, the nomad be seen as strategists of survival, as men and women of knowledge. Our informal economy is a knowledge system of its own that we are loathe to appreciate. The democratization of knowledge has to be part of the democratization of democracy. This demands that we be a knowledge culture first before we are a knowledge economy.

The Knowledge Commission actually did not work. India has no current equivalent of the Kothari or the Radhakrishnan report. We need an overall statement which links education to new ideas in science, ecology and culture.

Our paradigms of education are nineteenth-century and our policy is only a collection of add-ons. What we need is a new 'Educational Report' which is as ethnographically rich as a colonial gazetteer, which connects to other critical reports like the Sengupta report and the Sachar report on minorities. A theory of the knowledge economy cannot be a nation state document. It has to be simultaneously civilizational and community and civil society oriented. A project that links all these into a vision of the future is a project whose time has come. Do our politicians have the will to create such a vision and implement it, or is obsolescence and illiteracy the strategy of our populism-seeking elite?

The Asian Age
16 July 2010

Public Policy in a Knowledge Society

Imagine you are a citizen racing across newspapers. As you flip the pages you run into events like the Vedanta mining case, the Kudankulam nuclear controversy, the debate on poverty and reports about climate change. Each of these can be a life-threatening event and none of them has a life-support system of knowledge which allows them to be debated in the open. The basic information comes from the state and the media which are often in the grip of powerful interest groups. It is almost as if our society has no research systems of its own. Sadly, NGOs have specific interests and function as short-term entities. There is literally no school of public policy that can function with a degree of autonomy.

Public policy in India has been a twice disadvantaged subject. It is located in management institutes which see public policy as a secondary subject of tertiary importance. For management schools public policy is a polyglot subject, a second chance for economists. No public policy school in India can claim any major study in policy management. What management schools trivialize, think tanks in the control of government marginalize further. Our Knowledge Commission is too illiterate to ask why there is no school of public policy within one of our Central universities. The university is the home of autonomous ideas and yet stays silent about generating a school of professional talent that has the skills, the vision and the methodologies to look at governance in a kaleidoscopic and transformative way.

Public policy is an attempt to create public knowledge about governance as a process. Ask yourself a simple set of questions: How is science policy made? Is it an open process or is it a construct of a coalition of scientists who are not subject to public scrutiny? Science often claims to be public knowledge but science policy seems to be captive to private processes which often operate backstage. It is almost as if science shuns democracy, often confusing illiterate claim with literate critique. Science is so intertwined with security and state that any critique of science is seen as anti-national or labelled as anti-secular. Given this cordon sanitaire around science, debate becomes a risky affair, and opposition is seen as being influenced by a foreign hand.

Consider the twists and turns of the Anna Hazare affair where its critique of parliament is seen as merely insulting parliamentarians. The philistine parliament seems to think civil society needs to be taught a lesson in table manners. The tragedy is that there is no public institution to mediate the debate and argue how a legislative process can be built by a movement. Consider a second example. Time and again *India Today* and other magazines rank a bevy of chief ministers in terms of their governance record. These carry a great deal of weight and yet few seem to ask or even question the validity of these rankings. The public does not know whether these are by legitimation efforts or a serious exercise in public policy. It is time now that we considered ourselves a knowledge society and not just a knowledge economy and build institutions that can understand the making of public policy.

The idea of public policy needs to take the idea of the public seriously. The public has to become a domain in which the future of governance, the making of laws, the dynamics of audit, the philosophy of well-being are debated. To facilitate this, we need academics who can demystify the policy process, showing how a group of experts can become captive to vested interests or prey to their own methods.

Public policy cannot be merely about the state and the corporations. It has to be a space for the understanding of the informal economy as an agency for subsistence, for creating imaginations, for demystifying official and expert knowledge. Public policy has to demystify science and show that governance has to speak a variety of dialects that can comprehend a variety of solutions.

We are today a society caught between the arrogance of expertise and the threat of populism. Third-party forces like trade unions or NGOs have not built the expertise and the systems of research to analyse policy processes. Besides paucity of institutional investment, the failure of imagination is also necessary to recognize. One can think of the budgetary process but can one add new notions of ecological audit, new ideas of well-being, a civil-society approach to the future that turns foreign policy into the civics of everydayness and demands that war and peace be studied as everyday facts? Can we create a right to information system that makes all think tank reports public? Can we syndicate columns which explain major studies of the Planning Commission? We need to desperately bring knowledge under the Essential Services Maintenance Act and stop treating it as the cultural preserve of technocratic shamans with PhDs.

Public policy has to be an intellectual commons open to access and innovation. Our current flock of institutes are servants of power and not the servants or munshis of public discourse. Democracy desperately needs not just an inclusive society but a vision of inclusive knowledge. Ask yourself why is it that no major university has a centre for science studies. I am not referring to idiot centres for science policy or centres for policy innovation but open-ended attempts to exemplify knowledge as expertise as it works for corporation, state or coalitions. There is a need for playfulness about power and what better beginning than a public policy institute serving as a commons for civil society.

The Asian Age
5 April 2012

The Craft of Survival

Protest today has to be more than a dramatic performance, an act of defiance or even a demand for justice. It has to become a reflective act, sensitive to the past and future. Protest, especially when it concerns livelihoods, has to understand the linkages between life, life world, lifestyle, life cycle and life chances. Battling for ways of life demands that one understands the full nature of politics and bureaucracy. One is penning these lines not out of some sociological pomposity but from hearing about a recent protest by handloom weavers at Gajendragad, the epicentre of weaving in Karnataka. The town is an old Chalukyan site and was once the centre of the Vijayanagara Empire. If one draws a circle with a 30 kilometre radius, almost all the handloom communities of Karnataka would be included in this space.

The battle over handlooms is a complex one. At one level, the government projects it as a sunset industry which keeps eating up subsidies. Yet, as handloom weavers and activists show, handlooms can be the fabric of the future. Handloom workers, they claim, do not need charity. All they want is dignity and a clarity about the norms and sincerity of government intentions. Unfortunately, handlooms are being destroyed by the Shakunis of governance, when policy itself has become an act of deviousness.

The recent protests in Karnataka sought to emphasize this paradox. At a concrete level, it was an objection to the Karnataka government's decision to hand over the production of school uniforms to the powerloom sector. What looks to be a simple bureaucratic act, an innocuous welfare measure, now threatens the livelihood of the handloom weavers.

Leading the protest against the government's decision are institutions like Dastkar and non-governmental organizations like Desi. I also met Prasanna who helps a rural women's handloom co-operative called Charaka.

It was a few days after the protest. Prasanna was relaxing, reading Dashiell Hammett's *The Thin Man*. A one-time student of IIT Kanpur, he is a graduate of the National School of Drama. For six years he was involved with Samudaya, a political theatre group he helped found in Karnataka in the mid-1970s. As he talked about theatre, one saw weaving and theatre as the two strands of his life.

He talked of his mentor, Fritz Berkowitz, who was director of Max Müller Bhavan. 'Fritz was a great influence. I remember he enacted Bertolt Brecht's *The Caucasian Chalk Circle* with tamasha actresses without knowing a word of the local language. Yet, it was a hit.' He added sadly, 'Politics destroyed Fritz. He was an East German, who did wonders for theatre in India, and was looking forward to changes in his country. When the Berlin Wall fell, he went back to his country. But the West Germans surrounded him with a cloud of suspicion and virtually obliterated him. Berkowitz died broken-hearted.' Fritz Berkowitz's story almost seemed a prelude to the handloom drama.

Prasanna explained that handlooms in India suffered from a classificatory politics. At the root of it is the Handlooms (Reservation of Articles for Production) Act, 1985, which prohibits around twenty-three items of clothing from powerloom manufacture. These items include lungis and dhotis, among others. It was this Act that the Central government sought to surreptitiously undermine. (The roots of this Act go back to the colonial era, to 1905, when the British had tried to protect the handloom weavers from the cotton mills).

Prasanna pointed out that all it took was a few backstage alterations to undermine a life-giving framework. His comments pointed to a folklore distinction between pathways and 'conways' in policy. A pathway is policy with ethical content. It is life-giving, while a conway undermines livelihoods by destroying the ethical content of a legislation.

Conways in the handloom industry operate through classificatory tricks which blur differences between powerloom and handloom while pretending to be protective. One way is to change the definition of what constitutes handloom. A handloom remains a handloom as long as three processes including the pulley and the shuttle are hand-operated. All one has to do is meddle with this list and declare that any process where at least one of these processes is hand-operated is a handloom industry. With this Trojan Horse of a manoeuvre, even powerlooms become handlooms. Several consequences then follow.

First, powerlooms can claim contracts and subsidies previously limited to handlooms. The allocation of school uniforms to powerlooms under the 'Vidya Vikas' scheme is one example. But such an insidious politics goes beyond classification.

Our governments perceive the handloom industry to be pitiable and define it as a sunset industry unable to deliver large orders. Prasanna explained how the government policy kills handlooms through malign neglect: 'The trick is to place large orders with the handloom industry at the last minute. For example, orders are given as late as December or January to supply 35,000 uniforms in fifteen days. This ultimatum creates the escape clause for the powerlooms to take over. As a result, the powerloom invades the handloom industry. This creates a whole set of spurious handloom products which alter the identity and integrity of the industry.' Prasanna added that many powerloom owners add 'defects' to their products to make them appear authentic handloom.

The members of the All-India Federation of Handloom Organizations objected to the government's strategy. They went on a padayatra, a 254-km walk across three districts in north Karnataka. Prasanna explained that these organizations were not trade unions, but were buffer groups between weaver and market, merely seeking to enforce the Handlooms (Reservation of Articles for Production) Act. He added that with the 'Vidya Vikas' scheme for uniforms, the handloom weaver was at least assured of 250 days of work a year.

While reflecting on his protest, he made three other observations. He pointed out that apart from Dastkar and his organization, there were very few NGOs in the handloom industry. Oddly, it was a result of the problem inadvertently created by Mahatma Gandhi.

Gandhi carved out khadi from handlooms. 'As a result', Prasanna explained, 'the Gandhians perpetuated a Brahminic distinction between khadi and handlooms, which left the handloom weaver neither here nor there.' In both khadi and handloom, while the weaving is common, the spinning is separate. Yet, khadi is handled by the Khadi and Village Industries Commission, and handlooms by the textile industry. Khadi has a halo, a touch of the sacred, even the pious, while handloom is seen as everyday.

However, Prasanna added, one learns from Gandhi. Gandhi was shrewd enough to realize that it was the middle-class consumer who could protect handlooms. The middle class has the monetary surplus to sustain it. Prasanna was shrewd enough to realize that the weaver was too vulnerable to be at the forefront of the struggle.

He made a second point. He claimed that the handloom industry was not a sunset industry. Its members were not an endangered community. India has more handlooms than the rest of the world. Handloom, he said, is the fabric of the future. All the weavers needed is clarity, dignity and honesty and the consumer to recognize his responsibility in sustaining this world. The consumer has a right to authentic fabric, but he has to be a trustee of such a world. Sustainability is eventually about trusteeship.

He added that handlooms have their own goddess of weaving in Bhimamma. There are *mathas* in Gadag district, where the priests are married women. The offering to the goddess is always a cotton sari and the prasad received is a bundle of yarn.

One hopes that the goddess will be benign and turn handlooms into the fabric of the future.

The Hindu

20 October 2014

A Reductive Reading of Santhara

Courts, as institutions of interpretation, intrigue citizens, and often awe them. The dignity of their ritual, the imprimatur of the official, the detailed litany of textual interpretations before a judgment is arrived at, are often impressive. Judgments often have the moral gravitas and the narrative power of a novel. Yet, a badly done judgment, even if it appeals to the secular mind, lacks conviction. One felt that about the judgments around nuclear energy; equally, one senses these limits in the judicial reading of Santhara.

I refer to the Rajasthan High Court's verdict against Santhara, the centuries-old Jain practice of voluntarily starving to death. On 10 August 2015, the court's Jaipur bench ruled on a public interest litigation (PIL) filed in May 2006 against the practice. It held that Santhara would henceforth be treated as 'suicide' and accordingly made punishable under the relevant sections of the Indian Penal Code: Section 309 (attempt to commit suicide) and Section 306 (abetment of suicide). It made its absolute rejection of the Jain philosophy underlying the practice unequivocally clear. An appeal challenging the order has now been filed in the Supreme Court.

The word Santhara means a way of life and encompasses a

way of dying as well. In Jainism, the body is seen as a temporary residence for the soul which is reborn. One must remember that a word can embrace a multiplicity of worlds and meanings. As a result, translation is one of the most difficult of acts and demands a delicacy of understanding the nature of language. Finding linguistic equivalences is welcome when we seek unity but we need a unity that can sustain the multiple senses of difference.

The critical word here is suicide. One is almost tempted to be facetious. I remember that moment of epiphany in the film *Sholay* (1975) when actor Dharmendra, as the character Veeru, standing up on a water tower, tells Basanti's mother (Hema Malini plays Basanti) that he will commit suicide. An old man in the crowd asks, 'What is suicide?' The answer is profoundly wise. It says when Englishmen kill themselves, the act is called 'suicide'.

I was reminded of this scene as I read the high court judgment on suicide in the case of Nikhil Soni vs Union of India. There was an element of irony to it. The scene in *Sholay* is straight from the classic 1969 film, *The Secret of Santa Vittoria* and yet, in the very moment of mimicry, the movie emphasizes the essential drama of difference. The court judgment, while playing with the cultures of difference, eventually succumbs to a reductive act which is hermeneutically disappointing.

There are critical nuggets of information in the initial part of the judgment. It claims that the Jain attitude to the body is different from the Christian attitude to the body and that Santhara is a ritual farewell to the body; it is an act of non-violence performed as an ethical response to the nature of old age. The court hints that for the petitioners, Santhara cannot be suicide. The etymology and the cosmologies are radically different.

The English word 'suicide' means a deliberate killing of oneself. *The Oxford Etymology Dictionary* cites W.E.H. Lecky, in *A History of European Morals* (1869) where he writes of the stigma attached to suicide. He claims that even in 1749, 'a suicide named Portier was dragged through the streets of Paris with his face to the ground, hung from the gallows by his feet and then thrown into the sewers'. Right from the time of its etymological origins up to the French Revolution, suicide was a mark of stigma of criminality and pollution.

Santhara encapsulates a different narrative. It is a ritual act of purification, done in consultation with a guru, and follows the most detailed of procedures. It cannot be an impulsive act or an egoistic one. It bears the imprimatur of theology and the approval of society.

As India became colonized, many Indian rituals came under the critical Anglo-Saxon lens, and translation and interpretation became a critical part of legal exegesis. Is Santhara a giving up of life or of taking death in one's stride? For a culture that believes in rebirth, is Santhara philosophically or ethically suicide? The frame widens as the drama becomes sociological because then a differentiation between sati, suicide and Santhara will have to be made.

As one looks at the colonial interpretation, the critique of sati, where a woman sacrifices herself for her husband, brought condemnation. Santhara was read in a different way by the Jain community. It was seen as an act of non-violence tuned to the deepest norms of Jain culture. Scholars of Jainism indicate that it adds a dignity to dying, where death is in continuum with rebirth.

Santhara is a multivalent term which cannot be reduced to the dreariness of suicide as closure or a termination. The English term, suicide, cannot comprehend Santhara in terms of being a ritual exit and a rite of passage to a different world. Santhara, performed correctly, is ritual of non-violence. In fact, I would feel that the court's judgment misinterprets both the word and world.

Doubts about Santhara exist. Many have pointed to the coercive, even aspirational aspects of the practice. Since the families of the individual who wishes to observe Santhara get respect and status, they tend to advertise the act. Witnesses claim that families whose reputations are at stake often refuse to let a person change her or his mind. Here, Santhara is often presented as sati. Its voluntariness is forgotten.

The court had to differentiate between Santhara and euthanasia, sati and suicide. It has made brief and superficial attempts to do so. And in its abortive act of comparative sociology, the ritual dignity of Santhara has been lost. In the confusion between the literal and the symbolic, between a construction of fact and celebration, the meaning is lost.

The court – after its abbreviated move through philosophy, ethics, language and law – has reduced the whole to one narrow issue, namely the test of essentiality. It asks whether Santhara is an essential tenet of Jainism and declares that it is not. Such a litmus test might work in a chemistry lab but it fails to work in the contextuality and polysemy of culture. The court could have been strict about preventing aberrations or deviations from Santhara but to reduce the ritual act to suicide amounts to a display of illiteracy. The court seems more worried about the debates on euthanasia and sati than about looking at Santhara as a cultural practice with its own repertoire of meanings.

The court claims that some rights can encompass their opposite. The freedom of speech does not compel one to speak. Yet, a right to life does not include the right to die under certain circumstances. Ethics and religion lose out to the wooden definitions of Santhara, which, as a ritual, has qualities of a controlled experiment. The court has held that extinguishing life, sacrificing it or effacing it cannot be considered as acts of dignity. A right to die cannot be a part of the right to life. In constructing such a judgment, the court's ethno-centricity becomes obvious. It enshrines a piece of Christian theology and Anglo-Saxon law in its response to the logic of Santhara. Eventually, the judgment creates a monologic sense of life and a standardized sense of death and dying. In fact, it has missed an opportunity to look at life and death and the ethics of dignity and dying in a creative way. In instituting such a standardized theology, the fact of justice becomes secondary. This has wider implications because words in one culture cannot lose their meaning in translation. Language and justice die or are diminished when language is deprived of its right to a multiplicity of meaning.

The aridity of a reductive secularism often comes out in displays of language. In fact, translation becomes a test of justice. This is the epic tragedy of the Santhara judgment. It conveys the fact that nation states that can inflict and adjudicate death, often feel lost in the complexity of religious phenomena that they mechanically legislate over.

The Hindu
24 August 2015

Part 9

The Gossip of Knowledge

The Fate of Gandhian Scholarship

I am not a nationalist. You can call me a lazy patriot. I am Indian because of my celebration of food, dance, Bollywood. I love Indian ideas but I also love the way Indians internalize and compost ideas from the external world. I think there is an Indian approach to diversity, rights and democracy. I am proud of our originals, men like Jagadish Bose, Srinivasa Ramanujan and Gandhi. I celebrate the way we have exported them but I am concerned about the fate of Gandhian thought and scholarship in India. My concern stems from the fact that Gandhi represented not just a mode of thought and code of conduct but a way of life.

The original Gandhi had a double circus of disciples. One group was very Indian and included such stalwarts as J.C. Kumarappa, N.K. Bose, Ghaffar Khan, Indulal Yagnik, Maganlal Gandhi, Vinoba Bhave. The other group had foreigners like Madeleine Slade, Henry Polak and C.F. Andrews. There was a balance and reciprocity between the creativity of the two groups. But both groups were marginalized within the first decade of Independence. Both felt the official power of the Nehruvian dream marginalizing Gandhi into an extra-curricular ethics. Even the ones who were creative were exemplars rather than paradigms. One loved them for their integrity and the way they lived but few bought their theories about life, livelihood and technology. With marginalization, came a certain museumization. Worse, Gandhian thought became politically correct or a pursuit of memorabilia. The final seal came when one of the greatest of the Gandhians, Vinoba Bhave, personally approved of the Emergency. The fact that Jayaprakash Narayan led the opposition did little to add to the Gandhian imagination.

And yet abroad, Gandhi became intellectual yeast to a whole generation of thinkers and activists. Danielo Dolci in Italy, Petra Kelly in Germany, Steve Biko fighting apartheid in South Africa, Martin Luther King leading the civil rights march in the USA, each added a different dialect to the Gandhian imagination. What was true of activism was also true of scholarship. The finest interpretations of Gandhi as a philosopher of technology came from abroad. Think of E.F. Schumacher's *Small is Beautiful*, Gene Sharp on pacifist techniques, Erik Erikson's *Gandhi's Truth*, Martin Green's *The Origins of Nonviolence: Tolstoy and Gandhi in their Historical Settings*, Ivan Illich's ideas on energy, equity and locality, Paul Ricouer's essays on Gandhi or even that little fragment of half-lost letters we call the Buber–Gandhi debate. In comparison with this the best of Indian work is still diasporic. One thinks of Bhikhu Parekh's *Colonialism, Tradition and Reform* or Ved Mehta's irreverent journalistic foray, *Mahatma Gandhi and his Apostles*. In my opinion only two Indian texts can match this array of scholarship: Ashis Nandy's *The Intimate Enemy* and N.K. Bose's critically affectionate study, *My Days with Gandhi*. Most Indian scholarship was banal or regurgitative. Read the pages of, say, the journal, *Gandhi Marg*, to understand that favourite Indian technique, the hyphen, the use of the word which yokes Gandhi to ethics, international relations, globalization, violence, technology, feminism, ecology, reducing the Gandhian imagination to a banal catechism. In fact, these works remind me of a Ford car which Jamnalal Bajaj gave to the Ashram. It broke down soon and was pulled by two oxen. Gandhi happily christened it his Ox-ford. It is these 'oxfords' of Indian scholarship that have alienated a generation of new thinkers. Gandhi excites more in Attenborough's film than in reams of *Gandhi Marg*.

But if the imitative Gandhian faded away, Gandhi as a heuristic, as an inspiration lived in the efflorescence of social movements of the last three decades. The Chipko movement 'led' by Sunderlal Bahuguna and Chandi Prasad Bhatt, the Narmada struggle, many of the human rights and anti-development struggles made Gandhi the text, pretext and context of their efforts. Interesting insights into Gandhi and Gandhian struggle emerged from the writings of Vandana Shiva, Claude Alvares and Dharampal in this context. But this was a generation that reinvented Gandhi for itself. Probably one of the most creative ideas thrown up by this group was to reinvent and rewrite *Hind Swaraj* to suit the metaphors and imagination of a new generation. But in a strict sense these ecological, feminist, human rights, anti-development critiques of science imaginations were not Gandhian. In fact the official Gandhian imagination got a new lease of life from this political activism.

The danger was we tended to officialize Gandhi as an imagination. Every police station has a picture of Gandhi looking benignly on the dramas enacted there. Departments of Gandhian studies became too theological in a non-playful sense. Worse, the spate of communal violence, the death of factories like the cotton textile mills of Ahmedabad and Bombay evoked no Gandhian imagination. The recent riots in Gujarat signalled a further disempowerment of Gandhian ethics. Gandhian scholarship was a cut and paste. The role of Gandhi in simultaneously challenging the eccentric, the dissenting, and the marginal imaginations was not a task Gandhian scholarship was ready to undertake. Probably the one exception was the lone, hopelessly misunderstood voice of the historian Dharampal. However, his partial hijacking by the Right drove this scholarship into a cul-de-sac. Whatever the drawbacks he remains a scholar who is inventively Gandhian in a civilizational sense.

Globalization has caught activism and scholarship in India flat-footed. Gandhi was once asked what he thought of Western civilization. He replied, 'It would be a good idea.' We need that same confidence to answer new questions. What is the crisis of agriculture today? Can the charkha and the chip meet in dialogue beyond digitalization? Can Gandhian movements create new methodologies of technology assessment? What is the new site for the satyagrahi – food, water, disasters or new forms of obsolescence creating new slums of marginality?

A few days ago I read a report that Narayan Desai was about to enact Gandhi as a Katha, as a folk narrative. Desai himself was worried that it may be boring to the audience and was therefore seeking to personalize it. But Gandhi needs more than these acts of storytelling by outstanding Gandhians like Desai. We need not just acts of memory but new sources of reinvention. Gandhi as ideas has to be applied to new questions, the problem of IT, the issue of biotechnology, or the way we think of our cities or our villages. Only then can we create the possibility of new futures, new theories of emergence. An exciting domain awaits Gandhian scholarship awash in mothballs.

From the author's files
Publication details unavailable

The Failure of Political Theory

I want to begin with a basic proposition. I believe that political theory in India has lost its moorings and become utterly flat-flooted vis-à-vis globalization. Psychologists refer to babies repeating sounds and words in meaningless babble as echolalia. Echolalia, the meaningless and continued repetition of old concepts, marks the domains of Marx and Gandhi. When socialists and Marxists took over the World Social Forum in India they reduced globalization to cliché. Even those who transcend cliché and struggle with the everydayness of vulnerability find that the concepts they use are highly overworked. The tiredest of them, in a Stakhanovite sense, is the idea of human rights.

The notion of human rights works for torture but subsides into silence before collective atrocities. A right, as a central word, becomes a pincushion of spokes to security, health, employment, energy, livelihood and property. Even given the suppleness and the transformative power of language, the concept of rights seems tired, overworked, overused and often sounds misplaced and redundant. The domain of rights cries out for an amniotic set of concepts around it, to sustain it and render it less vulnerable. One needs a new set of life-giving terms, and language of politics, after struggling unsuccessfully with security, sustainability and marginality. Worse, the rhetoric of rights seems hardly persuasive. PUCL (Peoples' Union of Civil Liberties) reports are written as in-house documents for the believers. Reports of Dalit atrocity subside without a murmur despite awesome evidence. Such defeat beckons to the power of hegemony where dominant groups appropriate dissenting concepts and put them to drawing room use. If the World Bank and G-7 and feminist and ecological groups use the same word, do they mean the same thing or does the meaning in use change with contexts which are different at different thresholds of power? Does a stakeholder's dictionary need a larger thesaurus of terms to be inventive? It is here that political theory has failed.

It has created an activism that separated political economy from image and succumbed to political correctness. By removing the historical smell and political taste of concepts, it created an antiseptic blandness that could not grasp the globalization of evil. By being oblivious of innovations in other fields, it failed to comprehend concepts like obsolescence, emergence, triage, entropy or complexity. By submitting language and society to reductive concepts it failed to understand paradox and irony.

Look at the concepts we have today – sustainability, development, rights, community, secularism, rationality. As a list it lacks diversity, as concepts they lack vitality, and as metaphors, they evoke, at best, weak drama. It is not just that we have secularized our concepts, we have desemanticized them paring down varieties of meaning to one or two connotations. Political concepts have become unmusical, incapable of chiming with a variety of meanings.

To grasp this one must look at one of the major expressions of political theory today: *The Human Development Report*. It embodies several major contributions to the understanding of welfare and well-being. There is sensitivity to gender, to ecology and it evidences a movement from GNP to GDP. The UNDP reports also operationalize Amartya Sen's idea of entitlements. But there is a basic split between what the German philosopher Habermas has dubbed the distinction between system and lifeworld. System reflects disembodied abstract connection. Lifeworld is a lived world, where concept is a dwelling, something lived through, embodied and implicated in time. The UNDP report's idea of well-being is systemic rather than lifeworld. It is a world of indicators, not a dwelling which calls for autobiography and storytelling. The report realizes the dichotomy and uses boxes to frame anecdotes and stories of success. Suddenly the UNDP report appears both like a corporate annual report and in phases like a Christmas card spreading the good news of development. Yet there is little doubt about basic concepts like development, democracy or expertise. The sheer facticity of the trends hides the mothballing of crucial concepts. What does sustainability really mean and how does one link it with vulnerability and justice? How does one address these issues as part of the reigning paradigm and not as back stage, not as externalities. How does a report like this respond to the writings of an Ivan Illich or an E.F. Schumacher who argues for a Buddhist economics of scale and harmony?

What one witnesses with development, one observes also with the idea of security which has graduated from a fixation with the nation state to a proliferating conceptual regime of food security, health security, etc. Does the politics of security understand well-being or vulnerability? What does security mean in a subsistence economy? A nomadic tribe or a subsistence farmer in a drought area needs a different idea of security. Can our current concepts, many of which cover macro domains, understand the micro-sociology and the micro-ecology of coping? Do we understand what coping with drought means as agency, knowledge, as a form of expertise living at minimal conditions? The Italian philosopher Giorgio Agamben recoined the idea of *Homo sacer* or bare life. He was of course referring to the concentration camps. But bare life has broken out of the concentration camps and marks large areas of Africa and Southeast Asia. When are we going to produce a political theory that grasps these facts rather than create cheerful UNDP reports?

One major problem with political theory was ideology. Ideology as a corset of values provided consistency and perspective. But where it had to be protean, it remained Procrustean, immune to new knowledge, dead to new facts. Political theory today has to balance between the security of ideology and the temptation to be scientifically value neutral. One needs openness and a sense of dreaming about the future. Oddly, few political scientists wish to do that. They pretend to be overwhelmed with battles fought a few decades ago and indulge in stories that stem from that era.

Oddly the best political theory in India is emerging from management scholars. Read C.K. Prahlad's *The Fortune at the Bottom of the Pyramid* or Sumantra Ghoshal's *Managing Across Borders* or Raghuram Rajan's *Saving Capitalism from the Capitalists.* They deal with management and governance in the global world. The books are matter of fact, constructive with a deep sense of the possibilities of power. They combine critique and constructive ideas, something which political theory seems incapable of. The ghosts of Hayek, or Lenin, or Mao, or Lohia, haunt the work of political theorists, reducing politics to an act of irrelevance. The real challenge before us is to invent a new lifeworld for politics to understand riots, disasters, drought, waste, genocide and hospitality.

From the author's files
Publication details unavailable

Cinema vs Social Science

Today Bollywood has arrived. It is the stuff of cultural studies courses at Stanford and London. It is a brand name. Most people recognize that this process has been a strange journey from contempt to adulation. Yet the rite of passage from object to subject is still incomplete. Hindi cinema is treated as a serious subject of study. Yet people still have to recognize it as a framework of analysis, a critical view of society that challenges and matches critical social theory in India. To put it simply it is time we recognize Aparna Sen, Govind Nihalani, Shyam Benegal, Karan Johar as social theorists at par with Ashis Nandy, T.N. Madan or Rajni Kothari in their understanding of the critical changes and tensions India is undergoing.

Consider three simple facts. When the social sciences were wrapped around the Procrustean nature of class, Hindi cinema played creatively with the opposition of town and country. Town and country were not only opposites but their connections were creatively expressed through the idea of the double, of two brothers long lost reconnecting towards the end of the narrative. The social sciences were more wedded to the state, more committed to socialization, while the Hindi film realized the tension between formal law and familial affection, once again captured through the idea of the double. In fact no cultural agency has employed the psychologist Otto Rank's trope of the double as profoundly as Hindi cinema.

Even today it is Bollywood that has successfully sketched the scenario of current society caught between the creativity of crime and the material success of the diaspora. The diaspora is the Indian version of the American dream, a statement of possibilities, which would be mere fantasy in India. One should emphasize that the freedom is not just material but sexual, personal and occupational. An ironic scene in *Kaante* captures it. A group of diasporic Indians gather together to mourn that while the Colombians have their cartels, the Italians their mafia, the Indians sadly have no crime rings of their own. The diaspora is not a distant country. It is not exile but home. As a film star in *Stardust* once claimed, 'When I am homesick I go to Birmingham'.

Hindi cinema was more forward-looking at a time when the social sciences were desperately trying to be 'progressive'. Bollywood through Subhash Ghai, Manmohan Desai captured the creativity of the urban sphere, the dynamo called the city when the social sciences were wallowing in village studies. It was an odd irony that failed to recognize that while Bollywood was considered crude and illiterate, it had in fact a greater cultural confidence, a cosmopolitanism that eluded the social sciences still trying to write the obituary of colonialism. Strangely even in post-colonial times, when the social sciences are trying indigenous categories, carrying local concepts like sacks, Bollywood is experimenting confidently with hybridities.

The question one inevitably asks: Why did the social sciences lose out as a frame to cinema? There were, I believe, three reasons. Firstly, there was a search for scientism in the social sciences despite the penumbra of subjectivity. Ironically the social sciences, in being objective, missed crucial social facts. Hindi films, in enacting fantasies, captured fragments of reality.

One thinks of language. The vocabulary of the social sciences was heavy and imported, while film celebrated ordinary language. In fact the social scientists who wrote simply and elegantly are the ones who survived. One thinks of M.N. Srinivas's *The Remembered Village*, the closest equivalent to Malgudi in social science or Ashis Nandy's *The Intimate Enemy*. The latter in fact can easily be converted into a film script. Thirdly, Indian social scientists were surprised by violence and naive about evil. Bollywood might stereotype the corrupt politician and the mother-in-law or landlord as bully but it always struggled to describe evil.

The real tragedy of the social sciences is strangely witnessed in their approaches to film. Reading the pieces with their excruciating attempts to deconstruct, to season their articles with the concepts of French social theorists like Gilles Deleuze or Christian Metz one wonders whether the writers ever enjoy cinema. Reading the monographs one can't even guess whether the author is watching *Raja* or *Roja*. Contrast this to the interviews with Mrinal Sen or the recent interviews with Javed Akhtar. The latter are elegant, modest and insightful. Of course, one must admit that not all film-makers can write on film. Ray on Ray was quite pedestrian, distant from the genius he displayed in his films. A Pauline Kael or a T.G. Vaidyanathan captured what Ray did better.

Basically what film succeeded in doing was capturing both individual agency and social structure better. The social sciences in India are still struggling with the dialectic of individual and society. However, the new reflexivity in the social sciences, and their encounters both with film and literature as comparative genres might trigger something new. A generation of social movements has already given them a new vitality. What remains to be seen is whether the social sciences can capture the new dimensions of evil, and the ironies of globalization. One hopes one does not need a Rohinton Mistry to capture the Emergency or Bollywood to create a new understanding of Partition as in *Panjara*. One dreams of a new social science, classical in perspective, supple in language. One hopes it emerges as something more mythic, more filmy, where the reader celebrates analytical insights as enthusiastically as a film spectator reciting dialogues in sheer ecstasy.

From the author's files
Publication details unavailable

The Coming Decline of the Social Sciences

The other day a friend of mine complained about the lack of gossip about the social sciences. He claimed that when an institution like the Planning Commission is scrapped there should have been protest, debate, mourning because planning gave the social sciences a focus. Planning demanded a new interdisciplinarity among the social sciences, and yet almost no one felt the need to debate its departure.

He said in an odd way the sources of social science were dying out. He cited three in particular. Civil society which provided the setting for many debates on energy, citizenship, democracy is silent. Even the debates on NREGA were more an act of accounting and budgeting than about citizenship and entitlements. Despite the best efforts of Jean Drèze and Aruna Roy, the NREGA debate, so symbolic of an approach to poverty, faded away. The problem exists but there is no problematic within which to discuss it fruitfully.

My friend claimed that TV had created a jingoistic, speeded-up social science. The social scientist lacks the telegraphic language of TV and, worse, lacks the space for debate. Apart from an occasional economist, TV hardly invites the social scientist.

Even if it does, it pays court to the diasporic expert vacationing in India, pouring out his pound of nostalgia. Even newspapers have little that is academic, theoretical or philosophical. Print debates policy, confusing policy as as everyday plumbing with the symphony of social science. Newspapers are content with catchphrases, instead of detailed analysis of how the craft of policy is conducted. They talk the language of smart cities when there should be full-blooded debates on migration, slums, the informal society, violence and unemployment. The bowdlerized social sciences relying on a few UN reports, substitute for critique. Indicators are the new substitute for ideology, and social scientists are content with rankings, ordering societies in terms of development, education, gender and violence. It is as if someone memorizes a Wimbledon seeding list as substitute for understanding the creativity of tennis.

The third threat is hardly talked about. It is the new effervescence in literature where Indian writing and publishing houses have made literary writing a profound source of power. Literature from U.R. Ananthamurthy to Aatish Taseer is more reflective, wiser about society than social scientists caught in the tired categories of modernity and postmodernism. Social science has become a tutorial college, a parroting of ideas while the freshness of thought comes from the novelist. What is true of the novel is also true of journalism, especially journalists writing on the city, who have produced an excitement about migration and urbanization one cannot sense in the social sciences. To understand the city, it is easier to read Jeremy Seabrook than plough through a tired academic sociology of the city.

The fourth threat comes from politics and politicians especially from the Right. The Left guards its ideological purity like virginity, afraid of debate but the Right has begun acquiring a custodianship over key terms like secularism, patriotism, well-being, development, nation state. Modi, Amit Shah or Bhagwat seem to provide the new correctness while social scientists watch helplessly. This reappropriation of terms and their transformations into an official vocabulary sends no warning bells into the academe. Even the few social scientists, especially historians, who object are of the Congress variety. Their academic sensibilities are as tired and faded as the political acumen of the Congress party.

Another trend which is less noticed but critical is the fact that social problems like travelling facts tend to migrate into new domains. Questions of technology, ecology are deep-seated questions about society and not just management and cost–benefit analysis. The recent debates between the Madhav Gadgil and Kasturirangan reports on the Western Ghats are debates about how society constructs nature and about how people's knowledge about livelihood has to be part of the democratic imagination. In a different way, the power, presence and durability of an agricultural scientist like M.S. Swaminathan lay in his ability to hybridize the natural and social sciences in his work on bio-villages. Sustainability in that sense is a concept that has to include new notions of times, nature, memory, invention, justice to be viable. Viewed this way, Gadgil and Swaminathan are as important to the social sciences as traditional scholars like Ashis Nandy and Andre Beteille.

One must emphasize the importance of the market as a frame for the social sciences. Marketing surveys have become as important as electoral surveys and in fact contain a whole range of information on choice, desire, the body, sexuality and urbanization which an ordinary academic sociologist is starved of. In fact, experts on the market like Santosh Desai and Rama Bijapurkar become philosophers of choice and desire and need to be taken seriously in this context.

I realized that one is facing a situation where social science is being emptied of social questions. It is as if society has seceded from the social sciences and is content with folklore concepts from management, new spiritual gurus and spin-offs from cybernetics and ecology. Caught between mediocrity and irrelevance, the social scientist realizes that he cannot be a mere establishment annexe, that he has to dig deep into his roots and explore the fresh sources for eccentricity, dissent, creativity and insight. He has to realize that many of the concepts he employed, like nation state and secularism, sound faded and he needs to build a new philosophical dictionary of concepts, case studies and even methodologies. Firstly, there has to be a return to storytelling, to ethnography, to case studies with thick description that the anthropologist Clifford Geertz talked about. The diversity of lived experiences has to come alive. Sociology, which once prided itself on village studies and participant observations, has few classics like M.N. Srinivas's *The Remembered Village* to offer. A density of case studies gives the scholar something to fall back upon, to renew his sense of the classic, to feel at one with great examples of the field. They are the equivalent of the epics for our discipline. To write such books, the anthropologist has to become a listener, allow for the varieties of time to enter his study. Quick visits and speed are no longer necessary. Sociology, like a Russian novel, must allow for the complexity of time and diversity of characters who add nuance to narratives. The social scientist has to become a munshi, a recorder of the memory of cultures which stay in the oral imagination or disappear in the course of history. Not only does memory become crucial but varieties of time beyond history and development have to be captured. The body and the sensorium have to return to the society, and a social science that celebrates the senses return to the senses. Colour, taste, smell, touch add a different dimension to sensuality, suffering and memory. A disembodied sociology becomes an abstract sociology. Sociology needs a range of micro-sociologies to retain its sense of diversity and agency which often get lost in the impersonality of structures.

Stuck in history, our social sciences need a sense of the future. Dream, imagination, design should now become a part of sociology as we link the question about the fate of the city with the future of democracy, the fate of technology. The social sciences under the Modi era have become a dismal science preoccupied with the narrow idea of India. Sociology can create new imaginaries beyond the current dreams of the RSS and the VHP. It must imagine new worlds, new bodies so that we escape the dismal science of development being created by the regimes of today.

The social sciences must recognize that religion as metaphor, belief, theology is creating world views and encounter them in playful debates especially around new technologies, new visions of the city, and new heuristics for ethics. Reality is not just out there, it needs to be constructed.

The idea of India in its current forms as technocratic, managerial, behaviouristic is dull. As an imagination, India is being out-thought and outfought while we hide behind derivative ideas from China and the USA. Unless the social sciences create a new imaginary for India, our middle class will become dull, aspiring to a mediocre competence, playing a secretariat to a more creative world.

Finally, as an aspirational society, we have little place for the displaced, the defeated, the obsolescent. As an ethics of memory, the social sciences must create a deeper sense of the possibilities of diversity, whether it is a dying language, craft, a species or a way of life. By constructing new realities, new possibilities, new critiques, our social sciences may reinvent a new playfulness which can rescue India from the grimness of its current future. Diversity is not just about difference but about how the logic of difference creates new grammars of democracy in India. India needs to surprise itself if it needs to be a creative force in the future.

The Tribune
9 February 2015

The Future of Our Cities

In 1913 Rabindranath Tagore published a paper in the *Indian Review* advocating a forest university for India. He claimed that the dialogue of India and the West could not begin till there was a dialogue of the universities. Tagore argued that the Western knowledge was embodied, in fact miniaturized in its university and that the Western university was also a microcosm of the city. But the mind of India, he claimed, always went back to the sage in the forest, for Indian civilization has its roots in the forest. Whether it was Tagore valorizing the forest or Gandhi rooting for the village, the Indian imagination has always orphaned the mindset of the city.

Even film, which was far more sensitive than social science, posited a dualism of town and country, played out as the dialectic between two lost brothers. In fact Hindi cinema makes the first breakthrough in the films of Amitabh Bachchan. Bachchan, unlike earlier heroes, had few rural roots. His was not a particularistic identity location in a nostalgic village. As icon and archetype, he portrayed a repertoire of urban coolie, cop, smuggler, bootlegger, paanwala with equal élan. Bachchan and Bollywood embodied the imagination of the city at a time when our political rhetoric was glorifying the village as a value. Eventually Manmohan Desai and Salim Javed were worth a dozen sociology congresses. For them the slum was the microcosm of the city and the problematic of the future.

In a fundamental sense Indians are obsessed with the past. They don't plan collectively for the future of the polis. They can think of sustainable agriculture. They cannot dream of sustainable cities. Agriculture renews the past legacy of soil and seed but a city has to keep inventing its future. Futures thinking, which the anthropologist Margaret Mead once suggested as a substitute for history classes, is desperately needed in India. We can think as a civilization with a thousand-year-old past, but we cannot project beyond a five-year plan or a business cycle. A city is a projection into future time but as the Indian imagination cannot hobble beyond five years, our cities have no future. Forget Corbusier, he was a bit of post-Partition absent-mindedness. Erase Patrick Geddes. Who has read his futuristic vision of the Indian cities?

In fact if one group has understood and celebrated the city it is our criminals. They have been our urbanologists, understanding not only real estate but the city as a knowledge system, as a desiring machine, as a cartography of violence. In fact, the only time the government displays an understanding of city is elliptically through its riot reports. The Srikrishna Commission Report on Bombay riots is read short-sightedly as an indictment of the Shiv Sena when it is an examination of the future of the city.

Democracy cannot survive if our cities do not survive. And our cities cannot survive if we cannot project into the future. Try a simple set of exercises. What would be the speed of car ten years from now on the main road of Delhi? Where do you think you are going to park your cars? Do we need flyovers or are we installing them – as Anil Laul once put it – because we want roller-coaster rides without going to Disneyland? How much of Mumbai or Delhi will be slum? Ten per cent, 50 per cent, 60 per cent? Who will run our city services? DDA? Ambani? Dawood Enterprises? Arthur Anderson? Stop any ten people on the street and ask them about the future of the city, they will have little to say. That is one Antakshari which will leave them woefully silent.

I think it is time the democratic imagination engages with the city and visualizes it in metaphors beyond idiot socialism, museumized Gandhianism or short-sighted Swadeshism. We have to stop thinking about the city as a den of vice or a collage of slums. Vice anyway is a form of marketable knowledge. Forget the old ideas of the city as a built-up environment. A city is a set of flows – flows of people, garbage, epidemics, information, terror, jobs, services, sex, water, transport. Civics then is the futuristic knowledge system for handling them. There will eventually be more democracy in a people-controlled systems theory than in a hundred World Bank documents. The tragedy is that Chipko and Narmada are in the wrong place. They should be battling in the cities. They would win at home rather than surviving in the syllabi of American campuses. Once the future of the cities becomes our politics, our trade unions, our political parties will stop being moribund. Mamata Banerjee senses this in a primordial way, which is why, the CPI(M) which has lost its sense of Calcutta, is doomed. If Gandhi were to come back today he would talk of the future of the cities. He would summon Kumarappa to survey slums to find out the time budgets spent on obtaining water or firewood. He would wonder with Patrick Geddes why Hindu cosmology has no place for human excreta. It has a poetics of cow dung but human shit is 'matter out of place'. His *Hind Swaraj* would be an interrogation of the cities. He would wonder why all our promising parties – Congress, CPI(M), BJP – began as urban inventions but then became apologetic about it. If India is to survive, we have to recognize our future as an urban civilization. Just remember Singapore is the size of a few Mylapores or R.K. Purams and it is out-thinking India. India is low on urban IQ. Where else would the capital of a country let a river die the way we have let the Yamuna die? Eutrophication is a lovely complex word for the death of a lake. What is the word for the death of cities? Lewis Mumford talked of Kakatopias. But we need something user-friendly. It is a pity that our ecological movements began in the forests. What we need is a vision of ecolate cities.

One city that had a sense of an urban and urbane vision was Calcutta. Calcutta despite being a colonial creation was the Indian city, a symbolic creation in the work and texts of Geoffrey Moorhouse, Gunter Grass, Dominique Lapierre, Satyajit Ray, Aparna Sen, the Naxalites and Mother Teresa. But Calcutta despite its cultural experiments was seen as a failed city, a site for sociobiology rather than an urban invention. Calcutta like Bengal was history rather than a continuous set of innovations. In a way Calcutta was like Nirad C. Chaudhuri.

Chaudhuri was an archetypal urban Bengali. He knew the maps of London by heart but first visited it only in his fifties. On the first day he was imperiously telling a London cabbie about which street to take. The cabbie in desperation told him, 'The street you are referring to was bombed during the war.' Chaudhuri was chasing a London which was already nostalgia. Calcutta too smacks of nostalgia. What one needed was a city with a future unburdened by a past.

Each Indian city today is offering itself as a metaphor for the future. Mumbai is the criminal future, Bengaluru the science city of the future, Hyderabad the cyber city. Each is an attempt to drag India in a different direction. But none has the durability of a rooted metaphor. Even Delhi offers itself as an urban imagination to be reread.

Sheila Dikshit as CM claims it is also a cybercity. But it is the Supreme Court legislations that might make it the problem city of the future. Delhi has the highest number of cars, more than the cities of Mumbai, Kolkata and Chennai. It consumes the highest amount of plastic and has created a nightmare of plastic waste strangling its sewers. In ten years the average speed of vehicles in Delhi will be 5 km an hour. Delhi is the most polluted city and the way it tackles pollution as a part of middle-class angst might be another model of the future. But no vision today captures the festival called the city. No city has a sense of its future drama. Our cities have lost their metaphorical power.

What India needs is a politics of the future with each city as a particular idiom for it. To do that we have to enter and invent a sequence of futures. The tired visions of garden cities, science cities, cyber cities, film cities won't do. By 2020, over 50 per cent of India will be urban. In our capital city, 43 per cent of our arrests are of homeless people arrested under the Vagrancy Act. Mumbai is virtually 60 per cent slum, and by 2020 Delhi will achieve a similar nirvana. As one senior DDA official put it, the choice will be between organized and unorganized slums.

Our thesaurus of cities is woefully incomplete. All India has to offer to the world glossary of cities is Bhopal. It is a failure of a society desperately in need of a Thomas Pynchon, an Andre Bely, a Walter Benjamin, a Lewis Mumford and a Joseph Heller. We are tongue-tied about the future because we are autistic about our cities. It is time to liberate our cities. What India needs is not a constitutional revision but a new manifesto for the city. The future is now.

From the author's files
Publication details unavailable

Part 10

Constructing Science

A Celebration of Difference

Science and Democracy in India

India today stands as one of the world's great clearing houses and compost heaps for ideas. It keeps alive some defeated ideas without consigning them to the museum and reinvents others through translation. This is best seen in the attitude to its three greatest imports: democracy, the English language, and modern Western science. For Indians these were not alien ideas to be handled with suspicion but celebrations, which they had to internalize and reinvent for themselves. Indeed, the confidence and openness with which India greeted and scrutinized science constitute one of the most fascinating chapters in the encounter between science and democracy. Unfortunately, the dialogues between science and democracy in India fell captive to the dullness of official science policy documents, which presented what was a festival as a set of thermometer readings. To grasp the drama of science as a cultural force I want to trace the development of Western science in India.

The institutionalization of Western science in India began with the establishment of the Great Surveys – the geological, the botanical, and the trigonometric – under the inspired impetus of the Asiatic Society of Bengal, which was inaugurated in 1784. This was followed by the establishment of universities in the presidency towns of Bombay, Calcutta, and Madras in 1854. As colonial creations these universities were not primarily concerned with improving the local culture and economy – such issues only became alive with the Swadeshi movement of 1905. In its aftermath Swadeshism produced the great tradition of debate on science and democracy, and it is on the continuities and discontinuities of this debate through the nationalist (1905 to 1947) and post-colonial (1947 onwards) periods that I shall focus.

As early as 1900, Mahendralal Sarkar, the Calcutta homeopath who established the Indian Association for the Cultivation of Science (the first science laboratory outside colonial control), claimed that it was a scientific India that would humanize the aggressive West. In 1912, the nationalist Har Dayal advocated a celebration of science and argued that the sacred cities of Benares and Puri have had their day: 'What is there in Benares but fat bulls and fat priests, what is there in Puri but cholera?' Har Dayal opined that Pasteur and Koch had done more for human welfare than all the nuns and monks, and believed that scientists would become the rishis of this era. But if hospitality to science was a hallmark of nationalism, there was also criticism.

What the Indian national movement did was to turn India into a theatre, or a series of thought experiments, where modern Western science would converse with other forms of knowledge. One can list a whole series of experiments in this context: the theosophist attempt to look at childhood and nature in a new way; the movement to allow equality and reciprocity between various systems of medicine, including allopathy and homeopathy; the endeavour to incorporate local systems of technology and architecture in cities such as New Delhi; and the effort to evade the use of synthetic fertilizers while modernizing Indian agriculture. This search for a plurality of knowledge, this attempt to evade the monoculture of modern Western science, constitutes modern India's greatest contribution to democracy and democratic theory.

The debates about science in the nationalist era were debates about the politics of knowledge. They were not restricted merely to the uses of knowledge, of what one might call the applied science of good and evil; there was a concern about the grammar of violence implicit in science and about how science appeared at that costume ball called Indian civilization. It was a pursuit of cognitive justice, that is, of the right of different forms of knowledge to coexist without being marginalized by official, state-sponsored forms of knowledge. What was sought was a living ecology of knowledge, as expressed, for instance, in the debate between indigenous and new medical systems in 1923. Indian nationalism took the principles of liberty, equality and fraternity and applied them to the world of knowledge.

It is within this tapestry of debates that Gandhi must be located. To portray Gandhi as anti-science or Luddite, as the technocrats of the Nehruvian era did, is superficial. His ashrams, a combination of hermitage and laboratory, were locations for scientific experiments, especially on waste management. His theory of khadi was a theory of technological innovation, of communities fighting obsolescence. For Gandhi, the modern innovator was a cultural idiot who did not understand the death of communities forced into obsolescence by technology. A democracy that talked about nylon and synthetic dyes without considering the decline of craft communities was amnesiac. Gandhi's *Hind Swaraj* (1908), a document to rank with *Rights of Man* or *The Communist Manifesto,* was one of the great critiques of science and technology. It was an attempt to create a technological and scientific conscience for modern India, which had no sense of the roots and tensions within modern Western science.

The symphony of pluralistic debates on science declined with Independence in 1947. Nehruvian India was committed to a civics of development, industrialization and, eventually, the national security state. This was a world where science policy and the scientific perspective were as important as the national flag. The Indian pursuit of scientific knowledge became bureaucratic, and science became a positivism without a sense of its genealogies of doubts. India proudly claimed that it had the third largest pool of scientific personnel in the world. The policy was technology transfer, embodied in the innovation chain with its three great links – invention, innovation and diffusion. Invention was the turf of the expert scientist. Innovation was the world of technology, which was locally adaptable. Diffusion was democracy incarnate. So the question of science in India shifted from cognitive justice to popularization, to science as consumption. P.M.S. Blackett, the British Nobel laureate who was a consultant to Nehru, had to warn him that science was no magic wand that could bring prosperity. Nehru's idea of expert science resident in the complex of laboratories called the Council for Scientific and Industrial Research (CSIR) and the Atomic Energy Commission was very different from Gandhi's vision of every man a scientist, every village a science academy.

Indian science became a bureaucratized grid of laboratories fumbling over import substitution. Homi Bhabha, the father of the Indian atomic energy programme, observed that the creation of these mammoth bureaucracies had emptied the universities of outstanding talent who could have served as seeds of creative dissent. The 1950s and '60s saw a celebration of official science where, to cite Nehru, 'dams and laboratories became temples of modern India'. The tragedy was that both were disasters. The CSIR laboratories basically produced second-grade research that was often a crude mimicking of some foreign paper, and the dams became a source of controversy, by creating a new generation of unrehabilitated refugees.

As bureaucratized science, knowledge lost its sense of play and was removed from the democratic domain. Critique was taboo, and even leading universities were ignorant or innocent of the works of Koyre, Kuhn or Bachelard. As a result, when science returned to the democratic domain, the great debates on science and technology came not from the scientific academies but from political movements. It was local struggles against trawlers, missiles, pollution, monoculture and industrial accidents that recreated the dialogue between science and democracy. These became the dissenting academies of Indian democracy.

Four events retrieved the debates on science, bringing it back to the democratic imagination. The first was the struggle against the Emergency, the imposition of dictatorship in 1977. The violence of the demolitions and the forced sterilizations were partly justified in the name of science, and this servile science began to be questioned by human rights groups. The second was Chipko, a movement against forest contractors in the Himalayas, which challenged forestry as a science, catalysing interest in ecology. The third was the Bhopal Gas disaster of 1984, and the fourth was the fight against the Narmada dam. They emphasized that the resolution of scientific controversies could not be left to experts, but was part of citizenship, especially when experts were tongue-tied or illiterate on technical issues. Only a few scientists, like C.V. Seshadri and A.K.N. Reddy, realized that these debates were grist for the innovative science mill and that Third World problems demanded front-line science, not third-rate research in the guise of renewal.

In a strange sense, Indian science had become allergic to democracy. What should have been a partnership of openness had become a dull civics, where 'the scientific method' as an ideology became a Victorian corset constricting creativity. What was worse was that scientific institutions themselves functioned undemocratically. Even a spate of suicides by scientists and the consequent parliamentary inquiries produced little change.

One remained content to cite the names of Nobel laureates like S. Chandrasekhar and Har Gobind Khorana or wax nostalgic about great physicists like C.V. Raman and Meghnad Saha. The fact that the latter two were the greatest critics of science in India was lost on the commentators.

The 1990s inaugurated the era of globalization and liberalization in which the social impetus for science in India has come from disparate backgrounds. There is the middle-class dream of a second-rate America of supermarkets and science cities, which clashes with the tribal scream against large dams (India has been producing more refugees from development projects than from war). Yet the very same dams that tribals were objecting to were part of Dalit demands which argued that modernity and science were ways out of suffering. Two ways of life, two modes of pain, are at right angles, catching each other on the question of science. The conversation between science and democracy cannot involve only questions of electronics, software and risk theory. The everydayness of politics demands that we find more inventive ways of solving scientific controversies. Whether it is shifting cultivation, large dams, reproductive health or the quarrel between urban environmentalists and trade unions, science can only survive if it faces these openly and courageously. In doing so, it will add not merely to the annals of creativity but to the imagination of democracy.

Science, Vol. 280, No. 5360
3 April 1998

History and the Costume Ball Called Science

A colleague of mine told me a story about the physicist P.C. Mahalanobis which I hope is true. It was in the good old days. A young Mahalanobis was travelling with his father, a good Brahmo, in a train. In those days like now, a child was entitled to a half ticket if he was under twelve. The train was chugging happily away to – let us say – Burdwan, carrying the junior with his half ticket. Suddenly the elder Mahalanobis jumped up and pulled the chain and insisted the son get down immediately. The flabbergasted passengers wondered what had happened. The father said this young man had turned thirteen ten minutes ago and was now falsely travelling with a half ticket. Luckily good sense prevailed when a passenger suggested the father pay the other half and the journey proceeded uneventfully.

This story about Mahalanobis, like innumerable others, shows that the story of science in India was not about method. It was about ethics, integrity, about how to construct a public space for knowledge. In fact, if one looks at the early autobiographies, there is very little on method. Science is seen as an ethical possibility. In fact, the autobiography itself becomes a method.

When one reads the memoirs of P.C. Ray, *Life and Experiences of a Bengali Chemist*, or M. Visvesvaraya, *Memoirs of My Working Life*, their life itself appears a statement on method. They are both exemplars and paradigms. Ray tries to construct science as a rishihood for the future. Sadly it is all front stage without back stage. There is nothing really private about Ray in these pages, except the admission that he had a difficult stomach. Reading Visvesvaraya is worse. You would think the whole man was constructed like a science experiment. In fact, Visvesvaraya's biography is the only personal memoir I know which ends with policy recommendations! The life of the man appears as a cut-out, like those dolls children play with. This view is heightened by the photographs of him. If you move from his immaculately polished shoes to sharply creased trousers, you realize that this is an Englishman till you reach the turban. Then you discover that he did not know how to tie it but hired a retired schoolmaster to do it for him.

One gradually realizes that science as a role didn't exist in India and had to be constructed. There were models from the UK and Germany but our science was a local quilt patch. Gandhi's *My Experiments with Truth* belongs to this genre. Gandhi, in fact, thought of himself as a scientist and unlike other scientists experimented on himself. His experiments were everyday – with his body, with food, with tools, with sexuality. But they were utterly candid and thoroughly transparent in the way a scientific experiment demanded.

The costume ball called Indian science was a variegated world. There was the mathematician Ramanujan who saw his solutions in a dream when Goddess Nammakkal rolled out her tongue. There was J.C. Bose who felt the Hindu hypotheses could be built into the mechanistic world of Western science without being dubbed communalist.

In fact, there was a confidence in the debates about science that one finds missing today. Mahendralal Sarkar who established the Indian Association for the Cultivation of Science stated as one of its goals – the task of rescuing science from the violence of Christian civilization. If the Indian national movement under Gandhi wanted to rescue the British from modernity, its scientists wanted to create an alternative science captive neither to dead tradition nor to mechanistic modernity. In addition, we had a whole bunch of creatively eccentric Englishmen from Albert Howard and Patrick Geddes to J.B.S. Haldane who wanted science to say things it could not say and dream in English and England. Howard is the 'father' of organic farming, Geddes the exponent of an agricultural thermodynamic view of the world and Haldane, one of the most original minds on science and diversity. All of them sought to create in India a 'post-Germanic science' based on biology. Geddes, in fact, felt that Tagore's Santiniketan needed a scientific extension to its aesthetic self. Tagore's conception of a forest university positing a different relation between science and nature is superior to current statements on diversity which are mechanical.

The Indian national movement was thus a celebration of a carnival of science. Its role players ranged from Raman and Bose to Haldane, Fisher, Chatterton and Saha. To Gandhi's 'Industrialize and Perish', Visvesvaraya had 'Industrialize or Perish'. The quality of debate was playful and literate.

It is with independence that a playful science becomes a dismal science. Science rather being one episteme in the repertoire of a nation becomes the solution. Nehru's poetics that the 'future belongs to those who make friends with science' is actually a prosaic epitaph to these grand debates.

Science became a statist effort which lacked both the ebullience of Bollywood and the aesthetics of cricket. Raman's arrogant statement that the laboratories of CSIR were tombs for the burial of scientific instruments became true prematurely.

Independent India did not see science as a culture to be celebrated. It was only a formula to be prescribed or a drug to be swallowed, not a dance to be performed or a philosophy to be lived out. There were exceptions – D.D. Kosambi living his double life of mathematics and history, Raman threatening a second Nobel Prize for his work on flowers, Haldane growling in Bhubaneswar about peacocks' tails. But eventually our policymakers saw science in instrumentalist terms, as a 'magic wand to create prosperity'. But science was never celebrated as a culture in itself.

Two examples illustrate it. One was the attempt to introduce the idea of scientific temper. During the debates that followed one discovered that none of the scientists who signed the declaration knew what it was. For some it was like a vaccine which one could inject to stop communalism. Even as late as the Babri Masjid demolition, one of our atomic scientists claimed that if we had the scientific temper the masjid would not have fallen.

The second example is the failure of our universities. The greatest innovation of modern Indian pedagogy is the tutorial college. The head of Brilliant Tutorials (BT) should have headed UGC rather than the Yashpals and other forgotten souls. BT was subversive and it subverted Macaulay, the 'father' of Indian education. Macaulay claimed that not all the civilization of the Orient was worth a shelf of Western books. The tutorial college was eminently pragmatic about it. It accepted the statement and reduced Western civilization to a mere shelf of books. Think of it. BT and Sultan Chand and Sons have done more for science than all the TIFRs (Tata Institute of Fundamental Research) and IITs put together. More importantly half of the IITs wouldn't have got in without BT, Agarwal or some equivalent enterprise.

The bureaucratization of science was a self-inflicted wound. The loss of play was devastating, so was the loss of confidence. Indian science legitimized itself by talking of expatriate scientists like Chandrasekhar or Khorana or some stray reference to India in *Nature*.

The sense of loss comes out better if we compare cricket and science. Few Indians have internalized the mythology or the method of science. But everyone from the barbershop to NIIT (National Institute of Information Technology) is involved in the discourse of cricket. Cricket is a part of our culture but science is not, except as a commodified set of goods. Where in India does one celebrate gene or fractal or crystal or the vision of Vavilov or the sheer beauty of entropy? Civil society should have a greater role in science. I am not suggesting that the cricket board run our science but science should have had more C.K. Nayudus and Mushtaq Alis. One wishes cricket writers like Neville Cardus and Jack Fingleton or S.K. Gurunathan had joined the celebration called science. They understood mythology and method, technique and rules in a way our Bhatnagars, Menons and Swaminathans did not. One can quarrel about cricket as public knowledge but our science was rarely ready to go public about dams, nuclear energy or gene technology. Science today is a creature of the market or the state. It is seen as the IT of Azim Premji and Chandrababu Naidu without asking how cyberspace and justice can combine. There is no sense of fun, no invitation to ask why the sky is blue, or why a top spins or why a boomerang is the way it is. We need to go back to our inventive history and bring science back into the celebrations called culture, to create a science as inventive as our music or our dance, a science that celebrates 50,000 varieties of rice and ensures that they do not become a monoculture of five to ten species. Next time you read the Mashelkars, the M.G.K. Menons or the Murli Manohar Joshis, remember the need for the Mushtaq Alis of science.

India Today, The Millenium Series, Vol. 2,
'Come Home to History', 2000

The Human Genome Project

Beyond Mapped Territory

The Human Genome Project (HGP) is presented as a spectacular scientific event, a fait accompli, a marvellous unravelling of nature rivalling Vesalian anatomy. The social scientist is then summoned along with the theologian to comment like bit actors on issues of inequality, diversity or the sanctity of nature. Such a sequence of events assumes that the social enters after the science is complete. But if we view science as a process, questions of ethics, equality, humanity, attitudes to nature enter at every phase.

The genome project was an act of 'big science'. Biologists were often envious of what the atomic bomb and elementary particles had done for physics. When Robert Sinsheimer of the University of California, Santa Cruz, put forward the idea of an institute for sequencing the genome, his dreams were twofold. One was the dream of big money for biology and Santa Cruz. The other was that physics's reductionism would yield similar dividends in biology.

Sinsheimer's project failed, but the Department of Energy (DoE) entered the act. DoE, a splinter of the Atomic Energy

Programme, had a long-standing interest in radiation, in genetics and mutation. The first big funding for HGP came from DoE. At that time itself, there were fears of Nazi eugenics and warnings about what insurance companies might do with the data. Many molecular biologists were suspicious of DoE forcing biology into the ways of big physics. One scientist who was sceptical of this trend was James Watson.

Watson is the HGP's icon. A Nobel laureate, with an adolescent competitiveness celebrated in the best-selling *The Double Helix*, Watson also realized that it was the interests of medicine that would drive the HGP. In the 1950s, antibiotics was the order of the day and genetics was a backwater. But as the old diseases were being wiped out, genetics and its relation to disease was making a comeback. Tom Wilkie in *Perilous Knowledge* notes that while Watson was sensitive to the genome project being part of the global commons, he brought to it his own unique style. He was also aware of the unequal division of labour in science, in the work and funding of the project.

The question soon arose around who owns the genome project and who owned which stretches of it, as Britain and the US began callously patenting sequences. While the political debate continued, patenting proceeded faster. Present in this disease-driven theory of nature was a theory of language. Genomes were read as linguistic sequences, and diseases were read as spelling mistakes. But when disease is seen as a spelling error, the notion of suffering changes. Nature is no longer seen as wise, but as making mistakes. It is a view of nature as a bumbler that is implicit in the HGP.

The question of privatization soon led to the question of privacy. The genome project required huge screening of select populations. But in such programmes, certain genetic traits were read as weaknesses or as stigmata. Screening then becomes a political problem which raises issues of psychological pressure and of privacy. Insurance companies wanted access to records.

The ethical question is whether the insurance agencies could access the genetic information in the medical records. Such access might stigmatize persons and make them even more vulnerable as insurance agencies often switch off coverage to certain areas of health care. What is coercive at the level of the personal becomes even more lethal at the level of the social. If the Emergency were imposed again, would a technocratic Jagmohan be more devastating with free access to genetic records of particularly vulnerable populations?

The life cycle of the genome project from conception to execution to completion hinges on issues of vulnerability, dignity and equality. How do we know when a life has to be terminated? The other question is what kind of knowledge does the genome project provide? Do we now argue as many scientists do that 'we are now what we know'. Francois Jacob once remarked, 'The only logic that biologists really master is one-dimensional. As soon as a second dimension is added, not to mention a third one, biologists are no longer at ease.' It is this lack of ease that underlies the HGP.

The genome is a map or, at best, a catalogue. Pushed beyond limits, it might magnify or overstate the power of biology at the societal level. We may reduce IQ to genetics. Also eugenics as an idea lurks in the recesses of every society. The danger is not of tyrants and technocrats alone but, as the records of the US and the UK show, of the susceptibility of democracy to theories of eugenics as well. Democracies have seen such theories as technical fixes to vexing questions of inequality and disease and violence.

Ivan Illich once observed that the concept of life was the last stronghold of Western humanism. If it is banalized, appropriated or equated with a reductionist theory of the gene, a whole system of philosophy and ethics collapses to obscenity or emptiness. The genome project is one of the great maps. But like all maps it is the less-than territory. It does not exhaust nature or the question of life which is bigger than its three billion base sequences.

The task before us is simple. While celebrating science, we need to realize that applying a map is an art form of its own for which science may not be the best answer. We need an ombudsman for the genome projects. We need civil rights teams to institutionalize referendum and recall of projects. We must institutionalize small groups to monitor screening of populations just as we monitor the fate of an election project. We need not be Luddites but we must rework it into the democratic imagination, as a challenge, as a morality play, as a philosophical marker to the ethical questions that originate at the beginning of the twenty-first century.

Outlook

10 July 2000

Fun with Science

The Indian Science Congress is a venerable ritual. It is an annual Kumbh of Indian scientists, a professional circus, though the Kumbh is better organized and has deeper memories. Today the Indian Science Congress sounds dated; but it has had its moments of romance.

The Science Congress itself is an outgrowth of the Asiatic Society of Bengal, one of the greatest scientific institutions ever created. It, in turn, also seeded the Great Surveys and the Science Congress, becoming that invertebrate anomaly, a group of amateurs that helped create a specialized, professionalized science.

Today the Science Congress is reported more for the prime minister's speech. What follows then is a series of editorials and op-ed pieces on how science must be made relevant, harnessed to productivity and made a vehicle of the nation state. There is a puritanical tone to the whole exercise. Science is seen as a special form of life requiring a scientific temper. And scientific temper is almost seen as an injection, an immunization programme against communalism and other various forms of superstition. Third, science is unilaterally seen as a productive system requiring investment. In all these readings, science is both a milch cow and a sacred cow, to be given special treatment.

Indian science and scientists rarely talk of the critical studies of the science movement, of the relation of science to modern violence. The works of Robert Lifton on the Nazi doctors (*The Nazi Doctors: Medical Killing and the Psychology of Genocide*) and Zygmunt Bauman on the Holocaust (*Modernity and the Holocaust*), the various studies of science projects or even the work of dissenting scientists like C.V. Seshadri and A.K.N. Reddy are happily ignored. The relation of science to democracy is never discussed and all we have are the predictable studies on investments in science and growth or hosannas to the new God, i.e., the innovation chain. Such an ignorance forces one to invoke John Ziman's statement that 'a scientist knows as much about science as a fish about hydrodynamics'. Ziman did not deny that the fish can swim. He only maintained that as the waters get murky, the fish get sluggish without sensing the cause of their sluggishness.

This particular illiteracy then produces a standard litany of science. This has several variants.

The first is the race for the Olympic medals of science and a complaint that India has not produced Nobel laureates in high numbers. As a country, we feel excluded from modernity without a place in the Who's Who of science.

The second variant is a kind of nationalist jingoism, particularly voiced by the diaspora, where science inflates their ego through nuclear power. Science is a way of commanding respect from other nations. It becomes a substitute for a collective machismo.

The third is what I call a bully's approach to science which attacks any mild superstition through a witch-hunt. It might be a Ganpati drinking milk or some dream of perpetual energy but no attempt is made to look at the new superstitions, for example, the relation between science and war.

The fourth looks at innovation chains, considers science as the root of invention, ignoring the everyday inventors who are outside science. I think it is a pity that scientists are unable to speak for themselves in more authentic voices. Few articles talk of science as a way of life, as an idiom of playfulness. One wonders why science is not seen as ecstasy or enjoyment, as musicians see music. Why do scientists refer to investment, recognition, evaluation but rarely ever to joy, sharing, conversation, the sense of surprise and the celebration of the unexpected? Few newspapers carry any clear-cut essay on science, or stories of a Bose, a Patrick Geddes, a Bhaskar Saha, a Krishnan or a Raman. My complaint is not that science is not a creative activity but that the joy of science, the music of numbers, the mystery of nature rarely comes out in the reflections of our scientists. The biographies of our scientists sound like good conduct certificates or hagiographies. One never gets to understand a scientific life or the evolving nature of scientific activity from them.

I think it is time we return joy and laughter back to science, go back to the openness of questioning. Let us teach our children to enjoy science, obtain a sense of mystery, feel a sense of puzzlement rather than feeling puritanical about science or spouting official clerical lines.

We need to be honest about science and tell our children that our scientists knew little about Bhopal when it happened, or that while we celebrated the Green Revolution, we did not understand the full ecological and sociological consequences it could spawn. In doing so, we create a more self-reflective science. We also realize that the mistake is as central to science as serendipity and surprise. Once we do that, we become less jingoistic about the nature of our heroes. We will not complain that few streets have been named after S.N. Bose but realize the brilliance and playfulness of the man, and celebrate the Boson that has been named after him.

What I want is a return to the cheerful science, not a dismal science that one sees in Science Congresses and editorials. I hope we create a knowledge society that is at ease with itself, which is tolerant, that is open to doubt and ambiguity. Once we acknowledge this, we create a science which is a way of life rather than a statement of method. My appeal is to celebrate science not for war or development but as a festival of enjoyment, a ritual for knowing and a celebration of adventure, wherever it is. I think this is crucial because in relaxing about science, a pompous India might learn to relax and enjoy itself. The question to me is not whether India can compete with China but whether India can enjoy life and science more than the Chinese.

The Asian Age
24 January 2013

Part 11

Popular Media

Misunderstanding *Chak De India*

One of the tragedies of popular culture in recent times is the appropriation of *Chak De India* by cricket. Ironically, it is Shah Rukh's presence in rooting for our T20 team that adds to it. In a way the message of *Chak De India* has been lost in the media. The movie was a window for a different way of looking, an alternative interpretation of sport which must be recovered and captured.

Chak De India is a story with clean lines: a little plot about a coach who wants to train the women's hockey team to a world championship victory. It offers revelations to an India celebrating the unity of nation, cricket and Bollywood. It is Bollywood warning India not to see Bollywood too simplistically, and aptly the message is from Shah Rukh Khan.

He plays a hockey star who goofs a final and is dubbed a traitor and driven to the wilderness. That fact that he is Muslim emerges in the moment of defeat showing that our unity is skin-deep. When we win, we are all citizens; when we lose, we are all secessionists who are suspect. Shah Rukh's efforts to set up a training camp also become a semiotic space which allows one to see the travails of hockey as a script of the problems of national unity. Semiotically, hockey is seen as a part of the public sector. A sport with a great tradition, it is still sustained as a failing government enterprise. Yet as a national enterprise, it guarantees minimal representation to all regions. Like Noah's Ark, you have a pair of players from almost every region: Jharkhand, Punjab, Andhra, Maharashtra. Hockey was a sport created by small ethnicities, including the style of the railways, the local varieties of Punjab, the resurgence of adivasi commitment to the sport. Hockey evoked the idea of a nation where unity was a coalescence of ethnic styles. Today, it is lost not just as a sport but as a metaphor. At one time the hockey stick was an instrument of defence in every household. You yelled thief and every householder ran out with a hockey stick.

What the movie *warns* is that cricket has become a homogenizing language flattened by corporate sponsorship and media standardization. What it does is to challenge cricket as a dominant discourse homogenizing the nation, state, market and culture. What it counterposes is an alternative unity based on hockey, gender and small-town loyalties which represents a different grammar. Here a set of ethnic mohalla styles confronts the homogeneity of the large city, women as gender confront masculinity as hockey confronts cricket. It is the story of four forms of marginality or minoritization seeking a different language for themselves.

The romance of hockey is the only romance in the movie. Apart from Shah Rukh as Kabir Khan, the rest of the team are bit players but of a cameo kind. The team is composed of a variety of feminisms, a collection of dialects of struggle resisting any master language. There is the woman driven to show her fiancé that she has professional dreams too, that her hockey is as vital as his cricket. And when the women's team challenges the men's team, it is defeated. But what follows is moving as the men raise their sticks in salute. Masculinity has its moments even if the ordinary male can be gloriously indifferent.

The movie builds up to victory and each little story struggles towards its own triumph. But the fable is more than the heroism of underdogs. It is a fable of unities of which Bollywood has offered two variants to the official unity of India. The first critique of unity comes from Aamir Khan in *Lagaan* and *Rang De Basanti*. These are movies that successfully challenge official histories to keep popular memory alive and embodied. But Shah Rukh's film is a quieter experiment. The softer undertones of *Veer Zaara* and *Chak De India* show that a nationalism as an official language can only be redeemed by its dialects, by parallel nationalisms that show you how to be Indian and that to love the flag is a small-town enthusiasm, a beauty and passion beyond official discourses and platforms. *Chak De India* is a simple love story of India beyond brands, where passion, vision, style still provide an alternative drama of modernity.

Sadly when people yell *Chak De India*, it has become a rubric slogan, a populist metaphor destroying the very message of the movie and its celebration of dialects. Watch the movie and you will realize when you yell *Chak De India*, one is forced to ask, 'Which India?'

DNA

13 November 2007

It's the Comedy, Idiots

The college community has finally arrived, in folklore, with the movie *3 Idiots*. Earlier, Bollywood recognized the college only as a site for the extra-curricular. Education was seen as a joke; the canteen was the theatre of activity. Hero and villain resolved key issues around the cafe. It was the site where boy met girl. Love was central, knowledge marginalized by common consensus. In fact, the good student was the standing joke of the campus, the butt of every bully. In *3 Idiots*, the college, even if arrogantly and naively called the Imperial College of Engineering, returns to the forefront. This shift is crucial because college education is recognized for the centrality it possesses in our lives.

For the middle class, education is everything. Failing an exam was the tsunami of our lives, where recovery was distant, difficult and doubtful. If you didn't make it to the IIT of your preference the family demoted you in their minds. I still remember a student who was berated by her family for missing a centum in mathematics, the poor girl had reached only 99 per cent. Yet for all its tensions, college education was a precious moment of freedom, the wild period between innocence and responsibility, the classic rite of passage in a modern middle-class society. The college was what we looked at in anticipation and then with nostalgia. The Aamir Khan movie captures this entire gamut of innocence, stupidity and ambition by building the story around a wide cast of well-delineated characters following different futures.

The picture reeks of stereotypes, but that is its power. Even the critique of education is predictable. The movie condemns rote learning, emphasizes the importance of choice, responsibility and freedom. But what holds it together is the riotous sense of fun, where the three idiots see college itself as the ritual of idiocy, centring on marks, hierarchy and rigidity. Most of us remember college for its cast of weird characters who had odd nicknames that captured a type. Memory was built around these types – the principal who would not listen, the professor who patented boredom, the student who competed ruthlessly for every mark and the roommate whose stomach contributed to global warming. These stereotypes were the stuff of education as theatre.

The emphasis was not on the abstraction of ideas. Ideas were derivative. They became alive only when lived through this kaleidoscope of characters, the panchayat of friends and the impossible people that made college education a thing of beauty. The theme of stupidity drives the movie, and slapstick substitutes for philosophy. For all its emphasis on change, the movie still plays on the standard themes of college life, hierarchy, rigidity and unfairness. The movie tries to show that laughter and a sense of play can still be winners in this ruthlessly competitive world.

The beauty lies in the intelligence of the movie. Comedy, as a form of intelligence, and stupidity as stereotype create the dialectic called education. In a tacit way, the movie shows that education is not embedded in the blackboard, the textbook and the exam, but in the friendships you make, the values you live out and the ideas sowed in college that might germinate later.

There are memorable characters throughout. The stereotype

of the ruthless diasporic who stops at nothing for his future Lamborghini is brilliantly done. The young boy from a poor family, the nerd who attempts to commit suicide because his project could not be completed on time, are evocative moments. Incidentally, the number of suicides in the IIT during the last three decades is still treated as a state secret.

At the centre of the movie is the question: Is success singular? Or are there plural definitions of success? The intelligence of Khan and his team lies in cataloguing this play of possibilities where boy gets girl, boy gets job, boy discovers himself and so on. This range of possibilities and varieties of success creates the openness of the movie and prevents any moralizing about success, values, ideology or intelligence.

Yet the weakest character cinematically is that played by Khan himself. He seems too original, too rascally, too generous. And when one discovers that he is an inventor, an Indian Edison who has created a school in Ladakh, one knows it is time to go home. While the logic of the story is unconvincing, it is details like these that keep the myth of college alive as an ever-present kaleidoscope where the difference between integrity and cheating, success and failure, is wafer-thin. Also, while in earlier generations of college life, the emphasis was on political ideologies, justice and social backgrounds, this movie emphasizes individualism, friendship and mobility, making it resonate with the contemporary generation.

The power of Bollywood lies not in refitting stereotypes but in playing with them to suggest new possibilities. This, *3 Idiots* does with laughter and intelligence, by treating lightly what we usually pontificate about, turning education into a world of anticipation and nostalgia that we enjoy and remember.

The Times of India
9 January 2010

The Fading Magic of News

I am a sucker for news and I think the newspaper is one of the most glorious things invented. As a child, I was fascinated by two things. One was the bioscope, a little machine that a ragged old man brought every week. One paid him four annas and watched fragments of old films where Nargis and Madhubala merged into a blur of fantasy.

In addition to this weekly desire, there was a daily need – the newspaper. In those days, waiting for a newspaper was a ritual of expectation. Sometimes the newspaperman threw it at the gate and my dog and I ran to fetch it. Adults had the first claim to it and then it was handed over to the children, who feasted on the sports page and the cartoons. These were worlds of action which a dreamy nine-year-old could never have enough of.

Reading a newspaper was an act of trust. I still remember men sitting on a khat in a dhaba reading the news aloud between slurps of tea. News, like the tea, was hot and strong. News was nutrition, it provided gossip, stories, reports, and the daily calories of democracy, as a wise observer put it.

Today news has lost that innocence. I admired journalists like Frank Moraes, S.K. Gurunathan, B. Shiva Rao. I always felt that an editorial was an act of integrity and the editor was the new shaman, the wise man who understood and interpreted the world.

My anger with the newspaper today is not just that news is tainted. The problem is deeper. Today tainted news and tainted journalists are seen as a part of the commodification of a newspaper. News and newspeak have merged and editors see little reason to separate the two. Earlier, at least, paid advertisements had a little footnote, like a medical warning. Today news and paid news have fused in the same lethal way that civilian and military violence have merged.

It is this taken-for-granted-ness that I find frightening. Owners of newspapers see it as an opportunity. Today a newspaper is seen as space to be leased out. It seems to make little difference whether the space is for editorials or advertisements. The latter are even hybridized as 'advertorials'. This questions the very integrity of language and the sanctity of the word which the world of news had done so much to sustain.

Today a leading newspaper establishes paid content services. It openly offers to send journalists to write about events. I see it as a blatant violation of the social contract between news and the reader. But I realize I am naive. The contracts have moved laterally. They are between politician and the news owner. News is produced in PR packages, written and canned by agencies. The journalist on the beat is often irrelevant and defenceless.

One thing that destroyed this world in a normative sense was the introduction of supplements. They were attractive inventions which added colour to the grey solidity of the news format. But the supplement blurred languages. It was corruptible space, open to experimentation, susceptible to trivia, a suburb of news to be leased out for less serious and more profitable concerns.

Today the disease has spread inward and news is becoming a supplement to power. Maybe this is why my students prefer comics and science fiction. These genres at least retain the quality of inventiveness and tautness of morality plays.

I have been reading about the Niira Radia episode and watching the whole soap opera. What I felt deeply was the rage of people who felt cheated. They looked up to icons like Barkha Dutt or Vir Sanghvi and then watched with horror as the icons became self-destructive iconoclasts. It became worse as people who one saw as professionals tried to put the humpty-dumpty of their reputation together again. One felt they could have been repairing a piece of plumbing or indulging in cosmetic repair. There was no guilt, no sense of ethical repair, no sense of remorse. But more than the journalists indicted in the Radia tapes, it is Niira Radia who is a sociological event.

One was stunned by her contempt for journalists and the way she cajoled and ordered the senior among them. She was demanding made-to-order news as she would a custom-made dish. The sadness is she was treated like a diva, the empress as procurer, imperious in her 'Roberto Cavalli gown'. This very description made her look like a cut-out figure, a creature from nowhere, so utterly brazen as if she represented the new icons and exemplars of our time. Her sense of power makes her indifferent to whether she is buying people or commodities. In fact, the tapes indicate she is more loving about her new Jaguar than some of the people she is damaging. Everything is instrumental, buyable and calculated. It is as if ethics has been sucked out of her.

By this time, the reader might ask if there is a reason to feel optimistic. I think there is. Individuals and their idealism have always made the difference. I think of Arun Shourie in the Emergency era and P. Sainath in recent times. I keep hoping the likes of Claude Alvares would return to journalism. They add sanity, ferment and integrity to news.

I still wait every day for my stack of newspapers, my TV news. Despite my jaundiced eye, I still have to hope that idealism and integrity are not dead, that there is still news which is unadulterated. All I can do is salute those who keep my hopes of idealism alive.

The Asian Age
18 November 2011

Satyamev Jayate

Mere Spectacle or a New Movement?

Aamir Khan is an actor forever reinventing himself. He loves India and is concerned with the tensions and divides that haunt it. *Satyamev Jayate,* the TV show, is his discovery of India as a civilization, as a nation and as a civil society.

There is something of the NCERT (National Council for Educational Research and Training) textbook about *Satyamev Jayate.* Like a true patriot, Khan begins by asking if Gandhi, Bose or Patel were to return today, what would we tell them? It is an old-fashioned question which he answers through a set of social dramas. His first report is on feticide. Feticide, along with incest, is a part of India's secret history. If Partition was the silent holocaust, feticide is our silent genocide, having eliminated over a few million female fetuses over the last couple of decades.

Khan's strategy makes him the most exciting sociologist on the horizon. When star power focuses on scandal, it can grow from a spectacle to a movement. What all of us know still shocks us when presented starkly.

The format is simple, and the script combines interrogation and listening. It states a problem and follows the ritual of problem solving. The entire kaleidoscope of pain, horror, resistance, investigation, protest is caught in a set of poignant vignettes.

Ordinary people, housewives, in particular, are the storytellers. A housewife is an incarnation of the Indian obsession with the mother. The mother as Durga or Kali is all-powerful, but the vulnerability of the mother comes with the dispensability of the housewife. As a child bearer, she is a form of bonded labour, condemned to bring forth only male children.

Bearing a girl child is a form of guilt, a stigma. Khan explains, almost pedagogically, that it is the man's sperm that determines the gender of the child and yet in India it is the woman who is blamed for it. The womb becomes a microcosm of hell as the woman is forced to abort again and again like an insane reproductive machine. She is beaten and tortured for carrying a female fetus.

This conspiracy of violence is twofold. At the level of the household, the husband and the mother-in-law become the coercive machines. But as Khan shows his viewers, such murder cannot take place without the doctor and the lawyer as accomplices. The innocuous 'check up' becomes the site for murder. Doctors provide a double offering: the sonogram and the abortion become twin rituals.

The women 'drop' baby after baby as in an Indian version of a Greek tragedy. The narrative reaches intensity when a doctor as housewife is asked to abort her twins.

At this moment, Khan breaks another stereotype. He asks people on the street: Who would do something so repugnant? Middle-class responses create their own folk sociology. For them, such an event can only happen among the poor, the rural, the illiterate. The middle class sees itself as an Immaculate Conception. It cannot see the genocide at its own core attributing it to the other lesser self, created to absolve it of its own violence.

In the example of the woman doctor forced to abort, the husband is an orthopaedic surgeon, the father-in-law, a professor of history at Delhi University, the mother-in-law a vice principal of a school in Rohtak. One suddenly realizes it is the very people who buy Boost, fight cavities, use Godrej dyes, drive Nanos, and love Glucon D, who practise feticide. Feticide is the other side of a middle class in love with commodities.

The inevitable questions: Is there anything we can do? Is society only a mute or indifferent spectator? Khan points to the work of two journalists in Rajasthan who exposed the feticide racket only to discover that what doctors abort, the lawyers seek to abort further. Law itself becomes a violation as its labyrinthine ways prevent the conviction of anyone. Not one licence is cancelled. A judge in one case even reprimands a lawyer for pursuing justice. Feticide becomes an organized crime in India.

Khan confronts the audience by saying it is we who have to fight. A TV show can become the basis of a movement. One has to wait to see if this happens. Meanwhile the show goes on. It is a good social science class, wonderfully presented.

Thousands have known and lived the ugly truth. Does it need a film star to tweak our conscience? Is the show mere catharsis or the beginning of reform? Only time will tell.

Firstpost

7 May 2012

An Invitation to Al Jazeera

Watching Indian TV over time, the spectator senses voids, a shrinking of frameworks. Our media claims to be global and yet its global map is empty. We mention the USA, the UK, China and Pakistan, yet as far as TV goes most areas like Africa and Latin America are empty in our imagination. An ordinary travel agency is more adventurous and cosmopolitan than our TV channels. The weakness derives partly from the way we conceive our strengths.

Our anchors are confident and yet there is a trace of the jingoistic about most of them. Some channels often give you a patriot's test which you have to pass, to be allowed to speak. Our Delhi-centric sense of the world makes us insular. We are patronizing to the Kumbh and ignorant about the Arab Spring. The pity is we do not see Kumbh, the cosmic creation of a postmodern city almost in instant time, as a global phenomenon. We do not connect with Arab Spring as a sibling effort in democratization. We let American propaganda define our words and our world. As a result, TV for all its virtues insulates us from global events. If one wishes to understand global regimes, one has to engage with programmes on technology and biology.

The point is not to grumble but ask how a spectator can meet this knowledge deficit. Fortunately there is a quick remedy, a station described by Al Gore as a prelude to the Arab Spring, Al Jazeera. Al Jazeera is a perfect complement to Indian TV. It is a mirror to what we should have done. Firstly, Al Jazeera does not merely cover the Arab world; it locates itself in an Arab perspective and covers the world. Unlike our TV which confines religion to spiritual channels or reports it as communalism, Al Jazeera can look at politics and religion in the eye and report their myriad connections. It does not become less secular because of that but more open-ended.

Every time our TV reports corruption or communalism or terrorism as a global phenomenon, we get hysterical about it. We are obsessive for a week and then drop it indifferently. Anna Hazare or Kejriwal disappear after being the flavour of the week. They are presented as monadic events. Contrast the way Al Jazeera presented Tunisian protests or even the vagaries of the Egyptian fight for rights. It is balanced but optimistic. It shows how our TV reports discrete events with no continuity. One has to also mention that Al Jazeera's coverage of Bangladesh and Afghanistan is superior; it captures struggle, pain and suffering. Our TV shows too often share Delhi's view of the world.

The question one then asks is, does Delhi care about the violence done to the Kachins in Myanmar or does it understand the debate in Bangladesh around the war tribunals? Or does it think that a wider geocentric strategy springs from indifference or self-obsession? Our TV merely reflects the insulation or pomposity of our elite. The TV channels of Al Jazeera might be therapy for this indifference. They might create a systematic curiosity about South Asia, about Africa where China is out-thinking us or Latin America which seems farther than Mars. If TV is a map of our middle-class world, our global concerns do not extend beyond our diaspora. There is a need for a new imagination. Learning from channels which are more creative than us could be a beginning.

Ahmedabad Mirror
9 February 2013

Part 12

The Stuff of Sports

Football vs Cricket

A Diversion

And Calcutta
where the women love the men
and the men loved only football
– Anonymous

I recently bought Bernardo Atxaga's award-winning novel, *The Lone Man*. It's the brilliant story of a Basque activist, Carlos, who retires to run a hotel near Barcelona. One day two gunmen come to him seeking refuge from the cops. Carlos must spirit them away using the Brazil–Argentina football match as a diversion. Chewing on the novel, I wondered how such a scene would have been enacted in Calcutta. Would the climactic background be a football match or a cricket game? With some hesitation I must admit thinking that cricket, despite Sourav Ganguly, would lose out to football. So why does Bengal still prefer football to cricket?

The standard answers are well known. Cricket, until Independence, was a colonial tradition, a game for junior princes and nawabs while football in Calcutta was a working class obsession, a mass game. Legend still celebrates Mohun Bagan's victory over the East Yorkshire regiment. It is fair to add that the only sharpshooters Bengal had then were not terrorists but footballers. Its assassins always missed.

Folklorists like Ghanshyam Dutt observe that while cricket was high-brow, football as a working-class game was a perfect accompaniment to communism. Football provided the carnivalesque complement to its idea of the revolution. Every move on the field was as hotly contested as a party manoeuvre. It is not that Bengalis did not love cricket. But no Indian would call cricket a team game. Cricket in India, from Mushtaq Ali and Hazare to Gavaskar and Tendulkar, has always been an exercise in individual heroics. It was a scrapbook of solos but never a symphony. As behaviour, cricket in India was closer to liberalism and individualism.

One has to think of the group solidarities each game offers within the framework of political economy. The key word is not nation but club. Cricket clubs in the presidency towns of Bombay and Madras were popular middle-class entities, but those in Calcutta were a different species. They were snootier. My colleague Sujit Deb claims that a person often had to borrow fine clothes to report in one's Sunday best for a cricket match. Oddly football clubs like Mohun Bagan had as addendums cricket clubs that were high-brow affairs. Eventually, the bhadralok played cricket but watched football. Cricket was a colonial indulgence, the other a mass ritual. If you think of solidarities that range from club, ethnic group, state and nation to the globe, cricket in Bengal only dominates at the level of the nation state. Let me add that if *Lagaan* were a Bengali film, it would be scripted around football.

We have to ask one more question. How come football is so popular although we play so badly? The revelation came when the World Series came on TV for the first time in India. We discovered that an analysis of our deficiencies was like 'memories of underdevelopment'. But it didn't matter for two reasons. Firstly, because football is about primordial loyalties, an enactment of a mythical play. Here, it is the feud that is important with the occasional heroics. Some anthropologists have argued that the encounter between East Bengal and Mohun Bagan is a ritual replaying of the partition of Bengal, an enactment of the division and unity between the two lost halves, with Mohammedan Sporting adding to the multicultural drama.

Football makes us realize that the real hero is the spectator. It is not the player but the spectator who has killer instincts. Quarrels between rival groups can be more lethal than the match. Next to our crowds, even British hooligans are pale Barbie dolls. It is the creativity of the spectator and game as text that we celebrate. We can afford to play bad football as long as we play at football. It is the dream that counts.

Calcutta's split level love for football and cricket may be a cultural solution. Football represents the ethnic, the local and the global. Cricket represents the national. The complementarity between the two represents the unity of opposing forces that Calcutta and other cities are struggling with today.

Outlook

20 May 2002

The Missing Middle Class

The Indian Premier League (IPL) auctions and the prices paid for the Pune and Kochi teams were both impressive and depressing. What was impressive was the money paid. What was depressing was the response to such payments.

To say that cricket is business does not explain everything. Cricket for all its hypocrisy was a wonderfully middle-class game which captured a whole set of values from gentlemanliness to sportsmanship. Oddly, I was waiting for someone to say that the price of the teams was 'just not cricket'. Cricket in a classic sense was also an appeal, a particular code, a vision that went beyond business and the practical. I do not want to say that the investments were obscene. I want to make a different point.

I want to make sense of what I am calling the absence of the middle-class response. It is a bit like the Arthur Conan Doyle story where the mystery lies in the fact that the dog did not bark. Has something changed in the middle class?

I am not making a case for the middle class. The Indian middle class was terribly repressed, supine during the Emergency, happy if the exam results were above the pass line. But the same corseted community created a sense of social work, a pride in professionalism, the romanticism of old protest. It had a sense of proportion, a music of values.

One could dismiss all of these as a legacy of socialism. One could explain them away as the remains of the ration-card economy which had turned us into scavengers and foragers. Maybe, scarcity and shortages create a sense of limits, a sense of this much and no more. It made the middle class reasonably ascetic, committed to saving. Consumption was limited to target goods; the body was a bounded entity. Life centred around exams, competition and the dream of Indian Institute of Technology. Desire was a Lux soap and excess was foreign liquor.

Today consumption has exploded. We no longer have a generation that is afraid of debt, that believes in saving. It wants to spend. Conspicuous consumption has become a sign of success, or even excellence. Cricket in a sense expressed the transition to branded goods. It was a game which was middle class and started expressing the new sense of excitement about upward mobility and small towns. The Dhonis, the Tendulkars and the Irfan Pathans told the story of cricket as a cornucopia of opportunity. Cricket was a middle-class game. Its combined individualism and nationalism gave India a sense of style, of standing up to the world. But our cricketers like Gavaskar, Sardesai, Contractor, Venkataraghavan, Prasanna and Viswanath, were wonderfully middle class. Restrained. Modest. Disciplined. Professional. Understated except in their achievements. They lived buttoned-down lives. One could never associate these names with consumer frenzy, luscious beauties and cheerleaders. Cricket has turned global, even diasporic. Every Indian, Australian, West Indian and Pakistani in Silicon Valley is an avid weekend player. Cricket provides a sense of roots. There are, I believe, around 700 clubs in California alone. Cricket signals symbolic power. It is hyphenated with Bollywood, and now with money. In that sense, cricket is no longer cricket, that old fashioned game where we challenged an empire in a ritual game of competence and sportsmanship.

It smells of money. It drinks up investments, and suddenly the middle-class sense of proportion and the limits we associated with cricket have disappeared. What I am bemoaning is not IPL, but the framework of values, even goodness and responsibility that surrounded both cricket and the middle class. Cricket was once a symptom of the best of middle-class values, from play to fair play.

If an act of conspicuous consumption like IPL took place, one would have added a few buts to it. This was a generation that would not waste food as people were starving. This was a generation that felt investment in education was a prime goal, that exams were priority over sports. In that scale of priorities, excess was always frowned upon. Excess was attributed to the nouveau rich and the last page pin-up. The achievements of Gandhi, Baba Amte and Mother Teresa were recited with pride and belief. Even communism as a style was part of the middle-class lifestyle. Today, that framework of values that stood for justice, limits, penny pinching, repression, and restraint is silent or has gone underground.

No Gandhian is there to condemn it. No socialist leads a protest march. One misses an official condemnation from the communist party treating it as capitalist excess, even if it enjoys the game. Coffee house conversations and office-goers on bus rides would have clucked in contempt instead of remaining silent in awe, indifference or acquiescence. A value horizon has suddenly disappeared.

One wonders why. Is it that globalization has legitimated consumerist excess, so that a middle-class sense of limits appears both apologetic and a failure? Does the old middle class which created the nation seem anachronistic? Are our models only the upwardly mobile and the new rich? Can we have core competence without values?

This does not call for a spoilsport attitude. We celebrate success but we create a framework of values and limits for it to operate within. Let me put it another way. One can expect the Tatas or the Birlas to back a research institute, a temple, but the IPL is not their style. Or at least not yet.

Today, the ecstasy of vintage or classic cricket seems different from the high that IPL provides. Cricket which glorified its narrative slowness suddenly glories in the machismo of speed. Narratives change, but should values disappear with it?

The middle-class man was a spectator, a knowledgeable witness, who saw in cricket part of his heritage of values. The spectator had power. He was a commentator but today his comments say little about the nature of the sport. The spectator seems to have ceded his claims to the expert and it was the spectator in cricket that kept it a middle-class game. Cricket no longer feels middle class. Does this change in essence convey a fading of middle-class frames and values? This loss would be a tragedy and the vaudeville called IPL cricket is an early warning signal that something precious is fading away.

Deccan Chronicle

26 March 2010

Life in the Middle Order

Cricket has become one of the greatest soap operas of our time. A soap opera has three qualities. First, it has a stock of memorable and identifiable characters. Second, it creates a corpus of conventional values and vices and then summons melodrama as the mode of resolution. Without a sense of epic battle, a dose of hysteria and a touch of climax, week after durable week, a soap opera as an epic cannot survive.

The World Cup was high excitement but what was more moving and sociologically interesting was the aftermath.

An aftermath is a chorus, a tuning fork that tells you whether the battle has been fought in the right way.

India won and won as a team. The nation state felt it had come of age. It was no longer a collection of talented individuals. Today, no one can say one Pakistani is equal to three Indians. We have found our sense of synergy. We are Team India. The nation as a cricket team sounds right. The euphoria is unbelievable. Crowds flow into the streets, strangers greet each other. The sense of tribal ecstasy is complete. The performance continues but at a different level.

Once the nation has been sufficiently affirmed, it is time for family and professional values. The first tribute is to Sachin

Tendulkar. Tendulkar is an exemplar. He is a genius at cricket and a repository of all the right values. His autobiography is a collection of good conduct certificates. He is the good son, the good father, the loyal husband, friend, mentor prankster – the stuff of moral science books we read as children. His is a middle-class goodness, conventional in its religiosity, predictable in its loyalty, generous in its sense of good work. Tendulkar is a man who can do no wrong, a legend untouched by scandal. He does not climb Everest. He is Everest – as the peak of achievement. As a cricketer, as an Indian, as a person, he is the ultimate Guinness Book of Records.

But the exemplar as exemplar can only survive if the values he upholds and represents are collectively resonated. This, the Valhalla of heroes around him will quickly do. Yuvraj Singh is no longer prince in waiting. As Man of the Tournament he is quick to salute his guru and his mother. The guru as the peak of renunciation and the mother as the epitome of sacrifice represent our traditional values and sustain them.

Next to them is the teacher as coach, as mentor. The teacher is more secular than the guru, but he represents knowledge to the guru's wisdom. His is the logic of everydayness, the rules of craft, forging the bundle of skills and tactics every cricketer as warrior needs. Enter Gary Kirsten. As coach he is the real Dronacharya, demanding in his discipline, accessible through his advice. Kirsten knows Tendulkar is his Arjuna and treats him as such. Fortunately, there are no Ekalavyas off the field.

Then there is the chorus of cricket, which comes in three magic circles of validation. First, there is the family, middle-class to the core, thrilled at the son's achievement, excited that it is a fragment of history. The scene is always the drawing room; the act is usually the sharing of sweets. The family, as the spectator, waits for the hero's return. The scene could be middle-class India anywhere where an anonymous family becomes a predictable album of middle-class values – pride, faith, discipline, love, sacrifice, loyalty, sharing.

The family cannot be complete without the nukkad, the neighbourhood, the ecology of friends that watched the heroes grow. The nukkad is the witness. The nukkad of friends will testify to the making of the hero, his ups and downs. No ecology of Indian cricket can do without the nukkad of storytellers, regaling one about the first six, that special stroke, or the art of bowling brewed in the streets of some small town full of Gambhirs and Sehwags and Pathans.

Family and nukkad have something organic about them. The third circle is more virtual, more artificial – this is the circle of commentators, the mercenaries of gossip and expertise paid to dissect every move, retail every blow, the circle of discourse that keeps cricket as a normative framework alive. As experts, as former exemplars and as socialites, they enact the tacit rules of cricket, analyse every game, every move, as if cricket owes its origin to an anatomy class. They are cricket's genealogists, judges, scribes, its oral historians, keeping alive stories and values in memory.

Cricket as middle-class nationalism survives because of them. They combine state and market, and nation and individual into that creative dream that sustains us. Cricket as myth would be lifeless without their tireless efforts. They create cricket as a middle-class morality play. They are the sutradhars of middle-class values that no management school can match.

Yet, such a picture, moving as it is, hides a more discordant reality. The innocence of cricket as a middle-class reality is anchored between crime and commerce. The latter provides tension to the value frames of the game. It is not advertising that pathologizes the game. Advertising only enacts the dream of middle-class desires and success. A Tendulkar advertising Boost or a Dhoni's ode to Orient fans does little harm. But cricket as commerce gets obscene when the scale of money involved loses all sense of proportion. It loses its sense of being middle class. One wishes there were more symbolic forms of reward and a wider sense of distribution where groundsmen and less successful players get a share, emphasizing that cricket is not a zero-sum game of modern mobility. Between money as commerce and money as betting, cricket has a touch of evil. One realizes that India won but, what one wonders more about is how much the punters took home. This nagging question makes the 20-20 World Cup a bitter-sweet story, reminds one of the other face of cricket, of a brittleness where values are still fragile. This is the shadow looming over a fairy tale called cricket. Excess destroys the sense of the middle that keeps cricket such a sane and lovely game.

The Asian Age
8 April 2011

Cricket's Lost Innocence

Cricket must regain the innocence of childhood tournaments and break free of the embrace of brands and bookies. Cricket today is a blend of nostalgia and the future, innocence and worldliness, which demands a different kind of storytelling. On the one hand, it is only cricket and the English language that have achieved the transition from colony to commonwealth. On the other, cricket inevitably conjures up memories of childhood days, where on a little nukkad, armed with tennis ball and bat, groups of friends enacted the great battles of life. Nukkad cricket created a bunch of local heroes, little legends who inevitably faded away later. This is the innocence captured in R.K. Narayan's *Swami and Friends* (1935), in which a gang of urchins form the Madras Cricket Club, evocative of the legendary association of the same acronym.

For people throughout South Asia, cricket was childhood fantasy. *Swami and Friends* might sound remote, even naive, today. But it is that nostalgia, that magic of nukkad cricket, that today sustains the World Cup. For all its paraphernalia, its commentators, its bookies, its branded creations, stripped down to the essentials, it is still a nukkad battle between two sets of warriors – the dreams of childhood enacted on a different scale.

The little warrior who had carried his bat to battle is now a plump spectator, commentator and connoisseur of a world in which sport has become a model of life. Sitting back, he realizes that the world and sport have changed in a way he might not want to understand. The innocent flavours of childhood have become a bitter-sweet lozenge.

At one level, what sustains cricket is the South Asian diaspora. For those who make up these communities, cricket is no longer a colonial game, but rather a fragment of their childhood carried along wherever they go. The other day, a friend told me there are 600 cricket clubs around Berkeley, in California, where Indians, Pakistanis, New Zealanders and West Indians regularly enact one of the greatest rituals they know. Cricket has become the identity kit of thousands of students and professionals abroad, a marker they live out and are proud of. Earlier, one would hear stories of diasporic families inviting musicians or religious leaders to sustain that touch of culture we call South Asian. Today, these groups think nothing of inviting a Venkatesh Prasad or a Javagal Srinath to spend a week playing with them. For them, the World Cup is a way of keeping in touch, living out battles that sustain identity.

If the diaspora is one element of the cult of cricket, the second could be thought of as the 'minnow effect'. This is the inclusion of a whole array of new cricketing countries in the international sport – Holland, Ireland, Canada – which has added to the cosmopolitanism and, generally, surprise element of the game. Watching the recent World Cup, the rise of Bangladesh is immediately reminiscent of the rise of Sri Lanka twenty years ago. For several decades, the only widely known cricket that Sri Lanka produced came from players based in England. Today, Sri Lankan players are legends; the Sri Lankan minnows are now killer sharks. Just three decades ago, Tamil Nadu would send the Jolly Rovers, a local team, to play in Sri Lanka, with the exercise being viewed as low-level 'club cricket'. Who remembers the

Jolly Rovers today, as a Muttiah Muralitharan spins his way to history?

There have been local changes too. Today, between the Indian Premier League (IPL) and the World Cup, one is seeing a split between nationalism and the market – perhaps these are just the two strands of globalism? At one level, nationalism provides the spice, the catalysts for combat, preventing cricket from becoming too amiable a game. Nationalism and professionalism, meanwhile, provide the edge to a game that good manners and a class system had turned into a set of exclusive clubs. Nationalism also creates nostalgia, a 'what if' feeling about historical events such as Partition. As a child, I still remember that after a game of cricket, we would assemble and quarrel over the selection of a hypothetical combined Indian and Pakistani team, which we knew would be world beaters. Our selection committees quarrelled over choices as if they were life and death issues.

Nationalism also created a sense of pride through cricket. A whiff of sporting spirit has always prevented nationalism from turning jingoistic. The fact that the Dutch team is sponsored by the dairy giant Amul is itself a hallmark of a new globalism. Likewise, Pakistani legend Javed Miandad has coached the Chinese cricket team. He and other cricketing legends such as Gary Kirsten, Garfield Sobers, and Mushtaq Ahmed have also served as coaches for teams from other countries. Globalization has created a space for this circulation of expertise and wisdom, which also gives cricket a hybrid touch of nostalgia and generosity.

Memory is also a crucial part of cricket. Memory is not merely recollection, a recitation of an epic game with all its poetic appeal. Memory demands a comparative perspective, a sense of judgement. It breaks the structure of jingoism or provincial fanaticism around cricketing skills and performances. When commentators were talking of Shane Warne as the greatest spinner of all time, a comment from Garfield Sobers restored some perspective. Sobers briefly said that Warne was good, but Subhash Gupte was the best spinner he had encountered. It was as if a morsel of memory had bubbled up to do justice to an almost forgotten legend. (Incidentally, Gupte settled down later in the West Indies.) Memory also gives cricketers forced into exile by politics a new lease of life – paying tribute, for instance, to Graeme Pollock and Barry Richards, South Africans whose best playing years were lost because of apartheid boycotts.

Beyond the framework of memory, though, what haunts the World Cup today is money. Between brand and bookie, the World Cup has changed irrevocably. It is not just that the IPL is the market end of the spectrum and the World Cup the nation end. The market has today made millionaires out of cricketers. Cricket as a spectator sport has become a consumer semaphore. From a sport, it now embodies lifestyle; a game that once had heroes now produces brands.

Brand and lifestyle read cricket differently. Although advertising in cricket goes back to the days of C.K. Nayudu, in earlier times the cricketer was stiff as a scarecrow in most advertisements – grace on the field yielded to rigor mortis before the camera. As brand ambassadors, Sachin Tendulkar and M.S. Dhoni are today as successful as top film stars. In fact, between them the two represent the old and the new middle class – Ranchi and Mumbai – respectively, in the marketing imagination. Sachin represents an older generation of professionals like Rahul Dravid, Sourav Ganguly and Anil Kumble, while Dhoni embodies the new generation's sense of speed and success. He possesses a James Dean–like cool, evoking the grace, mobility and speed of a new generation of small-town boys who have taken quickly to cricket and the lifestyle it involves. Meanwhile, it is hard to ignore the massive new presence of women as spectators and, increasingly, as commentators. Some add verve to the game while others, such as Sharda Ugra of *India Today*, are probably amongst its most meticulous chroniclers. For younger women, the game is interesting in itself; but for many older women, one had to know about cricket simply because that is all the men talked about. When the World Cup comes around, life revolves around it and all else is relegated to the background. To not speak cricket in this context is to choose a kind of aphasia, a loss of speech, about a major ritual of everyday life. As one woman told me, 'When your husband, son and son-in-law speak only cricket, something of the game seeps into you.'

Cricket demands a continuous narrative as commentary, but it is this commentary that is nowadays often disappointing. In earlier eras, the radio commentators were the eyes and ears of the populace. Today, with television, commentaries have become literal, even mechanical. The use of gimmicks, the introduction of electronic gadgets as referees, and the efflorescence of malapropisms add little charm. The narrative is too literal, a weak echo of what one can see, or too hysterical or nostalgic.

Cricket as commentary needs to create a fresh narrative. What made cricket a game to be discussed were its writers. The likes of Neville Cardus, S.K. Gurunathan, Jack Fingleton, Norman Yardley and C.L.R. James were not just storytellers; their writings were like judgments sustaining the normative power of the game. Between advertisement and hysteria, cricket has lost its linguistic competence, leaving a huge gap between the excitement of the game and the canned narratives to which one is subjected. Maybe one needs more economical, Hemingway-esque prose to capture the excitement on the field.

All sport enacts the body as metaphor. But while wrestling or boxing exhibit an immediacy of physicality, cricket has a mediated sense of the body. The body is always at a remove – or almost always. When Ganguly removed his shirt at the Natwest finals in 2002, viewers were witness to an aggressiveness and machismo rarely seen in cricket. Cricket does demand physical skill, yet the body is always secondary. Speed, agility and stamina are certainly required, but cricket, for all its ruthlessness, is a ritual form of battle that hides animality in a way no other sport does. Its warrior's code is a sublimated one, and its narratives always create a screen where culture dominates nature.

But the battles are changing. When one reads the cricket reports today, there is a sense that corporate interests guide the story. The feeling of the fairy tale, the sense of epic, that cricket once had now seems largely extinct. Between brand, commentary, advertising and reportage, one misses the original innocence of the game. The anecdote is not quite anecdote when the same game is played on television a thousand times over. There is something lost when the imagination cannot reclaim the power of the story, the immediacy of battle.

Today, cricket is a multibillion-dollar enterprise, a corporate sport. But one hopes that the link between the World Cup and the drama of nukkad sport remains. It is that fantasy, that magical hope of fame, that innocence where every child can dream of being a Tendulkar or a Muralitharan, which keeps the game alive.

Himal

April 2011

Why We Will Never Allow Anand to Surpass Sachin

I am a couch potato. We couch potatoes live life and sport through others. As spectators, we have our own ecumenical way of looking at things. We are armchair anthropologists who celebrate differences, make comparisons and connect impossible questions. Let me tell you it is not just the old imaginary games of putting together the best Indian team to beat the best Pakistani team. We look at more fundamental things. As spectators, we are both witnesses and consumers; we compose discourses, examine evaluations. In this imagined anthropology, strange questions pop up.

This week Viswanathan Anand, Vishy to all of us, won the chess world championship for the fifth time. As an exercise of skill and stamina, it is a stunning achievement. It matches Sachin Tendulkar's century of centuries and yet I wonder why we downplay the former.

In terms of spectatorship, there was one thing that was similar to both achievements – the cry of relief that greeted it. Waiting can be a gruelling act for a fan and one had to wait almost as a test of faith for both events to come true. Gelfland stretched Anand to the rapid fire. Sachin's detour of a year was an ordeal for every spectator.

Yet the two achievements as stories are so different and so differently consumed. For cricket, and the world of advertising, Sachin is fable, legend and hero. Whether mouthing 'Boost is a secret of success' or sipping coke like a magic drink, he is the middle-class dream of success. He seemed to advertise everything and anything. A hundred centuries gets him to parliament as a Rajya Sabha member. Sachin seems all-pervasive, a visual excess, and Anand seems a background figure. His only consistent connection with advertising is his NIIT contract. Both Sachin and Anand seem to expound middle-class values but from radically different angles.

Sachin is disciplined, honours his coach and his father, but for all that represents middle-class consumption. He is the consumer as hero, a model of conspicuous consumption that every upwardly mobile dreams of. His lifestyle demands a Ferrari, a palatial house. His discipline as a cricketer justifies an excess of consumption. He is the prime example of the guiltless success that India dreams of. Sachin is a floating signifier. He works to valorize any commodity. He combines that tacit masculinity, the clear-cut professionalism with that cornucopia of consumption that India dreams of. You cannot think of Sachin without a Ferrari. He looks a familiar of the Ambanis, he is courted by all from Bal Thackeray to Aamir Khan. Corporate India celebrates his hundredth hundred like a night at the Oscars with Aamir, Salman and Abhishek saying the right things. They are all his fans. Every spectator understands the nature of his achievement.

As a chess player, Anand is among the greats. He probably earns a fortune. Yet if Sachin is at home in India, Anand appears to be in exile in Spain. People celebrate the rigorous physical adjustments that Rahul Dravid and Sachin make. The mental adjustments that Anand has to make to battle both the Russian chess mafia and the later open age of chess are amazing. At a time when chess is seen as a game of twenty-year-olds, Anand appears a gerontocrat. He is king. Yet he is king without a crowd. When his victory was announced, politicians spewed out certificates as if they were for good conduct. There was no discussion, none of the replays that followed Sachin's achievement. If Sachin's was a style of conspicuous consumption, Anand's was one of ascetic restraints. One attracts the crowd, the other barely summons the aficionado. Sachin is consumed by the fans but Anand appears like an alien dish, an act of production which sees no future in the consuming act.

It is as if consumerist India does not know what to do with Anand. Sachin is still the boy next door, an image he shares with the wilder Salman Khan. However, Anand sounds alien. It is like a Nobel prize winner dropping in during his travels. Anand will never be the barber shop hero to be discussed along with Aishwarya and Amitabh. Sachin is history and fable, Anand the genius is a footnote. He does not seem consumable. The ascetic Brahmin going home after his success sounds either alien or too everyday. He summons neither hysteria nor excess. India is a consumer society first and still not a knowledge society.

The spectator goes hysterical over Sachin. The commentators sanitize Anand. Sachin summons excess, while the Anand label almost says 'for limited use only'. There is sadness here because the celebration is one-sided. It is as if an achievement is an achievement only if it is consumed. Advertising decides the consumable and Anand seems fit for window shopping. There is a cultural one-sidedness that one must confront. Sachin and Anand are two types of genius. Both deserve the noise of celebration, the exuberance of spectators, and the ecumenical sense that sees the power, the integrity, the athleticism of chess. Invented in India, chess is subject to amnesia, in the overflowing hysteria called cricket.

Times New Crest
2 June 2012

Milkha's Glory

Racing against History to Create History

This essay is a personal tribute to a man who defined an era. It is inspired partly by the rumour of the film, *Bhaag Milkha Bhaag*, and partly through all the fascinating interviews one has read about the man. It is a small attempt, a little fragment to add to the mosaic of greatness being assembled around him.

To write about Milkha Singh is to write about a different era. It is to evoke a different set of emotions, a different philosophy of life. To see Milkha as a runner is not enough. The sociology of sport is not enough to explain the man. In a new and independent India where our heroes were Nehru and Patel, Azad and Gandhi, Milkha represented a new kind of hero – as the athlete, as the earthy son of the soil.

Milkha, like many of his time, was a child of the Partition. Partition not only divided a nation but tore into the heart of a people. Surviving Partition and exorcising it were two aspects of many an Indian biography. Milkha had to race against history to create history. He saw his parents, brother and sister killed in front of his eyes. As an orphan, he had only his siblings to take care of him. Milkha tried to join the army and was rejected three times. Finally, he joined the electrical wing of the army and then raced into folklore. The army in India is a great institution, but a sociology of the army and its relation to villages in India has never been written. The army is a Keynesian genius, creating employment, a career, an honourable way of life for millions of Indians. For the honour and codes it provides, the army becomes a form of therapy. The Flying Sikh was a flying soldier. He realized he joined the army feeling like a lost orphan, he graduated as a patriot. Milkha, like many villagers, could have been a dacoit or a thug if the army had not become his home. Milkha was never to forget that the Flying Sikh was first a flying soldier.

The journalist, Archana Masih, tells a wonderful story of Milkha's home. There are no galleries of medals, no memorabilia of victory in the house. Only two pictures adorn the walls, one of the American doctor who saved his wife Nirmal Kaur's life and other a picture of Havaldar Bikram Singh, a Kargil martyr. Few know that Milkha adopted Bikram's son and today the boy is in a boarding school.

To paint Milkha as a soldier, a patriot and a citizen is critical. He once complained that today we honour our cricketers, not our martyrs. Our cricketers behave like ungrateful mercenaries while our martyrs stand forgotten. Today we forget how the army created a sporting nation, became the nursery for the sporting greats in athletics and hockey. In an odd way our middle-class obsession with cricket has blinded us to the role of the army. It has created a strange split in the Indian mind. Cricket, the gentleman's game, proud of its value frame, became over a period of time a mercenary exercise, while the army maintained the original DNA of cricket, the codes of honour. The army, in fact, is the first act of therapy for a Partition victim sublimating his pain to a greater discipline.

Milkha lived with the pain of the Partition through his running career. Pakistan was that empty painful space in his heart, a home which could no longer be home for a child born in Lyallpur. It was towards the end of his career that he found his cure. The Pakistanis had invited him to run against their best athletes and Milkha was reluctant to go, unsure of his feelings. It was Jawaharlal Nehru who persuaded him to go telling him, 'Son, we don't want more Milkhas to happen on either side. You are a soldier and your job is to fight the battle within. So do it.' Milkha, who was afraid to smell what he called the blood in the air in Pakistan, ran and it was Ayub Khan, the president of Pakistan, who gave him the sobriquet 'The Flying Sikh'. This vignette also illustrates Nehru's closeness to many an athlete, the warmth and understanding shared between them. In that deep sense, Milkha was a child of the Nehruvian era.

I began with a sociography of Milkha rather than with his athletic career. Today we have a diminished sense of sport. We see it best in cricket where IPL has reduced sport to an organ with statistics. Anyone who reads the early history of cricket in the works of Neville Cardus, Jack Fingleton, Ashis Nandy or C.L.R. James would realize cricket was philosophy, an attempt to create a way of life. One could not reduce a Ranjitsinhji, a Learie Constantine to his score. These players used cricket to create an alternative world view.

There was something ethical about running at that time. It was the body, a pair of shoes running against the limits of oneself. The body stands as its own truth. Technology has little role to play. Almost anyone can run. Jogging and running are among the democratic sports. Before jogging became a lifestyle thing, one just ran around the compound or the maidan barefoot or in plain canvas shoes. Running is philosophy in motion. You run to create a different world, a better world.

One has to understand Milkha in that perspective. He was a runner. He just ran. He ran at a time there was little science to running in India. One trained by racing against the elements, by running on sand or running till one bled. There were coaches but they were not the time and motion managers, the biophysics experts we have today. One just wore shoes. There was no Nike, no prosthetics, one just ran. One trained the body but running was never the scientific experiment it is today.

I am saying this to understand the poignancy of his greatest moment, his defeat at the Rome Olympics.

Milkha, like our other Indian runners, never won an Olympics medal. Our athletes just raced into the hearts of our people who understood the sheer drama of a sporting event. A few seconds can separate the hero from the anonymous herd.

Milkha was expected to win at least the bronze. But he ran a badly strategized race. He opened out too fast and then realized he had to slow down. He, however, slackened at the wrong moment to see three runners race past him. It was bad timing and then he could never catch up. There was a tragedy of defeat and regret here. For Milkha the real defeat was that he could not plant the Indian flag at the Olympics. He had the tears of a patriot.

It was a race he was to run and rerun in his mind, unable to forget or forgive himself for that burst of rashness. Yet even that event revealed the humility and greatness of the man, a legend reminding himself that he had feet of clay. Greatness is a power to look ruthlessly at oneself.

Milkha is today a legend and he showed us that legends have etiquette. One can be larger than life as a hero but one can be a simple man, pursuing life with the same focus as running. He brought dignity to sport even by his acts of refusal. An absent-minded government awarded him a Padma Shri and then presented him with a belated Arjuna Award. Milkha refused the latter quietly chiding the government by saying that they gave him his BA degree before awarding him his matric certificate. For pure economy and sheer simplicity, he was devastating.

Bhaag Milkha Bhaag reveals another part of the man. For me, these are stories about the making of the film. The interviews with Farhan Akhtar or Prasoon Joshi revealed that the sheer simplicity of the man makes him larger than life. Milkha could not be a biography because he was a part of folklore and the challenge lay in capturing a legend who smacked of everydayness.

I am sure Joshi and Akhtar and Rakeysh Omprakash Mehra will succeed at it. Therein lies the genius of Bollywood. It has always captured the defining moments of India better than social science, journalism and literature. It has a sense of poetic justice but it validates Saadat Hasan Manto's argument that the Bombay Talkies institution was the real answer to Partition. The title says it all. The plea, 'Run, Milkha, Run', was not the command of the coach but his father's last plea begging him to flee so that he could save himself. The double poignancy of the title gives one a new understanding of the man and his era, a generation that outlived the Thanatos of Partition to live life itself. Akhtar was profound when he said, there was Milkha in all of us. It was a reminder that all of us are runners, running against ourselves and history.

Times New Crest
13 July 2013

Reflections on Lalitgate

Psychologist Ashis Nandy once gave a classic definition of cricket as an Indian game, accidentally discovered by the English. In his playful way, Nandy tried to show how cricket as a game was a dream of the values of fairness and correctness sustained on colonial turf by the likes of Ranjitsinhji and Pataudi.

Today Nandy's thoughts on cricket appear like a fable, a period piece from a different era. In fact, if he were to rewrite it today, Nandy might have to say that cricket was an English game systematically reinvented by the Indians. For the English, cricket was a bit like table manners, or breakfast, but for Indians cricket was a way of life, a festival of everydayness to be enacted again and again. Today, when one looks at cricket, one does not think of Bradman and Larwood. It is not a sublimated war between nations, a struggle for the Ashes, or an encounter between India and Pakistan. Today cricket is a club game, a commodity, a ritual for aspiring classes. One man made the change, transforming cricket as a myth – an entrepreneur called Lalit Modi who made the earlier impact of Kerry Packer sound like small change.

Lalit Modi created a monstrosity called the Indian Premier League (IPL) which changed the ecology of cricket. When one reads the classics of cricket from C.L.R. James to Neville

Cardus, cricket was a canonical text of values. Today Modi and his ilk have transformed it into an extension of matka. When one reads the news today, one would think he is wrecking politics. What one has to see is that he wrecked cricket to play politics.

Modi's IPL globalized cricket and transformed the Indian cricket board into a global player. Cricket was now a marketing game. The IPL gave an intensity to cricket which changed its value frame. Players realized they were not mere heroes but legends who could be created as franchisees. A Tendulkar or a Dhoni replicated themselves through advertisements, while younger cricketers realized more could be earned from one ball than through an entire series. By introducing speed, spectacle, obsolescence, the IPL changed the everydayness of cricket. The slapstick quality of the game was disguised with the trappings of entertainment, slicker commentary, starlets, Public Relation events so one could not decide whether more was happening on or off the field.

Cricket is no longer a game. A game now takes place in a maidan where barefoot kids enact old rituals like high priests. The IPL is an industry; cricket is no longer an art form. Between bribes, brands and investment, cricket had become a commodity. Words like conflict of interest would have sounded alien four decades ago. Dhoni earns more in a day than a Dilip Sardesai or Polly Umrigar earned in a lifetime. Umrigar used to cycle to the match and earned a princely sum of Rs 25 per match. I imagine Dhoni cycling and one senses it can only be for an Adidas advertisement.

Lalit Modi represents the downfall of cricket magically elevated to a millennial event. Cricket has now become a continuation of politics by other unfair means. It has allowed politicians to exert power through India's most successful multinational corporation – the IPL. Indians controlled the game and the game corrupted politics.

As one watched the pictures flashing on TV, shots of Narendra Modi and Shilpa Shetty, Lalit Modi and Sushma

Swaraj in a cricketing cap, it was clear that these domains were at ease with each other and allowed for reciprocal flows. Power seemed to be mutually convertible.

An observer stated that IPL left cricket with a choice of corruptions. One could now choose between Dalmiya, Lalit Modi and Srinivasan, the forms of entrepreneurship which make the game what it is today. What one is watching is a merger of matka, betting, fixing, Bollywood, money laundering with cricket providing a site for all these activities.

In fact, as one watches Modi and his lawyers release document after document, one realizes that the behaviour of the man is a violation of the norms of cricket. He has no sense of values, fairness, transparency, loyalty. For me the crime is, he destroyed a fairy tale without playing even Robin Hood. Yet, in a way, he represents the new global Indian, playing socialite with discarded stars and retired bureaucrats. Worse, he shows how the world of non-resident Indians (NRIs) has added to the corruption of the Indian elite.

Our overseas Indians pretend to be holier than thou when they corrupt our elite further. Modi is the 'gigolo of cricket', a man who senses power and commodifies it. Yet Modi is also the new aspiring Indian desperate to succeed in the global world. Years ago we showed our weakness for Rajat Gupta believing the former Indian Institute of Technology don was merely being a Third Worlder in the First World. Modi extends this concept showing that corruption is the only truly global game that the world loves to play.

There is also a cynical sense that nothing will happen to Modi. One realizes now that humanitarianism is strictly for criminals. It gives a new taste of evil, of cynicism, to the worlds of care, charity and cricket. That is Modi's achievement.

Daily O
28 June 2015

Part 13

Persons, Personae and Personalities

Sachin Tendulkar

In a Class of His Own

One of my great dreams is to possess a picture of four cricketers together, the four legends of Bombay. The first is Polly Umrigar, tall, wiry, hitting a century with quiet competence, retiring with equal quietness. He was paid Rs 25 for a day's cricket. The second is Dilip Sardesai. Equally competent, equally understated, Sardesai epitomized the middle-class competence of India of the 1960s. He was outstanding, but there are no monuments to him; he would have been surprised if there were.

These two men just did their job. They produced heroism without heroics. When you watched them play, you realized the odds they had mastered. They were Indians of another time for whom honesty, national pride, teamwork were the building blocks of everyday imagination. These were virtues one could not live without. There was an as-is-where-is quality to their life and cricket, which made them seem deceptively prosaic, disguising their achievements by making them appear almost dutiful.

They were outstanding individuals and personalities, but there was nothing individualistic about them. They challenged no paradigms, led no trade unions. Their only answer to racism was good manners. They were content to live within and with themselves.

The third figure is different. He is larger than life. To competence, he adds defiance. A legend in his lifetime, Sunil Gavaskar demands more for he created more. Gavaskar created a collective mindset. He demanded a different form of respect. He looked the white man in the eye, could stand alongside a Viv Richards or a Garfield Sobers with assurance. He oozed professionalism, and an impersonal competence that demanded more in recognition. There was a toughness about Gavaskar and Sardesai which was path-breaking. They used their competence in sport to argue for a wider dignity. They were great players who wanted more from sport, and demanded more for sport. There was nothing understated about either. Their competence broke through colonial obsequiousness. Indians began getting used to victory. There was a touch of Bombay about each of them and an urbanity, a middle class that captured the Bombay of each period. Gavaskar represented a middle-class-ness ready to take on the world. He exemplified an attitude that defied the nonsense of authority. There was something industrial about him.

He rewrote record books to show India had arrived, that the team was no longer invertebrate, that the tenor had changed. The language was no longer of survival; it now spoke a dialect of victory. Gavaskar was exemplar and paradigm of a new Indian cricket where we were no longer also-rans. You don't write Calypso songs for the defeated.

In a predictable way, Umrigar, Sardesai, Gavaskar created the cultural humus for a Sachin. They were a prelude to his genius, the ancestors of his competence bred on middle-class values, the ritual protocols of urban life which sought dominance through professionalism. I began with this long-winded sociology of cricket personae, because I want to see cricket as a metaphor and look at Sachin Tendulkar in a wider sense. Genius for all its individualism reeks of sociology. Cricket is one game that belongs to the oral imagination, and commentary for cricket is as important as hermeneutics for the Bible. Retelling is reliving, and both religion and cricket have that in common.

School and street are an integral part of the urban imagination. They are models of life and frameworks of mobility. Here, exam and game create two parallel worlds. The legend of Sachin begins in the playing fields of Shivaji Park. There is a Drona of the cricket field, Ramakant Achrekar. There are no Ekalavyas on the scene. But there is a Kambli.

Vinod Kambli is important not just for his talent but for his zest for life. Kambli is talent that refuses to discipline itself. He is the exuberance of the street that refuses to yield to the school. Kambli is desire without discipline. He is the exuberance of the here and now that the middle-class envies and despises. Kambli is the short-lived Sachin; the cameo of exuberance unlimited. Sachin and Kambli are a middle-class fable that needs more attention. Kambli treats cricket as a site for desire, for the short-lived joy of politics, of cinema, of TV.

He is the middle-class boy who lacks a centre. Intensely appealing, he is the other, the friend who humanizes Sachin, creates other rhythms which would otherwise render Sachin a metronome. Kambli and Sachin are foils from school. Kambli is the other who burns out, because he burns too fast. He is the Sivakasi cracker to Sachin's blowtorch. He is the partnership that went wrong between exuberant talent and focused genius. Kambli is the child who forgot to drink Boost, who did not have Aviva insurance, who forgot school creates a timetable for life, who happily jumped on to the escalator of life without realizing that it was speeding down.

Kambli is the noise of part success facing the silence of success; he is the friend who remains though he got left behind. But he is still Kambli, the only hyphen in the Sachin legend.

The fable of Shivaji Park would be incomplete without Kambli; the shade of regret in a saga of success. The middle-class history of Shivaji Park is less ruthless. It has a place for him too.

As the legend grows, the fables diversify. Sachin appears relentless. He looks perennial at thirty, which is old age in cricket. While others move to graceful retirement, turn from heroes to storytellers, our legend grows. Ganguly, Dravid and Laxman are virtually gone. At thirty-six, Sachin is naturally the grandfather of the team. He commands respect and the young ones sense he might still be playing when they are gone. What makes Sachin a legend is the way he has mastered time.

A cricketing career occurs in escalated time. It represents speed. It is demanding. Injuries recur and the body screams. A middle-class, middle-age stodginess is tempting. Even the perennial Sachin realizes he is no longer young. His brilliance lies in the way he reconstructs himself.

The middle-class suffers from the midlife crisis of nostalgia. Sachin is a twice-born genius who reconstructs his game, reinvents himself for a new era. The Dhonis and the Harbhajans know his body is a match for theirs. The discipline is almost spiritual. It cannot be reduced to diet, or exercise, or to any technique. It is a mindset which distances the sentimentalism of nostalgia, the hypochondria of the middle class. It is not a hunger for runs; it is a hunger for perfection. Sachin challenges the mental arthritis in every middle-class Indian, the urge to settle down and be slow. A mindset where success turns into the fatty tissue of contentment. Sachin is Indian cricket's only perpetual mobile. He is the body fantastic.

Sachin might be a millionaire many times over, but he represents middle-class values. In fact, the advertisements provide the cultural frame for him in the public domain. The advertisements almost seem to provide a prosthetic of speech for him. Boost, Pepsi and Aviva emphasize energy, mobility, prudence, skill, a social framework for middle-class success. It is an ode to children growing right, whose dreams come true.

He is a childhood dream incarnate. Sachin, the name sounds right for desi values, desi competence, for success in a global world. Boost plus Shivaji Park propel you into a world beyond what IIT and IIM can prepare you for – the leap of fame. To blue-chip security, which the middle-class dreams of and advertisers can only offer as scenarios.

Advertisements create the substitute sociology of family life, professional knowledge and financial prudence that accompanies this genius, banalizing him through middle-class ambitions. A genius is caught like a fly in a third-rate sociology. But it is only such banality scented with consumerist romance that allows us to reclaim him. This is the sadness of genius and the irony of sociology.

The Times of India, The Crest Edition
14 November 2009

Deciphering Sonia

A friend of mine once tried to identify the difference between Prime Minister Manmohan Singh, and the Congress party president, Sonia Gandhi. He said that it was more than a question of persona. A persona stands between mask and face, individual and role. Sonia Gandhi, he claimed, was an ecology. She was also a translator. If Singh represented government and economics, Sonia stood for governance and the human face of the economy. He added Sonia could not be understood alone or monadically. She is a value frame of connections. Her meaning like any linguistic term moves with context. She conveys different sets of messages to different sets of people. He advised me not to seek individual biography as one might with Indira Gandhi but seek a sociography. 'The woman is a circuit of connections.' I think the advice was both guarded and wise. To understand Sonia, one shifts her from party to government, from mother to politician, from woman to nation, to understand the multiverse of Sonia as a travelling fact. The negative and the positive then combine in a kaleidoscope of fascinating angles.

Let us begin semiotically. She is picture perfect. Yet her politics is never a costume ball. Her clothes are right. They convey sophistication, an ease about surroundings, a body under control. She moves like an icon and knows it. She conveys thoughtfulness and a sense of having thought through issues. Sonia never impresses as a hoarding. She is never larger than life, an inflation of herself like an N.T. Rama Rao or a Mayawati. She is lifelike, life-size, in fact, true to life. She is more of a photograph but never a still life. She begins as noun and graduates to be a verb, creating a transition from presence to decisive action. The colours are always right, the combinations subtle. It is as if dress and the appropriateness of dress reflect the wider search for correctness. She has arrived and knows she is a presence. She is able to make her own Hindi jokes, laugh quietly in a way her husband could not. She has a vintage quality which Rajiv never conveyed and Rahul is far from acquiring. She represents the outside as inside, the prodigal as family, the stranger who worked at being at home in a world she never dreamt of domesticating, a backstage mind as a public imagination.

One realizes that one is outlining an almost cryptic character certificate. But character she is and has and it is this sense of character that has helped her transform Indian politics. Calling her Italian or international or a doll or even a puppet makes little sense. She is a leader and knows it. In fact, Peter Drucker's distinction between manager and leader could apply to Manmohan and Sonia. Singh as manager does things right, Sonia as leader guarantees that one does the right things. But between the correct and the true there exists a gap and the challenge before Sonia is that the gap should not become an abyss. To understand this, one has to look at party politics.

Sonia's control of the Congress party is not in doubt. Her cabinet is a team, a collection of deputies. The ones who dissented have faded away. Arjun Singh or Sangma appear like forgotten footnotes. She has mastered the power game but not yet the ironies and paradoxes of power. Like all Congress members, both men and women, she carries in her life the ambivalence between the logic of the party and the logic of the family. The Congress has made nepotism into an institutional necessity and a fine art. It is the party of the epigones where genealogy functions like a PAN. A kinship chart could function like an organizational chart and genes provide a tacit code of membership. As a result, the Congress is an embedded party and a powerfully populist one. Yet its real grammar of internal party democracy moves across the fault lines of hypocrisy and sycophancy. Dissent is rare and fated to fail. Oddly and paradoxically, Sonia might approve of critique from outside but dissent inside is a form of sacrilege which triggers the hunt for the scapegoats. The uniformity within is seen as a sign of loyalty, whatever the level of anarchy in performance. Plurality, diversity, tolerance are what one extends to one's allies. A Prakash Karat can be subversive, a Lalu problematic or a Mamata, hysterically contradictory. They will be greeted with patience but God help a Congressman who dares to take the cue from them. This creates what I call the Janus face of Sonia and the Congress, a hybridity of tolerance and uniformity which one senses as tactical but which leaves in doubt the integrity of the final gestalt.

In a legislative sense Sonia is an adept. She bears a large part of the credit for the Women's Reservation Bill, and she provided a large part of the stamina whereby the Congress survived the nuclear deal. The women's bill is fundamental and took over a decade to patch together. At one level, it was a national agenda, a vision that other parties shared. At another, it was a personal obsession, a commitment that she felt she had to honour, a search that began in fragments with panchayati raj, with the appointment of a woman as president and as a Speaker. It is a radicalization of the fate of politics few have achieved. Suddenly the OBC or Dalit politician sounds like a crotchety patriarch or an absent-minded Marxist. Also, there was grace in victory. She didn't personalize it but saw it as a commitment of all major parties. Rituals of generosity add to her reputation. In that sense, she understands the long run, and unlike Keynes who thought we would all be dead, Sonia realized that sustainability begins at home.

She handles politics with ease and threats with equanimity. She plays poker, understands the changing nature of trump cards, allows the Lalus and Amar Singhs their clowning moments in politics, waiting to make the right bids. Of all the Congress politicians, she is the one who has mastered the nuances of time and silence and knows how to use them as poker chips. When a smile can serve as a death sentence, why ask for the crudeness of a guffaw. She extends table manners into politics always honouring an Advani or a Vajpayee. Maybe, it is an act of reciprocity, a return for the courtesy they extended in her more vulnerable years.

To her political acuteness, she brings a sense of governance, a complementarity with Manmohan Singh, a jugalbandi which appears as a play of moves between governance and government. If Singh is the technocrat personified, Sonia selectively adopts the face of civil society.

One is not sure she understands everything that she nods about, but one can sense she has appropriated the image if not the content of many issues. Next to the women's bill, her greatest achievement, at least in sustaining it as an institutional idea, is the NREGA and the RTI. These two ideas represent the two great achievements of civil society as an imagination. By grafting them on to governance, she has amplified the democratic imagination. It is as if you adopt the two prime vaccines against poverty and corruption, even if you do not accept the overall theory of health which is at another level of complexity.

One is not sure whether the government will accept the full consequences of the Sengupta report on the informal economy, or how citizenship will get defined if one accepts the premises of the report of nomadic and pastoral tribes. The two reports are truly radical. One will transform the way we look at rights and the economy, the other, the manner in which we construct citizenship. But for the Congress, some sense of reform is preferable to a paradigm change. RTI and NREGA are humane alternatives which provide the minimum of hope and concern. The very presence of Jean Drèze, Aruna Roy and Harsh Mander guarantees that some of the best of the civil society imagination and its integrity are being incorporated into the government. The NAC with these individuals and also N.C. Saxena in its midst sounds like the 'kitchen cabinet' of the alternative imagination that the Congress so desperately needs. If Sonia creates an incubatory possibility for them, democracy might feel hopeful about the future.

Between meaningful acts of the political like NREGA and the women's bill, the Congress unfortunately creates the farce. The farce as a political skit can range across poverty to democracy. In reacting to the conspicuous consumption of its own members, it created conspicuous poverty, allegedly cutting down a few bastions of expense. But these have sprouted back revealing that combating poverty as a lifestyle is not yet the real idiom of the Congress. Sonia as an icon has added little here.

Finally, her silent messages of likes and dislikes turn her into a dummy of her own projections, while party men provide the ventriloquism. The recent furore over Amitabh Bachchan's presence at an inauguration showed that there are a thousand third-rate politicians mimicking Sonia. The epidemic of vigilantism and witch-hunting it creates is worrying. What adds to it is her silence, where reading her lips adds little to our sense of politics.

One final thought. While Sonia adds a lot to governance and the Congress, vitaminizing its politics, there is always a sense of disquiet. It is what linguists and literary critics would call a synecdochical failure. Synecdoche, as a part of speech, deals with the relation of parts and wholes. One must salute Sonia for revitalizing some of the parts. Yet by creating a penumbra of power, one always feels the whole is less than the sum of the parts. The system cannot stand because the Congress as a whole, as a mass and middle-class imagination, needs to rework itself. This will require a struggle of a different kind, beyond the power of experts and committees. This wider magic Sonia lacks. It needs a sense of the future as a different country, where the democratization of democracy will start taking place.

Governance Now

11 May 2010

The Cult of Jayalalithaa

Return of the Dark Goddess

In politics today, Mother India comes in three incarnations. Three metaphors of force, three icons of power. There is Mayawati, the Dalit queen; Mamata Banerjee, the noble savage of Bengal politics; and Jayalalithaa.

The first two incarnations are easy to read as psychosocial forces and are obvious in their tactics. Mamata is a Rorschach blob representing Bengal's wish to see the end of the CPI(M), while Mayawati represents the Dalit understanding of electoral politics. Each is a political vector powered by a societal force.

Jayalalithaa, however, represents herself, and has a sense of the inscrutable that is part of her power. She reflects no caste or class identity, no feminist force, no modernizing impetus. She is the persona as politics, the personality as pure presence, and therefore looks and feels like a hoarding. She is larger than life, and seems somewhat unreal. She could be a fair and lovely advertisement for the sixty-plus.

Jayalalithaa's isolation and authoritarianism are crucial elements of her mystique. The gates of her Poes Garden house convey that closure, that distance, that space around her which few can enter and only reverentially. Where Mamata and Mayawati are always seen surrounded by throngs of supporters, Jayalalithaa's power thrives on distance.

If the other two are icons because of their politics, Jayalalithaa creates politics out of her iconicity. Mamata and Mayawati are more immediately political in their appeal, but Jayalalithaa lingers in the mind as a powerful presence. The three women embody three different strategies of complexity: Mayawati is ruthless; Mamata populist and tenacious; Jayalalithaa is a Machiavellian waiting for the right moment. Here she is again, back in power, ready to forgive the Tamil masses for voting her out twice.

Propped up in the background is the figure of M.G. Ramachandran. MGR was no less than a political god, a semi-divine figure who dominated Tamil politics for ten years. When he died, Jayalalithaa inherited his mantle and his mystique, but with a difference. Her mentor represented the amalgamation of film and politics. The symbolism in his movies was obvious and overt, a wish list of Dravidian emblems. Jayalalithaa's obvious sociological persona goes beyond party and cinema, to the very roots of folklore.

There are stories of MGR drinking Fanta or some other soft drink and the remnants being sprinkled on the audience like holy water. Jayalalithaa, however, does not invoke holiness, but represents the awe of inscrutable power. She is more an elemental force than a human being. When politicians touch her feet, they seem grateful for merely being allowed close to her. She creates her own iconography through distance, isolation and indifference.

Unlike her political sisters, Mamata and Mayawati, Jayalalithaa exudes a sense of sexuality. There is, of course, her career as a sexy film heroine playing consort to MGR. Yet Jayalalithaa has transformed sexuality into a new untouchable iconicity, having renounced domesticity for the single-minded pursuit of power. She is that blend of fire and ice: the idea of power as sexuality.

But there is also a cold animality to her sense of power. She understands power, especially the symbolic power of violence, the politics of the threat. Her arrest of Karunanidhi at dawn on 30 June 2001 was a classic example. The wily politician was completely ambushed, screaming helplessly like a slum dweller victim before an indifferent bulldozer.

The act was reminiscent of the Emergency era and must have put the fear of God, sorry, the Goddess, in Karunanidhi. Her vengefulness, her authoritarianism adds to her imperious appeal. Power, which is irrational and unpredictable always appears more potent. An unpredictable, inscrutable, authoritarian goddess needs to be placated more than others. She demands unquestioning obedience. But this goddess contains no sense of spirituality. She does not convey sacredness but the *mana*, the awesomeness of power, the elemental rawness of power.

Where Jayalalithaa was ordained by MGR as his heir, all the DMK got were ideological scripts of Dravidian nationalism which have long run out of steam. Karunanidhi needs a political machine to be elected, while Jayalalithaa is the party.

Her politics is an egotistic projection of herself. Voting her in is like installing a goddess in an empty temple. She does not convey gratitude but a sense of fate and destiny. Next to her, Karunanidhi and his family seem everyday, mundane and quarrelsome. They look like Tamil soap opera while she conveys the iconicity of legend.

Electoral politics in Tamil Nadu has been a case of competitive corruption. In anthropology, one reads ethnographies of chiefs endowing gifts on their tribe. The ritual is called the potlatch where the more you give, the more you gain in status. The politics of tribes reached a new high in the DMK–AIADMK jugalbandi on corruption.

The DMK today appears like a political machine that

has been run down, banalized and criminalized by petty greed. Karunanidhi's politics has been a case of conspicuous corruption, while Jayalalithaa's is a case of the insidious and the invisible. They are occasional aberrations like her son's marriage but for the most part the flaps are down. Her crimes remain backstage while Karunanidhi's corruption has turned into an overt family spectacle enacted over two generations.

For all her goddess-like mystique, Jayalalithaa reeks of the modern, and understands governance. She likes the populism that votes her in but not a popular will that can defy her.

Oddly, it is democracy that produces this version of authoritarianism. Think of Narendra Modi or even Indira Gandhi. They are modernizers who exploit or channel democracy for their personal ends. All three treat democracy as a rite of passage that they have to occasionally resort to. It completes the irony that democracy as the will of the people gets forged into the will of one individual. A representative democracy gets subverted into an authoritarian polity by electoral means.

Of the lot, however, Jayalalithaa is the most Hobbesian figure in Indian politics, the sovereign as empress, the politician as a cult figure. She is the frozen hysteric, obsessive-compulsive about power. Power soothes her, thaws her, makes her forgive the occasional deviancy or disloyalty of electoral democracy. As the cult of Jayalalithaa engulfs Tamil Nadu, she exudes a power, contemptuous of citizenship.

She reveals the way in which democracy as a cult becomes doubly dangerous: first as populism, second as authoritarianism without feedback. How democracy produces such oxymoronic figures is one of its mysteries. One needs a new secular iconoclasm to go beyond such fatal idol worship.

Firstpost

26 May 2011

The Five Battles that Defined Jairam Ramesh

Jairam Ramesh is the odd man out in politics. It is a tribute to Sonia Gandhi or Manmohan Singh that they have the vision to keep the odd man in. He represents the new ideal of the Congressman: scrubbed, dapper, technocratic, managerial, happy in the give-and-take of politics but equally at home in an academic seminar.

Ramesh is a scholar at heart but prefers to use scholarship as a hammer to make a policy point. His originality lies in the consumption of data. He can smell an interesting trend, sense a promising problem. He reads, absorbs, sniffs out promising connections and synthesizes them quickly. He listens carefully, diligently and respectfully, but can smell a fake. He rations reverence like many intellectuals but can celebrate an idea like a child savouring a candy.

This is a proud man, proud of both his competence and his tradition, happy to rise early and listen to M.S. Subbulakshmi's recital of the '*Suprabhatam*'. The scientific method provides Ramesh a secular spirituality, a substitute for the traditional rituals of his background. It evokes objectivity, and makes no claim to sentiment, allowing him to go beyond ideology. For him, method provides clarity, rigour and a consistency that technocrats admire. Justice for the minister is a collection of indicators; method a virtual substitute for ethics.

Where the previous minister for environment, Kamal Nath, was a fixer, Ramesh is a problem solver. The power of Ramesh lies in his realizing that method, discipline and respect for knowledge can be a lethal force in politics. He knows he cannot be a populist and that he is too argumentative for it. Often he refuses to endorse collective wisdom when he knows the facts are different. He is a master at irritating the elite by demonstrating its ignorance while reassuring them of his competence.

This man is a duelist, his environmental career defined by five key battles, each of which reveal a different facet of his persona.

Bt brinjal: One of the first scientific controversies shaped by a public debate offered a rude revelation – and for Ramesh, a personal triumph. NGOs behaved like professional scientists, assembling data, coordinating arguments. The government's scientists were caught with their professional pants down, plagiarizing from easily accessible pamphlets. It was a case of self-inflicted injury.

The brinjal debates were sheer drama and Ramesh played listener, impresario and performer with great enthusiasm. He showed scientists that science had to be more open in accepting evidence, and helped NGOs recognize that cantankerousness is no match for organized scepticism. His ability to establish a public space created a sense of trust in the openness of the environment minister.

Ramesh was one of the first politicians to understand the power of electoral data, but he also realizes democracy is not a numbers game. It needs governance, the rule of law and a more inclusive theory of citizenship.

The POSCO deal: If the battle of the seed symbolized hope, the long-drawn-out war over mining soon defined the limits of hope. Ramesh's objections to the Posco deal triggered violent responses. Even the unflappable Montek Ahluwalia went apoplectic when 'economic growth', his baby, was threatened. The mining mafia proved more resilient and Ramesh was branded as an environmental outlaw. The mine prevailed, retaining its role as the fertility rite for modern industry.

Ramesh is a Tamil Brahmin to the core, with the strength, arrogance and weaknesses of one. He has faith in the power and discipline of knowledge and is still discovering that political bosses can be both contemptuous of constitutions and the logic of science.

Nuclear energy: Ramesh has been evasive – even a trifle silly – on nuclear energy, tarring anyone who objects to nuclear energy as fundamentalists. He will only speak to those who want to discuss safety or the quality of contracts, dismissing out of hand sixty-odd years of the sustained critique of nuclear energy. Nuclear energy is inherently risky. There are limits to our knowledge, and the time horizons required to ensure safety are virtually indefinite.

This sleight of hand – confusing fundamentals with fundamentalism – reminded us of the politician in him. It was a bravura performance that rang hollow.

The IITs: His comment that the IITs have made little contribution to major research was accurate and welcome. It was an act of truth-telling that worried the vested interests who summoned the usual character certificates.

Worse, it showed us that established scientists are poor debators and are probably more afraid of the facts than any sector of society. Indian scientists become hysterical, screaming foul as soon as anyone puts them up to scrutiny.

Ramesh is a technocrat, concerned about science as literacy, culture and innovation. It is silly to treat him – as Kapil Sibal did – as a loose cannon. He responds not to pompous reprimands, but to a counter-argument.

Climate change: Ramesh was devastating on climate change, and not because he took on Rajendra Pachauri, the Nobel-prize-winning chairman of United Nations' Intergovernmental Panel on Climate Change. What took insight and courage was his public indictment of climate change as not an objective domain of science, but a realm defined by an array of vested interests.

He exposed how Western regimes hide behind the alleged objectivity of scientific data which, in fact, serve as a screen for market interests. What we needed instead was research and quality data generated by Indian scientists.

If Ramesh's statements possessed a bluntness rarely witnessed in scientific matters, it's because he is matter-of-fact about science, and shrewd enough to realize that often expertise is only a sanctioned form of self-interest.

It is an exciting time for science and ecology with a minister who understands science and cares for the environment. But Ramesh has opened up a can of expectations that may yet be his downfall. When his politics meets the limits imposed by current reality, the NGOs are going to scream for his blood.

And then there is the 'tragedy of the third paragraph'. When people went excitedly to scientist Amulya Reddy with a new idea, he would ask, 'What is in the third paragraph or the third issue?' Reddy realized that an idea has to have a career, a long trajectory that goes beyond the opening proclamation. By the third paragraph, a good idea shows genuine possibilities and one can sense its potential.

Ramesh faces the challenge of the third paragraph. His ideas are intelligently ethical, but they have to survive if he is to be genuinely significant. Sustainability requires a minister who will be durable. This Jairam Ramesh has to be.

Firstpost

15 June 2011

Rahul Gandhi

A Set of Collective Expectations, a Drama of Projections

Rahul Gandhi is one of the strangest phenomena of Indian political life. He is neither being nor becoming; even if he does act, nothing seems to happen. He is expected to be the legendary hero, the millennial leader of Congress and yet seems to play bit roles which lack even a cameo quality. I would not blame Rahul entirely for such a situation because Rahul Gandhi is an invention, a Rorschach test of Congress and its dynastic dreams of modernity. I would label Rahul as a set of collective expectations, a drama of projections.

History will begin the day we return to the actual individual as a full-blooded creature with his own wants, dreams, hurts and feelings. As a collective function, he seems irrelevant and inadequate. The political Rahul has to be peeled as a set of layers. Rahul was conceived as an initiation rite, a set of learning exercises which he has to enact in public.

The transitions were to mark his ascent to power and his public anointing as PM. Instead of being thrown into action or being bloodied by fire, Rahul became that infinitely extendable status, the student, the perpetual learner. I remember the first time I watched him from close quarters. It was at an IRMA (Institute of Rural Management, Anand) meeting at Anand in Gujarat. He listened studiously, his body language was respectful, he met all the right people and yet there was something disappointing in the way he spoke. At the age of forty, he gave the speech of an awed twenty-year-old, announcing respectfully that he was the youngest person in the room.

The rest was a banality of good intentions. The problem was that the audience was ready to adopt him. No one saw him as a leader. He was just a VIP student. The presence of Digvijaya Singh as mentor has been dampening. Digvijaya, in the years following his tenure as chief minister, plays the loose cannon training an expert rifle shot Rahul claims to be. If Digvijaya is politically provocative, Rahul plays the Boy Scout.

He visits villages, eats at Dalit homes, carries plastic buckets to show he respects labour, and yet one feels all these are simulations.

One is afraid he might become a politically interesting young man of sixty. After the Bihar elections, Nitish Kumar said that he would take Rahul seriously after he had served as a minister or a chief minister for a year. Rahul, he suggested, 'did not smell of real problems or experiences'. His rhetoric seemed to float above the realities of electoral politics.

This picture became clearer during the final stages of the recent Gujarat elections. The Congress party unleashed him at the final stages and all he talked about was genealogy and family to a Gujarat which often felt that the Nehru era had been lukewarm to the legacy and ambition of Gujarat leaders. The Congress with great fanfare set up a pre-emptive contest between Rahul and Narendra Modi for 2013.

Media loved it but spectators watching the event often asked about the political issues that Rahul would articulate but met with a wall of silence. Rahul Gandhi seems to have become a set of roles rather than a message. He is a Boy Scout, secretary playing gardening roles for the party, listener but he rarely speaks or acts in a memorable way.

The most memorable of his performances was his almost forgotten confrontation with the younger Thackeray in Mumbai. The collective wisdom around Rahul treats him as an event or a spectacle. He is not seen as an argument.

He needs to be part of current history rather than a piece of the future waiting to be elaborated. One needs more anecdotes, stories about him. Rahul becomes Rahul when he stops being the prince of possibilities and becomes the king of the real. In the next two years he has to articulate a vision of the political around real issues, and thereby escape being a cliché. Incubating him for some imaginary future will no longer do. Rahul needs to articulate perspectives, positions and policies around prices, poverty, MGNREGA, corruption and education. We need to have the sense of his team as players for the immediate future.

If Congress is setting him up as Mr Democracy over Mr Development played by Modi, he has to show how his politics links up to governance and growth. There is a wonderful opportunity here to break from the past. Will he be ready to learn from mistakes and have the tenacity to woo the future? Being part of the Nehru and Indira Gandhi family is not enough for a new generation which has no memory of them. He needs to step out of the past to create history. He needs perspectives which live and talk. The idea of *The Dynasts* makes for good opera, but it leads to bad politics and Rahul needs to be a politician. The question is whether Congress will let him or chaperon him into a guided future.

The Economic Times
9 January 2013

The Poetics of a Nation

Remembering Nehru

This week, India will celebrate the 125th birth anniversary of Jawaharlal Nehru. I must confess that I hate anniversaries when they turn out to be rote affairs; when memory, which hurts like frostbite, is presented painlessly. I hate this era that measures Nehru with calipers and titrates his foreign policy. It is a dull world today when memory turns inane and history seems empty. Life must indeed be meaningless when almost two decades of the Nehru era produce less meaning than five months of a Modi regime. When memories fade, icons die, and when an icon dies, something dies in all of us.

Nehru cannot be seen merely as an object of history, a fragment of policy. He was a dream, a hope, a claim to innocence, an aesthetic which gave to modernity a touch of elegance. I think that is why Gandhi opted for him. The practical Gandhi realized that one needed the impractical Nehru to survive the first decade of Independence. It is only the impractical who survive, who understand desire, hope and dream. Words like development and planning are dull words borrowed from a dismal social science. Nehru gave them a touch of poetry and it is only the poetics of the first decade that allowed us to retain hope and dream differently.

Imagine a country which suffers two genocides, the Bengal Famine and Partition. Imagine a nation sprawling with refugees and the bitter memories of displacement. Such a nation could have turned melancholic, bitter, even tyrannical. Yet, with all the violence, India of the Nehruvian years had a touch of innocence. Indians felt they had done the impossible, i.e., win freedom, and now wanted to repeat it. It was Nehru who gave India that lightness of being, that childlike innocence and yet that sophistication that came with a civilizational confidence.

Nehru inspired a generation to hope and believe. In fact, it was the first decades of Independence that could be called the Indian century because Nehru made India feel that Indians were special.

We used science as an enzyme of hope, an elixir of development. Where else could a nation talk of the future as belonging to science or those who make friends with science? The concentration camps were still a stark fact and the atomic bomb had been tested over Japan.

No other nation saw science as a dream. The Russians and the West saw it as a tool of economic development. Nehru insisted science was culture, a form of playfulness, providing a sense of discovery and excitement. This was a man who felt that science would prolong his discovery of India and even the world. For Nehru, science was not about productivity. It was a way of looking at the world. In fact, if one looks at Nehruvian scientists one senses that same elegance about science, whether it was P.C. Mahalanobis, Homi J. Bhabha, K.S. Krishnan, Vikram Sarabhai or Satish Dhawan. For all of them, science was not just knowledge. It was an aesthetic for approaching the world, an insight we have lost in this dismal age of the information revolution.

One is reminded of a story about the Russian scientist, Nikolai Vavilov, who spent his student days with William

Bateson at Cambridge. While recalling an English colleague, a nuts and bolts empiricist, Vavilov claimed that he was a good worker but insisted, in his accented English, that he had no 'Phi-lo-so-phee'. Nehru provided philosophy to the first years of India's Independence.

It had a touch of innocence. In fact, it was re-echoed in Hindi cinema by Raj Kapoor, who, like Nehru, was an incurable romantic. Both saw, in being Indian and in nationality, a dream of a different being. When Kapoor sang '*Mera juta hai Japani, ye patlun Inglistani, sar pe lal topi Rusi, phir bhi dil hai Hindustani*', he was reciting one of the new anthems of the nation, a country, a generation which believed it had a tryst with destiny.

Even ideology had a touch of romance. Today one laughs at socialism and the dreams of the Left when one watches the dreary rhetoric of the CPI(M). But ideology in that era was an aesthetic of justice, a poetics of solidarity with people. I know the words might sound empty today but when the Indian People's Theatre Association performed, or Nehru spoke ideology, Marxist-Socialist ideology made sense of the world. As an old Marxist explained, in India Marxism was not just about class. It gave a touch of class to the way we thought of the world. One misses that elegance, that aesthetic of democracy when we talk of secularism today as it gets viscous with political correctness.

One must remember that the first decade after Independence was an idealistic decade. When one thinks of one's parents or their friends, one senses the deep celebration of India. Every Indian felt his sacrifice was worth it. It was a moral, aesthetic and scientific world where character building, nation building and dam building went together. There was little cynicism, a great realism about poverty and yet a hope that nation building, Nehruvian style, was one of the great epics of the century. India has lost that epic quality of hope and innocence.

Maybe the Nehruvian era needed that touch of pragmatism we call Patel. Maybe Nehru could have absorbed the insights of Rajaji. At that time we had such a surplus of leaders, from Maulana Abul Kalam Azad, Rajendra Prasad, B.C. Roy and Rajaji that we did not realize that the first decade was a festival of leadership, with each individual adding to the richness of the Indian vision.

I remember when the Nehruvian era died. For me, as a child it was a composite of two events. India, invincible India, the India that gave us Dhyan Chand, lost in hockey at the Rome Olympics. For my biased mind, cricket, tedious cricket, only emerged into the limelight after that. Then, even more poignantly, India lost a border war with China. It was a collapse of a world view where India which had conquered colonialism was mired once again in defeat. Nehru, our immaculate Nehru, sounded old and vulnerable. There was a loneliness, a tiredness about him. When a legend is threatened, mediocre critics like termites creep out of the woodwork of history to recite his mistakes. The magic was gone and Nehru faded soon afterward. The question 'after Nehru who?' popped up soon and one then sensed the momentous nature of the loss. One realized that for all the mistakes, those were the last magical years of the nation.

Today, given the mediocrity of his epigone and the autism of the Congress party, we forget that the Nehruvian era was the great period of institution building, where we initiated community development, celebrated planning, built our great IITs, revitalized our science laboratories. India could not have been India without harvesting the achievement of the Nehruvian years.

I remember my old friend and teacher U.R. Ananthamurthy. Before he died, he left behind a great manuscript, a testament, a manifesto. He criticized the Nehruvian years but he made a more critical point. Nehru might have made mistakes but Narendra Modi is the mistake that India might regret making in its angry backlash against the family.

Nehru was a classic. Our current regime is a footnote. It can only become history if it destroys the Nehruvian years.

Today, there is an epidemic of seminars, conferences and newspaper articles about the 125 years of Nehru. Writers will give Nehru the good conduct certificates he does not need and praise his concern for poverty and his interest in science. The Congress is petty enough not to invite Mr Modi but pompously invites guests from overseas. It is an un-Nehruvian act in its aesthetics and one must condemn it. Yet, what will be even more depressing is the social science litany about a man who gave us the poetics of a nation. In our current politics, it is not memory and its poignancy we are evoking. Our anniversaries become dull timetables, empty acts of repetition. When the magic is gone, only an official catechism remains. It is simpler to open a book of photographs and travel down memory lane. I wish there was something simpler, more abstract, a simple poem that caught the magic of the man without shrinking it to nostalgia, because Nehru, our Nehru, deserved much more.

The Hindu

15 November 2015

The Missingness of Gandhi

I must confess I am an old-fashioned man. I feel out of place and even out of time. I belonged to an age which honoured the self and not the selfie. Yet I feel strangely relevant as I realize my anger and my memories, my sense of classic and craft has something to say. I have stories that are still worth listening to, yet I feel sad when I look around me.

I know my world has shrunk. My icons do not make sense. People have not heard of them. Some even call them my collection of eccentrics. But I want to talk about them. For all of them the hero was Gandhi. Nehru was the future, as deputy. I remember an old wag telling me Nehru dreamed and Gandhi prayed and it was Gandhi's dreams that came true. They were like two octaves in an invisible music we kept hearing. The last years of nationalism had a cornucopia of heroes. What was beautiful is that these ideals were also lived out in the first decade of Independence.

Today people say the Nehru or Gandhi era is over. The obituaries sound like celebrations and I admit my nostalgia sounds like hypochondria. When I talk Nehru or Gandhi, or all my other heroes, I sound like a list of ailments, their missingness seems part of a strange disease. This is not an Alzheimer's of forgetfulness, mine is the pain and joy of living so many memories.

Of late I have been reading pieces about Gandhi. He is called the first corporate guru. Some would even say he is the original pioneer of corporate social responsibility (CSR). But Gandhi never outsourced ethics. He dreamt it, lived it in the rhythms of the day. Ethics was not an extra-curricular activity, a piece of social work to compensate for corporate antics. Gandhi is also attacked for not being as radical as Ambedkar. Ambedkar is promoted as this week's flavour by politically correct radicals without understanding the matrix, the quarrel and the complementarity between the two. So from corporate don, he becomes a lesser Ambedkar. Then the RSS which faded away after assassinating Gandhi, says India needs a statue of Godse. Godse to them was not an epitome of hate but a service boy. Gandhi got in the way of the logic of the nation state and had to be dispatched. Godse to the RSS excelled in the line of duty and therefore needed to be redeemed. Gandhi's assassination was a clerical act and Godse, a mere functionary.

To this regime of forgetfulness and critique, we can add the obscene appropriation of Gandhi by Modi and his regime. Modi epitomizes the violence of hate and the instrumentalism of development, where there is no ethics of means and ends. Yet all these distortions of Gandhi are fashionable today.

Recently I saw Attenborough's film on Gandhi and fell asleep. I used to celebrate it and yet it failed to resonate now. It sounded too much like a white man's idea of Gandhi, a Gandhi made easy for the West. I realize there is no easy access to Gandhi. He is eminently quotable but there is no catechism of Gandhi. He is a continuous series of thought experiments. He refuses replication. He wants you to invent your own ethical world.

Yet the complex simplicity of the man, who allows no simplification, is seductive.

Gandhi to me is both craft and classic. He knew his Gita and his Ruskin. He knew the power of the book but understood that the life of the book and the book of life could not be separated. His sense of civilization covered both canon and folklore, the text and the orality of memory around text. To the over-literate Indian who read a hundred books, his answer was, 'My literacy consists in reading the same book a hundred times.' Exploring a book a hundred times is not repetition. It is reinvention and discovery. It is an act of pilgrimage discovering or renewing the source of the sacred. Out of this reading comes a strange book, *Hind Swaraj*.

We have to stop reading *Hind Swaraj* as an eccentricity. It is a manifesto and has to be read along with other manifestos like Rousseau's *Discourse on Inequality*, Thomas Paine's *Rights of Man* and Marx and Engel's *The Communist Manifesto*. It is as relevant, as important, and as incomplete as any of them. Gandhi's silent message is to tell the reader to write or live out the rest. Each man or woman has to write his or her own *Hind Swaraj* like U.R. Ananthamurthy did in his last book, *Hindutva or Hind Swaraj?*, or Ela Bhatt has done in her *Anubandh*.

Between Swadeshi and Swaraj you absorb the world. No Gandhian would say: 'Climate change is not our problem.' To claim it is a problem of developed countries is to be global. To insist it is a problem for every man is to be planetary. Swaraj was planetary. The last man is not just a putty, a piece of suffering. For all his vulnerability he owns up to the world. For Gandhi, a Pascalian wager is not enough. A Gandhian wager goes beyond goodness and has to out-invent evil. Gandhi would not want a justice where the Third World says to the First, 'It is our turn to destroy the world.' The new consumerism cannibalized the world. Remember Gandhi in his *Hind Swaraj* wanted to rescue the West from its violence. The new Hind Swaraj would include a critique of climate change. As C.V. Seshadri would say, the Gandhian truth should combine thermodynamic truth.

Similarly, a discussion of climate change would include both the social and the technical to encompass the ideas of life, lifestyle, livelihood, life cycle, life chances in one set. Here the technical, the ethical, the political, the cultural are not separated. A classic is a way of keeping things together and connected.

But Gandhi was perpetually for experiment. Walking, fasting, weaving, printing, cooking, protesting were all experiments. Morality was experimental because ethics needed to constantly transform itself, work within a range of contexts. Ethics and craft had a lot in common. One had to craft an ethics and make sure it never got outdated. In that sense every man becomes a craftsman responsible for his world. The idea of rethinking waste, repair, fasting are ways of dealing with the world. There are no throwaway cultures or human beings. Healing, caring and working are seamless. Craft as ethics has rigour and style and most of all the inventiveness of diversity. For Gandhi, ethics as craft has to be inventive enough to challenge the inventiveness of evil. Today genocide, the death of a waterfall or a mountain, the displacement of a people, the disappearance of culture are new forms of evil, where violence is seen as inevitable, and mass death has no rituals of mourning. Gandhi did not live to link nuclear war to ordinary violence, genocide to murder, or technology to the military industrial complex. In fact, in his way if Gandhi were asked, 'What do you think of modern ethics'? He would have said, 'It would be a good idea.'

For Gandhi, ethics could not be extra-curricular. It had to be every day. Protest had to link to lifestyle, caring to livelihood, passion to humour so that nothing got dogmatic. The body was the site of ethics and the ethics of the body provided the framework for an ethics of the body politic. The body as site and metaphor was becoming the tuning fork of a complex world and its problems. Non-violence for Gandhi was not something you associate with war, non-violence was something you brought in to mitigate your war with the world, the violence of everydayness. In that sense ethics gave you agency, not just the concrete, the face-to-face with your children, strangers; it gave you agency against abstract systems where cause originated somewhere and consequence emerged somewhere else. What we need today is a Gandhi of the concrete combining with the Gandhi fighting abstract systems, complexities which often make an individual feel fragile, futile and helpless.

In an odd way for Gandhi charity began with the world and public policy at home. The body set the rhythms of the body politic. Ethics set the tone for self-discipline and self-reliance and therefore eliminated mass discipline and surveillance. If you had a conscience, the panopticon, as a centralized system of management, was unnecessary. The citizen is never passive and pacifism has nothing passive about it. A pacifist like Thoreau was constantly reinventing society. In that sense civil disobedience was an attempt to restore civility and civic duty. The human conscience is the greatest cybernetic mechanism invented.

One has to notice that ethics is not only experimental but full of mistakes and it begins by redeeming the mistakes you make. In owning up to the mistake, you own up to self and world. A mistake is an incomplete conversation with the world. Mistakes, the relation between ends and means, the connectivity between life and livelihood, show a new ecology of ethics where the body as biology, as person, as symbol becomes the theatre for truth. There is both fragility and strength here as one discovers in vulnerability, the power of resistance. Many students confronting water cannons for the first time during the Nirbhaya protest felt empowered in their moment of vulnerability because they understood the brutality of the state. One wished they would have continued their resistance because protest would have gone beyond mere protest to arrive at a deeper sense of alternatives. Years ago, Walt Whitman, the great American poet wrote 'The body electric'. Our protestors similarly could have claimed, 'I sing the body satyagrahic', if they had addressed both violence and the truth of what causes violence. Herein lies the challenge of satyagraha today.

It has to challenge large systems twice, first in the locality and then as a planetary idea. Even in battling or creating work one must have an emerging theory of peace. Satyagraha cannot be sequestered as an applied social work project because ethics has to be political, responding to wider issues.

One must remember that Gandhi's satyagrahi was an imagination. Gandhi's ashrams were laboratories where one invented alternative possibilities while the world slept. It was the one place where everydayness as invention, as rhythm, talked to the future. Gandhi was no Luddite. William Shirer's biography of Gandhi mentions that the loudspeaker was introduced for the first time in a rally addressed by Gandhi. His charkha was not a traditional tool but something reinvented several times. But Gandhi's craft like his ethics followed a linguistic rather than a techno-innovative model. He was sensitive to displacement, waste, obsolescence. His technology spoke dialects rather than attempt to create standardized forms. In fact, it challenged us to return to ethics; he wanted ethics to be more inventive than mere techniques. His creativity demanded that innovation should be more than instrumental. Every man then becomes a craftsman creating a new commons of ideas to be shared. There is none of the hypocrisy of intellectual property rights which confuses need and greed.

Such a world goes beyond the make-in-India model which only wants to manufacture but fails to ask ethical, ecological questions, where productivity displaces justice. A cosmetic Gandhi threatens India twice, first as a farce and second as a tragedy.

The man haunts me. His experiments fascinate me. He demands the storyteller. I feel his magic. He made mistakes.

He knew it. He did not ask us to repeat them. His leadership appealed to the ethics of my generation. I feel it is time to reinvent it. One senses a world ready for the poetry of it. This essay is a prayer for that other world.

The Tribune
30 March 2015

The Dalai Lama

Celebrating a Very Special Man

As Tibet and the world celebrated his birthday on 6 July, I wish to celebrate the presence of the Dalai Lama, a Tibetan leader, who has added to the very civilization of India. One has to understand the nature of his influence. I love the apparent paradox of the man, a monk who understands the real world, a refugee at home in the universe, a presence in the very marginality of his location. He makes China look silly, one man's exemplary life against the power of all the battalions. He seems more real, more tangible. In fact, more memorable than Mao Zedong. He appears like history's jokes. One can think of Joseph Stalin asking, 'The Pope? How many divisions has he got?' to realize that this Tibetan monk needs none. That is the beauty, the everydayness and the miracle of this man.

His spirituality can touch the core of ordinariness. I imagined reciting Ogden Nash's limerick to him.

I can hear the monk chuckling hardest, maybe even seeing a Buddhist nuance in it, a special cowl hiding wisdom behind a touch of idiocy.

Yet he, as a religious leader and a Tibetan monk, means

China well. He knows it is a great nation, a greater civilization enamoured with the power of itself, and he wants this powerful state to find the right values. This man realizes that state and church may be separated. He may also realize that theocracies as regimes may not work best, that the Vatican eventually has a symbolic role. But he knows that one cannot doubt the spiritual, the domain of values in the rituals of the state. He wants the rule of law to be wise and benign and he watches like a citizen. He speaks both with the passion of a Tibetan and the quiet detachment of a well-wisher. No foreign policy analyst has that double-edged clarity.

The Dalai Lama gave Tibet a special place in the imagination. From the 'Forbidden City' – the last Shangri-La of orientalists – it became a place the mind visited to renew itself. People talk of Hollywood and the commitment of film stars looking for meaning in Dharamsala, but with the impact of Buddhism on science and ecology peace becomes a search for life, a philosophy beyond security studies and the torrid dilemmas of the nation state.

I also realized his truth is not bland; it has spice and salt to it. I remember a friend of mine, petite, charming, a wonderful rock singer full of life, met him and he greeted her warmly, like an old friend, calling her 'Oh Buddi (old woman)'. She laughed it off, but I realized his insight had cut through. Here was a woman who was almost anorexic in her efforts to stay thin and I think the Dalai Lama sensed it. In a quick way, he was warning her of the old woman in her, requesting her to celebrate that also. The economy and timeliness of the comment intrigued me.

The Dalai Lama marks the best of Indian hospitality – an openness to a defeated country and a way of life with no questions asked. The monk always called India his teacher. While the comment was a simple one I think it had layers to it. He was referring to India as a civilizational home of many religions, of India as civil society, about India as nation and nation state. Puckishly he asks or suggests that maybe today the Indians do not add up. A more immediate example would explain.

Today, South Africa does not add up. A country that fought for freedom refuses to host a conference in which the Dalai Lama could be present. Can realpolitik go so far as to damage a nation's sense of itself? In his silence, the Dalai Lama seems to suggest that the South Africa of today is not quite Africa. It has a sense of being a bit more 'white' than its neighbours. It is in this same context that His Holiness, watching George W. Bush rant about the axis of evil and the dangers of Islam, observed succinctly, 'George Bush brings out the Muslim in me.'

Watching the monk one realizes that three possibilities, each spiritual in nature, have played themselves out in India. One is the guru, the other is the saint and the third is the monk. All are ascetics, all seek to define and exemplify the cultural and spiritual in different ways. All three go beyond the priest as ritual specialist and bureaucrat in articulating the possibilities of a message. I have a layman's view of the three roles as forms of spiritual being, of the way in which they get constructed in folklore. The guru as teacher, as exemplar, as one to follow, is ever present in media. They have been fragments of charisma and popular culture. The guru is a teacher whether in music, dance or religion. He brings an element of craft to spirituality and spirituality to craft. The guru has become a more populist, even controversial, figure through the works of Asaram, Ramdev or even Sri Sri Ravi Shankar and Satya Sai Baba.

When one talks of saints, one thinks of Ramana Maharshi or the first Sai Baba. They lived lives of extraordinary spirituality. They are objects of worship for the way they lived their lives, for their teachings and their spirituality. Gurus are common, but saints are rare, each almost unique and singular in his own way. The monk is a more everyday creature. He is the mule of spirituality. For him, spirituality is work, a regime, a rhythm, and even a routine. While the guru or saint conveys a message, a monk lives out one. He embodies the everydayness of a spiritual regimen.

Between the three they carve out the spiritual space and I feel closest to monks because they need neither miracle nor charisma. Their ritual regimen does the speaking. When I watch monks in the Ramakrishna Mission or the Buddhist monks, I feel the everydayness of religions is intact.

The Dalai Lama is a special monk who combines religion and spirituality to articulate the wisdom of politics. As an ethical exemplar he needs to be celebrated. I am glad that the world is celebrating the genius of a man and his life.

The Asian Age
9 July 2015

Part 14

A Touch of Sadness

Footloose with P.K. Sethi

P.K. Sethi (1927–2008) became a legend in his lifetime and we did what we do to legends. We created a biography, encapsulated him as textbook copy, with a textbook life. But the life of a man is a text that demands several readings where each narrative is a fresh story.

This essay is a resume of Sethi's story not as a biography but as a reflection on four fundamental aspects of the man: Sethi's biography as embodying a nationalist type, his style of innovation, his acute sense of phenomenology and his reflections on medicine.

Pramod Karan Sethi was born on 23 November 1927, the sixth of eight children. His father was a professor of physics at Banaras Hindu University (BHU). BHU marked a patriotism and nationalism of a certain kind. It created a style that was swadeshi, ascetic and deeply devoted to scholarship, a framework that sought to achieve integrity through professionalism, and a generation that offered biography as a value frame. It was a way of life and living which was immaculately correct, open and wary of orthodoxy.

Professor Nihal Karan Sethi transferred from Banaras to Agra and it was in Agra that P.K. Sethi completed his education, attending Balwant Rajput College and Agra College. He obtained his medical degrees from Sarojini Naidu Medical College and capped it with an FRCS from Edinburgh. He then joined SMS Hospital in Jaipur as a lecturer and stayed on to become a legend.

Sometimes the bureaucratic norm as a standard or legal requirement can provide the contingency for an innovative, out-of-the box career. The SMS College, in order to comply with regulations, instituted an orthopaedics department. Sethi was asked to head it though he had no formal training in orthopaedics. He regarded this fact as fortunate because it saved him from encountering orthopaedics with a prefabricated mind. There is a touch of pathos to this phase.

Sethi realized he needed a plan for rehabilitation. The first requirement was a professional physiotherapist and all Sethi had was a masseuse, equipped with a monthly allotment of talcum powder. Sethi knew that as forms of competence, the traditional and modern could be brothers under the skin, a wisdom he followed throughout his career.

The physiotherapy section grew gradually, surviving on gifts from patients. Sethi needed parallel bars and other infrastructure and he found craftsmen to construct them. Sethi argued that physiotherapy was a ritual of competence, a system enabling the patient to recover his skills. He saw the need for occupational therapy and felt that such activities could be both creative and therapeutic. He created a whole range of activities from pedal-operated saws to exercises for manual dexterity, anything that would help a patient return to the citizenship of competence. Sethi sensed the need for a workshop to create such tools. A rehabilitation centre can be a craftsman's studio but what one needed was a traditional craftsman trained in rehabilitation techniques.

Sethi realized that one of his male nurses could be that craftsman. He sent Mohammed Khan to Bombay for a two-year training programme. Khan returned in six months and Sethi set up a workshop for him in an old tea room at the hospital. Christened 'The fabrication unit' it began making calipers and braces. The transition from making braces and calipers to limbs is an almost natural one, but every new stage brings with it a different complexity and a different orthodoxy.

In *The Pasteurization of France*, Bruno Latour, the French sociologist of science, argued that the heroic model of science which gives agency to one man adds little to understanding. Latour's story centred around the network where pasteurization was a compact between microbe, peasant, technology and the scientist. In Latour's narrative, the microbe has an agency of its own in shaping history and theory. In the history of prosthetic limbs, the SACH foot has a similar role.

SACH is an acronym for Solid Ankle Cushioned Heel. As an instrument of prosthetics, a SACH foot is an ode to ethnocentricity. It was a foot piece which hid its artificiality disguised as a shoe. A great improvement over the peg leg, the SACH shoe provided ease of walking. However, it had a rigid wooden heel from ankle to instep which made it impossible for the wearer to squat or sit cross-legged. It represented a way of life that anchored certain cultural and economic assumptions, which became ruthlessly obvious as its novelty wore off. The fabrication unit began with a SACH shoe and gradually discovered its limits.

Sethi understood the complexity of innovations. He did not merely create the Jaipur foot, he created the network of relations that made the foot a possibility. As a wag said, 'He knew when to put the foot forward and when to put the foot down. It was a case of footwork.' We often forget that an invention is an act of philosophy. To create a foot, you don't just sculpt a foot; you visualize and posit a phenomenology. One of the books Sethi loved to cite was Oliver Sacks's *A Leg to Stand On*. Sacks was an exceptional neurologist who wrote an essay on his own damaged foot.

A foot is not just an object, it is a presence. A foot is a theory of walking; it is, in a cultural sense, a theory of squatting. A desk-work foot and a hiking foot demand a different repertoire of actions. An amputated foot is a strange presence. Sacks, in one of his essays, talks of the phantom limb. When a person loses his hand or leg, it persists as a memory, an imaginary of nerves waiting to act it out. A phantom limb is a presence without corporeality. It is there and not there. Amputation as a word evokes erasure. It describes an absence. In an additive sense, a prosthetic foot completes the jigsaw called man. But a jigsaw as a puzzle is different from a symphony. A symphony is a collection of relations, a being and a becoming. A foot that lacks a phenomenology is an object without relations. Surgery, invention, care are all acts of phenomenology and this Sethi intuitively and tacitly recognized. He understood that a technologist is a philosopher and being a technologist and a doctor required both a philosophy and an anthropology. A foot is not just an embodiment of the body. It is a metonym of a culture.

A foot role-plays out a culture as a theory of walking, as a theory of dance and a prosthetic foot must simulate these aspects of culture. In that sense, technology is a set of dialects that call for creative translation.

The Jaipur foot was such an act of adaption, invention and translation. It embodied a theory of pain as a theory of culture. A sense that recovery is an act of discovery and that rehabilitation is not just an act of plumbing.

Invention as mimicry demanded a reframing. The sociological facts were simple. Ours was a society where the shoe is not an everyday fact. Villagers hardly wear shoes and, in an urban environment, women rarely wear shoes at home. As an economic fact, a shoe raises the cost of a limb and makes it more susceptible to breakdown. A stiff shoe is a miscast in a village where walking over rough terrain is essential and squatting is the first act of calisthenics. The logic was simple: Why pay one-third more for additional discomfort? Could one imagine a cheaper, more comfortable limb?

Poverty demands a subtle imagination. A Third World limb does not allow for a third-rate science or a first world imagination. One needs to translate or virtually contextualize the shoe. Sethi made a shopping list of requirements.

The shoe had to cease being a shoe. It had to look like a bare foot and yet be cosmetically acceptable. While being waterproof and durable, it had to allow for ease of walking over uneven ground and allow the wearer to squat and sit cross-legged. In a technical sense, it needed dorsiflexion for squatting, transverse rotation for cross-legged sitting and also allow adaptability over uneven terrain. This much more demanding object had to look natural and remain cheap, providing a challenge to local art and artistry.

Sethi sensed that formally trained technicians disabled themselves. They were men who made Sach's legs, who had internalized the technology and the shoe. It became a black box within which they lived. One needed some sustained out-of-the-box thinking. Re-enter the craftsman, this time one with a pedigree from another paradigm.

Sethi in his typically pragmatic, unsentimental way wanted his patients to learn a craft and possess limbs for it. Fortunately, the craft instructor he found was a curious and caring man, who watched with interest the first fumbling attempts to shape a limb for paraplegics. Ramchandra, or Masterji as he was called, got involved in the exercise.

Masterji had the genealogy of a master craftsman. As a boy, he was apprenticed to artisans working with the maharaja of Jaipur. But the world of patronage with which he grew up was dying out. The new state, as a poor substitute, appointed him a teacher of arts and crafts. When he was being sent off to a village school, Sethi arranged for his transfer.

Masterji was a crucial part of this transformative story. The jugalbandi between a creative surgeon and a master craftsman provided the frame for the rest of the story. Happily the best storyteller of these events was Sethi's son, Harsh, a political economist who wrote major commentaries on the world of NGOs, a world where new forms of innovation were hybridizing with new ideas of institution building. The Sethi–Masterji collaboration deserves every intricacy of ethnographic detail we can muster.

Innovation begins with looking and listening. It moves to an understanding of why the old solution might be the problem. Formal training can become a rail track where the mind chugs along in old grooves. A dissent that merely derails the mind is inadequate. It must persuade the mind to run on different lines. For formally trained limb makers, the SACH foot was bible and imported materials, sacred objects of fetish.

Our craftsman was not subject to such grammars. He thought environmentally in terms of local materials. But one must understand that our craftsmen are not parochial creatures. They love the gossip of the cosmopolitan and blend and experiment with it. Technology, like cooking, becomes open to new recipes.

Ramchandra set up his own workshop in a kitchenette. It, in turn, was part of a building, a servant's quarters that Sethi had converted into a dormitory for paraplegics. Masterji was also skilled in metalwork and die making and the agile Sethi immediately improvised a furnace in the courtyard. Using a plaster of paris model and the ancient sand-casting method of making statues, Masterji produced an aluminium die. Meanwhile Sethi, playing on the experience of the Sri Lankan surgeon G.M. Muller, had designed a variation of 'the foot'. Muller while designing peg legs for Sri Lankan farmers had packed the die with rubber. Ramchandra knew little about rubber. He approached the rubber producers but they were indifferent. He then approached an ordinary wayside tyre retreading shop owned by Chugabhai near the hospital. The latter not only vulcanized the foot but also taught the workers how to do it themselves. He became one of the guardian angels of the place, deriving immense joy and satisfaction watching patients walk away from there.

The first rubber foot was more natural to look at but it was still stiff and suggested the colour of rubber tyres. In fact, Sethi was so discouraged by the product that he suspended work for a year. He played around displacing some of the rubber. While lighter, the shoe was still Western and of little use for squatting or sitting cross-legged. Sethi and Masterji tinkered around trying modification after modification. They scooped out huge parts of the SACH foot, filling it with glued layers of sponge in a vulcanized covering.

A juggling of materials at the concrete level became a shuffling of concepts at the abstract level. The duo, in thinking of the shoe, were reconceptualizing the foot. A substitution of components became a resetting of relations. It was not just a substitution of imported design by indigenous design, it was an invitation to a rethinking. The checklist of changes bears this out. His notes record: 'The sponge rubber heel section of the foot acted as a universal joint allowing freedom of movement in all directions to the amputee. A single wooden block, later supplanted by layered rubber, provided rigidity to the forefront essential for efficient take-off. Both components were wrapped in a rubber casing reinforced with a rayon cord lining commonly used in automobile tyres. The flat sole of the foot was constructed from the rubber compound used for tyre treads and provided traction much like a tennis shoe.'

A new limb was born and it was in three colours. Later a slit was made between the great and second toes to facilitate the wearing of a sandal.

The Jaipur foot would have delighted an Edward de Bono as an anthropology of lateral thinking, where 'six hats' solved a variety of problems by posing the question in many ways. What Kuhn called normal science was not what Sethi and his group belonged to. They were conceptual trespassers, who sought answers where none existed. By not being constrained by the logic of the problematic or profession, they created a set of out-of-the-box solutions.

The Jaipur foot is now the stuff of history. But history took time to be recognized. An invention demands not only unconventional thinking but a way of running the gauntlet of stereotypes. Our Western-trained doctors still hold that quality emanates from research centres and that science as expertise cannot be emulated by the untrained craftsmen and an unorthodox doctor. What people took a long time to understand was that craftsmen grasp science in their own unique way. They may be indifferent to blueprints but produce a 3-D model and they can grasp and reproduce it with uncanny precision. This is not something rare. Any owner of a foreign car desperate for parts could relate stories of the ingenuity of local mechanics. Sadly such stories remain anecdotal and do not take shape as a theory of innovation. Colonialism as a grammar was much more subversive and subservient than we think. But new contents provide new sites and the foot became a global travelling fact in a world addicted to land mines. The foot spread as an ideal solution to the amputated in a world of unrecognized wars.

Awards followed – from a gold medal from the British Orthopaedic Society in 1973 to the Magsaysay Award in 1981. But I feel the awards isolated Sethi and made him lonelier. He was searching for understanding not hagiography or the silly gossip that grows in response to creativity and excellence in our society. But more deeply, he was disappointed at the way medicine itself was going, and was saddened at the decline of the doctor as the ascetic professional and the alienation of medicine from justice and healing. Sethi, as he confessed, was 'a disillusioned man'. His essay, 'The Doctor in the 21st Century', was an initial testimony to this disappointment.

Sethi was more than an inventor and a surgeon. He was deprecatory about himself, claiming that as he was poor at maths, he took biology. A further set of accidents transformed him into a doctor. He was a self-reflexive doctor, deeply aware that medicine without the matrix of philosophy and anthropology was incomplete.

A doctor trained in the colonial era at Agra and Edinburgh, Sethi saw the dreams of Western medicine go wrong. What was to be a paradigm of healing became mechanistic, commercial and iatrogenic. The healer was obsolescent and a medicine that sought efficiency discounted the human.

Recalling autobiographically, Sethi claimed that medicine, like science, developed within a framework of asceticism. Something about the colonial era drove a generation of professionals to excel, to be better or equal to their masters. A few wrote research papers, but their originality expressed itself in a multiplicity of ways. It was a profession that 'oozed wisdom, scholarship, goodness, concern and humility'.

These values made sociological sense in a profession 'that was more art than science', where the doctor was a listener speaking the idiom of the patient. Such a medicine as a dialect lost out to medicine as science under the patronage of the state. The latter sought a different objectivity, celebrated a different idea of measurement which sanctified laboratory indicators rather than a sensitivity to pain and emotion. It was a decline of different kinds of diagnosis and storytelling. Sethi felt like Oliver Sacks who captured this lost world in his works, *Migraine* and *A Leg to Stand On*.

For Sethi, the new medicine destroyed the old contract between man and bacteria, a symbiosis that disappeared in the new politics of anxiety that targeted them. In that process we lost the wisdom of the body. It became 'a fallible contraption in perpetual need of patching'. Medicine based on advanced technology became a medicine of images rather than a full semiotics of the body.

Sethi was no romantic swooning over a lost past. His medicine was a lifestyle and he saw this expressed in the work of some of his colleagues, the Aroles, Raj and Mabelle, at Jamkhed, N.H. Antia's work on leprosy, K.S. Sanjivi's community of doctors – The Voluntary Health Service – in Chennai. It involved one legend celebrating the everydayness of other legends. It is this that made his essay 'The Doctor in the 21st Century', an act of generosity, a reflection of a surgeon recognizing the wisdom of medical critiques, the power of an Ivan Illich, in particular his seminal *Medical Nemesis*, a Lopa Mehta and Manu Kothari and their amazing work on death and cancer, a recognition that medicine as science must dialogue with health as justice. He realized that a medicine for the poor was not a poor medicine but a theory of health that reflected on the poverty of medicine. It was an internal dialogue within Western medicine which was as critical for knowledge as the traditional dialogue of different medical systems.

P.K. Sethi died in early January 2008 of a heart attack. There were obituaries worldwide, all almost identical, as if following a standard sheet. Death as obituary becomes the beginning of erasure. We inaugurate burials with standardization and stereotype. What we need is a festival of storytelling, of celebration, where memory looks at such a community of reinventions. The fact that India had a Sethi, an Amulya Reddy and C.V. Seshadri is a fact for celebration. If a society is known by its dissenters, the last years of the twentieth century were blessed ones. One is grateful for that.

Seminar
February 2008

Remembering Chandra

Today, the astrophysicist, Subramaniam Chandrasekhar (Chandra) seems an almost distant and iconic figure. He is the stuff of legend, and unfortunately his family and friends have stuffed it further. He almost sounds like a theorem – formal, elegant and unapproachable. I want to draw the picture of the man. Elegant he was, and once approached, he was an interesting character that one had to discover, almost anecdote by anecdote; and these were stored like nuggets by his friends. Maybe that is the best way to talk about him.

Chandra was generous. The astronomer Arthur Eddington's opposition to his ideas virtually destroyed his career. It took him several decades of research to vindicate himself. I remember asking him with my political impetuousness, 'Was Eddington a racist?' Chandra looked shocked at the idea. Eddington was still the great Eddington. He might have forced him into virtual exile but Chandra, immaculately correct, treated it as a difference of two scholars.

Chandra was a nationalist, but I think he had little sense of politics beyond that. He read controversies in an almost antiseptic way which was revealing. Asked about Satyen Bose, Chandra claimed he was brilliant and went on to add, 'When

Einstein snubbed him, he retreated. Bose had one flash of insight. It takes two to make a genius'. He felt a sense of wonder and sadness about that early generation of scientists.

His favourite was Ramanujan. He would recite with inexplicable glee how Ramanujan told Hardy that his theorems came to him in a dream. Goddess Namakkal came to him in a dream, unrolled her tongue and offered the solution. Ramanujan the person fascinated Chandra. He was appalled that when Ramanujan was abroad, his mother hid all the letters he wrote to his wife. He would recite the story repeatedly to convey the tragic nature of the event. For him, Ramanujan was unique, a genius. He then added, Ramanujan was a self-taught genius. Solutions to many of the problems he solved were already known to science. Yet, there were others that science is still discovering. He added in a sad footnote, Ramanujan died young at thirty-two. He talked of Ramanujan sitting in a veshti, cooking rice in his room at Cambridge. It was almost as if that little act made Cambridge precious.

He once observed, 'There was Einstein, and Ramanujan and plodders like me.' There was a humility to the man, a sense of the greatness of genius. He used to make me recite Newton's remark that he was like a child collecting shells on the shore while the great ocean of knowledge lay unexplored before him.

His modesty before genius hid his impatience with mediocrity. He was completely impatient or helpless before the everyday, the mediocre or the inane. Chandra was utterly proper, correct to his Brahminic core. This made him formidable and sometimes intolerant. I remember he was once discussing his old favourite, the English author, Virginia Woolf, celebrating both the elegance of her language and emotion. His sister, Sundari, my aunt, was rattling away happily about her grandchildren being happy in their achievements. Irritated, Chandra turned around and said, 'Can't you talk of something serious?' Sundari, a formidable person, retaliated, 'I will talk about my grandchildren. You talk about what you like and let us also do the same.' Brother and sister stood in immaculate opposition, signifying two ways of life.

Chandra was ruthlessly systematic about work. He would master a new field every decade, grasp it with a comprehensiveness, a sense of mastering a musical oeuvre. He told me it kept him from going stale. His work ethic was awesome, almost obsessive. My father and he would write letters regularly to each other. Each set revealed the man. My father's letters were fresh, almost muscular, in their claim to life. Chandra's were honest but often had the delicacy and precision of a titration.

But Chandra had his struggles. The one thing he struggled with all his life was his inability to reconcile himself with his father, whom he found authoritarian.

I must confess he had little sense of everyday politics. He liked Indira Gandhi and found her an intelligent woman. When Emergency came he supported it saying, India needed discipline. It is just that he found the Nehru family more aesthetic, more modern. The opposition seemed inelegant and no amount of talk about human rights could convince him. Indira was different and he felt she was the right person to lead India.

There was an innocence and simplicity about him. He wished to visit his old college, Presidency College, Madras. He wore a dhoti and a white shirt and walked anonymously down the college as memory lane and came back grinning like a child.

I remember one meeting at my grand-uncle's place in South Extension, Delhi. My father, he and my grand-uncle had spread out huge sheets and were arguing about the monsoons, haggling over data, like it was a bazaar for science. My grand-aunt held my hand and said, 'Look at them, they are so happy. All they need is coffee and science.' It was fun watching the three scientists go back and forth. It gave one a sense of the pleasures of science. They were like three violinists in a mad performance revealing a sense of science as sheer joy.

There were other occasional stories I was fond of. One was about another favourite of his, Enrico Fermi. Chandra was editing *The Astrophysical Journal* and taking great pains over it. The great Fermi was almost dismissive of the journal, claiming he did not have time to read. He said he just talked to the leading men in the field and such conversations were adequate for his research. My favourite anecdote was about Yang and Lee. Chandra drove a hundred miles to teach them and when they got the Nobel, he would proudly and impishly say, 'My entire class won the Nobel.' He added sadly, almost cryptically, that Yang and Lee had drifted apart and no longer talked to each other.

There were moments of beauty and elegance about him. He worked at these but sometimes his sense of correctness was unyielding. I remember hearing about a cousin of mine who drove all the way from Princeton to see him and Chandra snubbed him because he did not have an appointment. I remember him complaining helplessly about a niece who insisted that her son had the makings of a mathematical genius. There was something Wodehousian about it.

I loved the man but as a man with flaws, tensions, elegant to a fault and yet difficult in many ways. One hopes that in celebrating the scientist, one does not separate and forget the man, his struggle as a scientist, struggling alone in an alien world. I wish one day the letters he wrote to his brother are recovered and published. They tell a beautiful story of a friendship and reveal the personal side of a wonderfully complex man. Let us hope he does not become the one-dimensional caricature during his 100th anniversary. One hopes biography can resist hagiography.

New Indian Express
5 November 2010

Dara Singh

The Last Action King

India never had a native Tarzan because we wanted something more than a noble savage. Our Junglee was a totally different creature, raucous, rustic or even autistic in a different way.

Our culture valued physical prowess but demanded some additives from it. He could not smack of the jungle but of the grace and power of folk prowess, folk remedies. We wanted a Punjab-da-puttar rather than Tarzan. We wanted the authenticity of culture rather than nature from our hero. Our physical hero had to have a touch of maturity, a whiff of intelligence. Humour could not hurt and nor would chivalry. A mere inmate from an akhada would not do. The akhada, despite its role during the Partition, was a narrow domain, and eventually an annex for elections. The wrestler as a hero had to wrestle with life, and in wrestling with life, had to paint a larger sociological, even civilizational picture. The image and career of Dara Singh, alias Deedar Singh Randhawa, was made to order for just this.

Dara was not a mere wrestler. He was a folk hero, a toast of princes and eternal joy of haats and melas. As a wrestler, he was victorious, winning jousts all over the Commonwealth. In that world of excess we called wrestling, he was the world champion, though one must confess the world was a smaller place then.

Dara was a piece of folklore dying to enter Bollywood. He did this as King Kong in 1962. He sensed he had to pick the right myths and the correct moments. He was a great fighter and his goodness blended the physical and the moral. He found his niche as Hanuman in Ramanand Sagar's TV adaptation of the Ramayana. This was an archetypical role. As a celluloid Hanuman, he knew he could not be a hoodlum, a goonda, a rowdy; at the most he could be a dada, well endowed, well intentioned, with the right mix of nature and culture.

Dara was an archetype of a heroic man who was sadly reduced to a stereotype of masculinity. What marked him was a sense of versatility, a readiness to experiment. True, he exuded the physical as he moved from being the Rustam-e-Hind of wrestling to the action king of the Hindi film industry. He discovered Mumtaz and worked with her in sixteen films. He was a Salman Khan in an age where a Salman Khan could not be thought of. But if the latter was a perpetual brat, the other was perennially mature. He was no sidekick. The authenticity of the man created versatility as he mellowed.

The BJP, which was always a shrewd judge of TV as folklore, made him a member of the Rajya Sabha from 2003 to 2009. Yet he was no Hindi heartland provincial. His appeal extended from Tamil to Hindi films and he played Rajinikant's father in *Maaveran*, a remake of *Mard*. He had a guest role in *Anand*. He acted in 118 films ending his film career with *Jab We Met* in 2007. By that time, the raw physicality had mellowed to a deeper authenticity laced with rustic wisdom. There was a Punjabi verve to it which one sensed in his last film where he played a grandfather whose juices were flowing. He did not have to act, he just had to be himself. His humanity comes out in his Punjabi interviews. When asked to play Hanuman at the age of fifty-nine, he hesitated, wondering whether he had the physical aura for the role.

Dara aged in an interesting way. He did not wither like Rajesh Khanna or Dev Anand. His moustache bristled, his muscles rippled, conveying a deep commitment to life. The humour bubbled and one realized that he would always be an archetypical Indian; local in values, global in impact. Dara's career was not just the life of a champion but what future legends would call a champion of life. He was the Bollywood ultimate where screen and life combined till one did not know the difference: the legend as the ultimate reality show.

India Today
13 July 2012

A Tribute to Political Scientist Extraordinaire and Teacher, Rajni Kothari

How does one talk of a man who defined a subject, determined its directions, was its dominating presence without a shade of pomposity or status? Rajni Kothari (1928–2015) was clear about some of the subjects of his studies, irreverently and pragmatically certain that the Indian elite was knowledge-proof, that the only changes it would accept were pressures from below or by mimicking its colonial masters. Here was a man far ahead of his times, a futurist in perspective.

Today the tributes will flow and embalm the man. Dissenting imaginations are best sanitized lest they destroy the hypocrisy and the current clichés of the establishment. The obituaries will recite how he started election studies, how he set up the Institute of Chinese Studies, founded journals like *Alternatives* and the *Lokayan Bulletin*. They will dub him the author of Indian political science's only durable classic, *Politics in India*. Oddly, Rajni was embarrassed by the longevity of the book and even tried to stall further publications but the book, like many of his inventions, had a wonderful life of its own.

To me it was not just the inventiveness of the man that is important. It was the vision he brought to his work. Rajni's enduring passion was his commitment to democracy, its sustainability, its creativity and its vulnerability. The sense of democracy was not an abstract one of formal definitions. He saw democracy as a way of life and wanted people to live it out and celebrate its everydayness.

This is what impelled him to create that wonderful institution, Centre for the Study of Developing Societies (CSDS). CSDS was a community, a perpetual adda built around the gossip of democracy. Without this passion for democracy his many projects would have made little sense. They were mere pretexts for sustaining the texts of democracy which in a holistic sense went beyond elections, data analysis, governance and grass-roots studies

Two things must be stated clearly. CSDS was a collage of friendships and Rajni invented many of his ideas along with his friends. He had an acute sense of the inventive and followed it up creatively. In that sense the idea often originally belonged to the others. Rajni's idea of the Congress as a coalition of competing confusions was Gopal Krishna's. The idea of *Lokayan* as a grass-roots experiment belonged more to Ramashray Roy and D.L. Sheth. Rajni took it and transformed it.

As a commons of ideas, CSDS was extraordinary. For me, CSDS is that wonderful pack of quirky incorrigible scholars like Ashis Nandy, Bashiruddin Ahmed, Sudhir Kakar, Giri Deshingkar quarrelling over ideas at every lunch as if democracy was a hypothesis that had to be digested every day. No group had a greater passion for politics, its myths, its facts and its folklore.

The style, the theory, was as important as the substance. Neither CSDS nor Rajni will rest in peace if I do not resort to a few anecdotes.

I remember how he recruited me. Rajni was chairman of

ICSSR (Indian Council of Social Science Research) and he had heard rumours about me as a rebellious and even problematic PhD student at the Delhi School of Economics. He dropped in one day for a casual chat and asked me to join CSDS. Some of my teachers warned him against it. And one of them even complained that I was a goonda, a gangster. Rajni smiled and said, 'I need a few intellectual gangsters for my new project.' He had an easy charm that soothed opponents and part of it came from his acute ability to listen. If you insulted him, he listened intently almost as if you were wooing him.

CSDS and Rajni became institutional legends during the Emergency. It was then that CSDS became home for every dissenting imagination: George Fernandes, Romesh Thapar, Arun Shourie and Kuldip Nayar were frequent visitors. This hospitality to dissent seeded the creative style of the future where CSDS became home to critical studies, social movements and the search for alternative imaginations. CSDS, which glorified the Nehruvian era and the initial creativity of the Congress, now became Indira Gandhi's fiercest and most obsessive critic. It became the hub of human rights movements, environmental struggles, and development battles that insisted that democracy had to reinvent itself beyond its electoral form. Civil society became the creative subject of study: a counter to the elitist preoccupation with the state and its development project.

The Left was the dominant intellectual imagination of the period. Rajni had no quarrel with the Left, only with Leftists who romanced with the state, infiltrating government committees as if they were party cells. Oddly, both the Left and the Right were obsessed with being legitimized by the state. During the infamous controversy involving history textbooks when ideologists went hysterical, Rajni observed quietly, 'Both sides wanted the state to approve of their version of history.' This intellectual dependency on state approval of scholarship worried Rajni. Did truth need to be approved by power?

Rajni had a playful response to criticism. I remember when an acerbic Marxist wrote a critique of his work claiming that Rajni had forgotten to mention the word class, with easy equanimity Rajni replied that he had not mentioned cucumbers either. This ease was important because the period of the 1960s and the '70s was dominated by a pompous Left which treated Marxism with a kind of idolatry. Rajni felt that Marxist critiques dealt more with the formal economy and had little place for marginal groups and the informal economy. Little protests did not acquire the officialdom of trade union struggles. The movements alone in the era, Chipko, Narmada, Balliapal and the fishermen's struggle in Kerala had to battle with the official radicalism which refused to go beyond conventional categories. CSDS became an archive and a sounding board for many of these struggles which linked ecology, livelihood and empowerment to the still life of electoral democracy.

Rajni had an easy way of pushing younger colleagues to stretch beyond themselves. I remember when the Bhopal gas disaster occurred. He looked at me and said, 'Let's see if your work on science helps. Pack up. You are leaving for Bhopal tomorrow.' When I began my work on science and violence, he sent me to Hiroshima requesting the mayor to take me around the city. He believed that projects should begin as pilgrimages; he was always nudging us to see linkages and connectivities. He never lectured, and wanted us to discover and internalize and share our insights. For him mistakes were something precious one owned up to. He was a great teacher who always taught by anecdote and example.

I must confess that in the final decade, many of us moved away from CSDS and Rajni. Quarrels are important because they mark the contours of a relationship. One felt that CSDS was now imitating itself rather than inventing ideas. In spite of having moved on, I realized how much CSDS had taught me.

In his final years, Rajni was a lonely man – ill and broken by the death of his wife, Hansa, and son, Smithu. Also, by then, political science had lost its flavour of dissent. It had become a game of think tanks and Rajni must have watched it with wry sadness, a prophet abandoned by his own community. The future however will no doubt celebrate the man.

The Hindu
21 January 2015

Nek Chand

Remembering a 'Rock' Star

Nek Chand, one of the world's foremost and self-taught artists, passed away last week. It felt as if an entire era had disappeared with him. Most readers, especially the younger generation, might ask who he was. He was not Maqbool Fida Husain, Hamidur Rahman or M.S. Subbulakshmi. But if one looked for an answer in the world of creativity, he was on a par with them; a legend who emerged out of folklore to create another volume of folklore around his notion of art.

To understand this great man and his work, one has to go back in time to Partition, Le Corbusier and Chandigarh. Tired with the violence of Partition, Jawaharlal Nehru wanted to create a new memory and a new sense of India and wanted Chandigarh to embody that vision. To enact the vision, he summoned one of the greatest international architects, Le Corbusier, to build his new city. Corbusier's Chandigarh is now legendary as India's greatest planned city.

Corbusier was a Swiss-born French architect who belonged to the first generation of the so-called international school of architecture. It was he who prepared the master plan for the city of Chandigarh and contributed specific designs for several buildings there.

In fact, Nek Chand appears as a footnote in the celebrated Corbusier story. He was a child of Partition, whose family moved to India. Later, he found work in Chandigarh by joining the Public Works Department (PWD). He was fascinated by the story of how the city was conceptualized and even talked in awe of having once sighted Corbusier by the lake. But what intrigued Nek Chand more was the debris from the sixteen villages that Corbusier's Chandigarh displaced. He was fascinated with the shapes of the junk. He loved the art of erosion which he called 'God's way of sculpting nature'. He felt nature itself was a great sculptor and called himself a mere collector.

Out of these mounds of debris, and remnants of waste, the humble PWD worker created a spectacle of art; at first surreptitiously, in the forests around Chandigarh. It was almost as if the selected debris from these villages was a counter-statement to Corbusier's manifesto of the city. Junk, as a record of memory, soon became an answer to India's great planned city. As news of Nek Chand's prowess spread, he managed to find space for his surreal fantasy and creativity in the form of a plot of a few acres of land in Chandigarh. Thus, the foundation for his fabled rock garden was laid. To call it a tourist attraction would be to undervalue it. It was a semiotic masterpiece that quietly restated the values of industrialism and urbanism. However, his critique was not sociological. It was a 'folklorist' response to urbanism. It was as if planning was being retold through tales from the *Panchatantra*.

There is an air of storytelling, myth and fairy tale about the rock garden. It is what the French would call a bricolage or something constructed or created from a diverse range of things and which makes a statement. Nek Chand's garden was structured at three levels. In the first, there was a collection of eroded rocks surrounded by little gardens that depicted nature as a spectacle. The second was a 'festival of junk' where shards of glass, bits of porcelain and the debris of a city were shaped into a giant menagerie of animals. It was a zoo where birds, lions and zebras enacted a carnival. The garden had a wall and on its turrets, Nek Chand walked every day, the lord of all he surveyed. The garden was a child's delight and an adult's wonder. All the animal species one could think of in myth and in the local forest formed a combination to stage this creation.

Nek Chand realized that what people saw as 'waste' and as something to be abandoned, had immense value as a form of entertainment. He came up with the idea of wanting the general public to slowly understand that their 'waste' was a philosophy, and even a way of life. 'Waste' was not something to be thrown away but was a material with immense potential that could be reworked and recycled as works of art. To him, an object did not die when disposed of in a garbage bin. It could be given life again and reincarnated to continue a new story. Soon, this idea of 'born again waste' fascinated people. He would travel around Chandigarh asking people to give him their rubbish. Nek Chand felt that terms such as junk, garbage and waste belonged to the language of materialism, and that generating waste as a culture was critical in understanding a society and how it worked. During one of my interviews with him, he talked about his foreign trips and the opportunities he got there to work on waste. Did it work? He wistfully admitted that 'their junk was not like our junk and spoke a different language'.

There was a leprechaun-like quality about the man as he took visitors around his castles created from 'waste'. One could see that he had breathed life into it; it was almost like a play being enacted before us with the subjects of folklore and fantasy. One felt as if his animal creations were speaking to him. On one of my visits, he proudly showed me a huge cartoon of the political leader, Lalu Prasad.

Walking around his garden, I sensed that Nek Chand was cryptic and even reticent about a large, empty space in his garden. He even went into a mysterious sulk when I asked him what he planned to do with it. I got no answer.

One day, I got to know that Nek Chand had been invited to attend a World Punjabi Conference in Pakistan. He decided to visit his village which I learnt had been obliterated after heavy bombing by the Indian Army. As he recollected fond memories of his place, Nek Chand became excited. While mourning its loss, he found his spark and moment of creativity. Nek Chand decided to recreate his 'remembered village' out of the waste and junk in his rock garden. Waste which people had discarded or forgotten would now become the basis, not of erasure and obsolescence, but of memory. For this, his village would be forged from and would rise from rags, cloth and plastic. The remembered village would be the philosophical answer to the new urbanism of Le Corbusier. Recycling would confront design, remembrance would be juxtaposed with planning and garbage would become a way of retelling a story – a bridge with lost memory, a city and its long-forgotten refugees.

In a way, it is tragic to recollect this. Nek Chand, for all his impish, playful genius, has today been reduced to the level of a secondary artist. His celebrated rock garden – which was even subject to attack by vandals – is almost treated with the same delight that one would greet a child's creation; a collector's toy that is seen at an exhibition. His sense of the classic did not stem from great traditions but from the easy everydayness of folklore. It was all about folklore and myth which came alive as animals and other creatures in his magic forest created from waste.

Yet, behind his creativity and representation was not just

folk wisdom but a deep philosophy, which many seem to have missed; it posed an intellectual challenge to an India that had, and has, grown out of urbanism, industrialism and design. By emphasizing the magical power and the potency of renewal in what the rest of the world dismissed as waste, he challenged – and still does – the popular and current culture of generating waste which treats both people and materials as being dispensable.

Nek Chand felt and echoed the philosophy of the great chemist, C.V. Seshadri. Seshadri, who came up with great ideas while working out of a small laboratory near a slum in Madras, once claimed that 'waste is the only resource of a wasted people'. He felt that the idea of a slum as such highlighted the desperation of creativity.

Slums, he felt, should not be treated as objects worthy of a pathological examination but as representative of a new citizenship of creativity. For both Nek Chand and Seshadri, recycling was a new form of storytelling; here, the material instead of facing an end, was transformed, reinvented and then told a different story. In his creation, Nek Chand showed that craft could, and still can, redeem the ill effects of industrialism by prolonging the life of a product long beyond its industrial efficiency.

There was also a deeper critique of the current ideas of what a city is – of an urbanism which ignores waste, that is illiterate about the informal economy, and which fails to recognize the citizenship of the marginal. With its sense of memory and the inclusiveness of waste, Nek Chand's garden suggested a more organic city, where the city represented growth and was not a mere artefact.

The city that he visualized is a more humane answer to the cities of today which have no place for refugees, memory, for waste or for a defeated people wanting to pursue a different way of life.

In that sense, he was more than just an artist. Nek Chand was a philosopher of technology who in turn gave technology a sense of pathos, irony and laughter. He provided technology a mirror in which it could laugh at itself and go beyond the hubris of innovation to reflect on its tragicomic consequences.

The Hindu
19 June 2015

Yellappa

The Last Trustee of Indigo

I often work as a historian of science, an ethnographer of social battles, seeking to capture the story of an age. I sometimes play storyteller, but often I am a mere munshi, a recorder of movements, who keeps their archives, their memories alive. The other day, a friend of mine told me in the middle of a lecture on weaving, 'Yellappa died.' The announcement was so matter-of-fact that it took my breath away. In the world of indigo dyes, Yellappa was a master craftsman, the last of the great dyers. It was as if a Picasso or Mozart had died. A genius dies in India and the news is met with silence. For me, as an anthropologist who is perpetually writing on the history of loss and erasure, it was as if Ishi, the last Indian of the Yahi tribe, had died. When Ishi died, a language died, a way of life died, and a set of dreams faded away. Today, ways of life are perpetually dying and there seems no way of remembering, recovering or redeeming them. I realize how the anthropologist Alfred Kroeber might have felt as he wrote Ishi's story. There is no Yellappa story, just a few fragments of recollection, but I thought I would put them down. There are a few who knew him and this is what they told me. I am not the storyteller; just a cassette tape mourning the loss of a genius.

Yellappa was the last of a family of great indigo dyers in Andhra Pradesh. Indigo was a legendary colour, a natural dye, which died when the organic chemists synthesized an artificial dye. Yet the natural colour was not the same as the synthesized colour. It was like saying that the glass windows of Chartres Cathedral are the same after we recreated the stained glass windows. When natural indigo died, a way of life began fading away. In India, however, nothing dies fully. People keep it alive in little silent pockets which struggle invisibly.

In recent times, the story of Yellappa started as a rumour, a fragment of a National Institute of Design (NID) thesis by Padmini Balaram. The dyer had invited Yellappa to come to NID and set up a vat, paying him a professor's salary. Yet Yellappa was unhappy. He felt no one really wanted to learn and that his colours were being insulted. He left NID and worked as a paid labourer in a chemical dye house. Yellappa was secretive about his skill and suspicious of outsiders. He was a scrupulous trustee, contemptuous of dabblers. He cropped up again literally when Uzramma, head of Dastakar Andhra, persuaded Guruppa Chetty, a Kalamkari artisan, to bring him back. Uzramma could be persuasive in a way NID could never be. She knew that her group of weavers were different. She realized that for indigo to be authentic, one had to have the right soul, the right soil, the right climate, but also the right people to listen, hear, and tune in. As Yellappa complained, his indigo 'was a delicate child: treat her harshly and she withdraws and swoons'. A colour has to be enticed to be redeemed.

Colour, any colour, contains the hues of dedication and sacrifice. Craft in that sense is a ritual of understanding. Yellappa was the last trustee of indigo as an indigenous form of knowledge.

Uzramma enticed Yellappa to teach the weavers of Chinnur. Chinnur was more to Yellappa's liking. It was a community of weavers, friends; and collaboration was not in an antiseptic professional institution. The weavers invited him to set up his vats, his large pots, in the village.

But things were not easy. Nothing suited Yellappa in the beginning. He grumbled about food, the water, the charpoy that wouldn't fit him. Yet the villagers played to his every whim. Yellappa's very intransigence was a part of the initiation rituals of indigo. Redeeming a colour was redeeming its rituals of memory, its practices, its craft and toil.

There were technical problems as the vats were set up. The local potters had a different style. They made smaller pots and they refused to make the large vats Yellappa needed. Finally an old potter agreed to make them. As the vats were built, old memories came alive, old routines thawed and hummed. Old fragments, discarded rituals, throbbed to life.

Building a vat is an art. To make a vat 'flower' was to create a cycle of fermentation. Each vat has a ruthless time cycle of its own. The vats arranged in Chinnur became a symphony of orchestrated time, where half of them were always at the right stage of dyeing. Yellappa felt at home. He had security, a salary of Rs 3,000. He invited his younger son to come and join him.

Teaching a craft such as dyeing was like recreating a miniature civilization. The body was the site of memory. One carried knowledge in one's fingertips. As Shakti, an NID designer from a craftsman's family, explained, 'The hand knows. If you want to gauge temperature, the hand will tell you.' Shakti once asked Yellappa, 'How do you measure pH value?' Yellappa replied, 'I smell it.' Smell is an index of pH.

Salim, one of the later dyers, explained that the colour indigo is not extracted; it has to be coaxed. You cannot force a vat to reveal its secrets. It whispers them to you when it is ready. Uzramma explained that Yellappa is a trustee of indigo. One is grateful one met him, and today one has a community of natural indigo dyers in Andhra Pradesh. She remarks sadly that the old red, the madder red, is lost forever. The art historian and geologist Ananda Coomaraswamy wrote one of his classic papers on synthetic red, contending that a standardized red is an inadequate red, and red comes alive in each village, each craft community adding its own quality of redness to it. The colour indigo would be lost without Kamaladevi Chattopadhyay, without Uzramma, Yellappa, Jagada and Salim.

Colour and indigenous dyes owe a moment of tribute and reverence to Chandramouli. Uzramma explained that if natural dyes had a master craftsman, a storyteller, it was Chandramouli. He was not a usual scientist but a chemist who spent his life among craftsmen. An India would honour a C.N.R. Rao, a Venkatraman Ramakrishnan, but that same India needs to honour a Yellappa, a Chandramouli. Chandramouli was a walking encyclopedia of indigenous recipes. He was a government chemist who, after retirement, repaid the gift of indigenous knowledge. He and Uzramma became a duo who revived indigenous colour. He recreated natural dyeing, keeping it alive while teaching Kalamkari artists and taxi drivers with equal enthusiasm.

The sadness is that Chandramouli died in 1997, just as Uzramma was going all out to trace Yellappa. There is a poignancy to this search as an older generation fades away silently. India needs to honour the Yellappas and all its great trustees of colours.

The Hindu
25 November 2014

PART 15

Afterthoughts
A Miscellany

Ahmedabad

An Imagination for a City

Ahmedabad has not been as lucky as some other cities in that it hasn't always had access to a bustling, thriving social imagination. It has had its great photographers like Cartier-Bresson, its great architects like Corbusier and Louis Kahn. They defined a few sites, created a few buildings, but they didn't weave the socio-drama of a city. Ahmedabad is a city pleading for a social science perspective, a sense of literature, art, space and colour that could define it more intellectually.

There are fragments of a social science language, the embryos of important experiments. After all, one of the great experiments in psychology was embodied in the B.M. Institute of Mental Health which can invoke major disciples of Anna Freud and the grand presence of Erik Erikson. BM has had great figures like Ramanujan, Ashis Nandy and Sudhir Kakar on its roster; but their totemic affiliations seem elsewhere. IIM produced fragments of a social science imagination. Kamla Chowdhry was the most outstanding as an early exponent of the Tavistock School, but she failed to create any effective nursery of social science. St Xavier's incubated the Behavioural Science Centre and possessed some outstanding teachers like Suguna Ramanathan. The city owes her a debt of gratitude. Our universities were empty. Nirma is too recent to have an impact. MICA's (Mudra Institute of Communications, Ahmedabad) effort to be a centre for media and semiotics research still needs incubation time.

However, what could not be created academically was reinvented through a proliferation of NGOs. SEWA (Self Employed Women's Association) under Ela Bhatt and Renana Jhabvala have articulated the world view of women and the informal economy, weaving around gender and livelihood an acute sensitivity. Through the Honey Bee Network, Anil Gupta has created not a museum of dead technologies, but living sensibility around local innovations. 'Bhasha' might belong more to Tejgadh and Baroda, but Ganesh Devy has been a roving presence at Ahmedabad, courageous in his idea of the tribe and its travails. The Sabarmati Ashram threatens to come alive again in the social science efforts of Tridip Suhrud. SETU: Centre for Social Knowledge and Action under Achyut Yagnik is indispensable for any political understanding of Ahmedabad. NID's craft catalogue hints at the making of an original social science imagination but sadly, as something partially unmade.

One might ask why a city needs such an availability of interpretations. These perspectives provide a common ground for discourses around which role, communities and responsibilities can be constructed and socio-dramas invoked. They provide frameworks of identity and sites for redefinition. This is crucial because a city is perpetually incomplete and constantly reworking itself. In moments of crisis, disruption or breakdown, the social sciences and the humanities are more than a Linus blanket. They can be life-giving, providing an availability of storytelling, analysis, therapy and also the crystal seeds of a new construction.

Such an availability of ideas was necessary thrice in recent times and each time the city shrunk because it could not access those ideas and their possibilities.

Ahmedabad was a great textile city, but when the textile industry died its slow but ruthless death, there were few to chronicle this story. The exception was in fact the Dutch sociologist, Jan Breman. Ahmedabad owes him a monument. When textiles declined, the soul of the city shrank in the absence of storytelling. The debate over the Narmada dam created an intolerance, a silence, an ostracism which the city has yet to recover from. Truth-telling is never welcome but it is absolutely essential in dramas of such scale. The carnage of 2002 produced the third failure. The standard stereotypes of fascism and communalism explained little of what happened in the city and to the city. Activist reports kept care alive, memories alive but not analysis. It was a fight for rights but without the classical understanding that should have anchored it.

There is a sadness here, a sadness compounded by the failure to understand the mall, the SEZ, the diaspora, the explosion of desire that rocks the city. A mimicry of social science through marketing and management terminology won't do.

What one faces is an intellectual and institutional challenge. One needs to create spaces for conversation, a hospitality for dissenting ideas and most of all that sense of conscience that keeps a city alive to its possibilities. A 600-year-old city without a cornucopia of theorists, analysts, interpreters would be undefinable sadness. One hopes one can avoid it.

DNA

17 July 2008

Will Advani Apologize for Godhra?

Dear Advaniji,

This is a letter to a man who represents my constituency and also to the individual many think of as a future prime minister. It is also a reflection on the fate and ironies of Indian politics. I am not a BJP supporter but I don't think I want to demonize the role of the BJP. I was a student during the days of the Emergency and I have admired the courage that many of you showed at that time. It was a period when Jaitley was a charismatic student leader and Arun Shourie galvanized a generation of young journalists. I also realize you are a fellow film lover, a Sindhi who can still feel a nostalgia and fondness for his home in Karachi.

Yet, today, I must make a small request.

I must ask you to step down from your seat.

I believe you are a man who understands violence and I know that you, your party and the RSS cadre have confronted it publicly several times. The first was around the agony of the Partition and the profound pain Hindus and Muslims suffered. I realize you have been unhappy with the idea of secularism.

You dubbed it a pseudo-concept but had little to offer as an alternative.

The agony of pain, especially as it marks history, needs an intellectually satisfying answer or an emotionally fulfilling one. I am afraid you have fanned much anger but not offered one word of consolation or healing. Does Babri Masjid become an answer to the emptiness or inauthenticity of secularism? The violence that followed makes one wonder how accountable you felt for the long-range consequences of your political rhetoric. One has to ask: Are politicians irresponsible wordsmiths or are they to be held accountable for the positions they take? If so, Advaniji, could you honestly tell me what the genocidal quotient of your speeches is? I acknowledge that there were times when the response of the party and your own stand towards violence have been courageous. Your stand against the Emergency was immaculate. The role of the RSS in sustaining everyday life in Punjab during the violence of Khalistan has not been given the attention it deserves.

Yet, when it came to the murder you appeared tone-deaf. Is a missionary less of a human being because he is Christian, a foreigner and a missionary? Having set the background, let me address the central issue of and the violence of 2002. Let us begin with a simple fact that violence began from your constituency. The dead bodies from the Godhra carnage were paraded here, triggering not a ritual of mourning but an orgy of the most obscene violence our country has witnessed in recent times. Yet you spoke as if a balance of murder is the only sense of justice you have. When you can mourn for what happened to the Kashmiri Pandits, what prevents you from acknowledging a moral responsibility for what happened in your constituency, or are you saying that ethnic cleansing is a permitted and legitimate form of political hygiene? Today, the evidence before the Nanavati Commission and the investigations of the SIT show that your party has been deeply involved in rioting, violence and genocide. Your attitude seems to suggest that majoritarianism exhausts the democratic imagination, that violence is an acceptable tactic for enforcing majoritarianism. Your close colleague and our current CM seems to suggest that it is part of the logic of development.

Violence negates politics and a party that banalizes violence eventually exhausts its own political imagination. One wonders whether the current emptiness of your party is a result of this indifference to the atrocities that so many citizens suffered. There is a difference I want to emphasize.

Vajpayee owned up to mistakes, even expressed frailty, doubt and error.

You stand immaculate in your disciplined competence and yet one gets little sense of doubt and uncertainty.

One would expect some words of regret and apology for what your party did after Godhra. When the German leader, Willy Brandt apologized for the Holocaust kneeling in a concentration camp, he accepted a moral responsibility, a humility before what had happened.

It was not an admission of guilt, it was a claim to responsibility. A leader has to have the courage to own up.

As Peter Drucker once said, a manager does things right, a leader does the right things. Does one conclude, then, that you managed the party, its organization and its election campaigns but leadership as a claim to the ethical high ground was beyond you? As a leader, you could have shown the way to Modi. Yet realpolitik demanded that you both become siblings in evil. A word of apology, a recognition of a wrong done, a statement of an alternative imagination would have been a true answer to the fumbling fuzziness of secularism. Trapped in your own sense of machismo, you now echo the language of security, creating a paranoid electoral style which is futile in the long run. And it is tragic that they cannot yet be Muslim and Indian. In a deep way, your behaviour shows you lack the power of a South Asian imagination that speaks for and speaks to different localities. If you stoop to Modi's level, you stoop lower than him as you are something he is not, or not yet, a natural leader. The irony is that, in emphasizing the emptiness of secularism, you actually elaborated the depths of evil your communalist politics was capable of.

Your constituency is today on its way to being a beehive of academic institutions.

We have an IIT, a leading computer and information science centre, major centres for design, fashion, law and petroleum. It promises to create an ecology of intelligence, a place in which your ideologies can be life-threatening to intellectual values and institution building. As an academic, a citizen, proud of the Gandhian tradition and its commitment to non-violence, I have a small request. Do own up to the violence you have created, or go. I realize that mine might be a futile, dissenting voice. But it is mnemonic that in the future one vote you will not win. A leader and a statesman is aware of his limits unlike a politician who clings to power even when it is counterproductive.

Let us hope you are leader enough to do that. You owe it to the democracy you once fought so courageously for.

New Indian Express
8 May 2009

The Fading Memory of Nationalism

One of the intriguing themes that Anna Hazare's fast threw up was the question of memory, particularly the memory of nationalism. As one activist explained, he had read about Rajguru and Bhagat Singh while studying for his exam. But it was only now they rang true.

It struck me how distant the national movement was and how simplified and even ridiculous it had become.

One of the things that destroyed nationalism was the arrival of the nation state. The nation state abbreviated the complexity of nationalism by defining the permissible options. It even ordained the permissible options. Its tutorial-college mind loved oppositions between Nehru and Gandhi or between Gandhi and the Left. But deep down, nationalism had a sense of civilizational gossip which the nation state did not. Worse, the Partition and the holocaust that followed, hollowed the nation state and its history. We were now a nation contra Pakistan.

Nationalism lives now only as a fragment. Yet nationalism as an imagination did not merely create imagined communities as the glibness of Benedict Anderson proclaimed. Our nationalism also dealt with the inventiveness and imagination of communities.

Just consider a single issue: science and technology. Let me describe the variety of debates that took place. Our nationalism was unique because it was always open to the dissenting British imagination. We saw the West as plural and saw some of these Wests as part of us. Our nationalism allowed for the other side of the Raj, a place for dissenters like Patrick Geddes, Alfred Wallace, C.F. Andrews, Annie Besant who helped shape a different West in India. India was not anti-West, it was anti-colonial.

Consider one paradigmatic figure: Captain Srinivasa Murti. He was an authority on traditional medicine, head of the Adyar Library, secretary to the committee that debated the future of indigenous medicine in 1923. He also translated *Merchant of Venice* into Telugu and was John Barrymore's doctor when the actor became an alcoholic. He warned about the dangers of nuclear energy in the 1920s and stressed the importance of mothers feeding their babies. He was a cosmopolitan.

Rabindranath Tagore was another such cosmopolitan. A cosmopolitan does not deny his identity. He only refuses to make a fetish of it. Tagore built Santiniketan as a university to dialogue with the Western university. He was sceptical of nationalism and yet felt we must be open to the West. Tagore was not an internationalist; he was a cosmopolitan seeking unities beyond the national. Tagore, along with Patrick Geddes, created a summer school for science in Darjeeling. He even attempted a textbook on science.

What I want to emphasize is that nationalism before the nation state guaranteed pluralism, demanded the availability of eccentricity. The question I then wish to ask is how this forest of imaginations turned into a flat land called the nation state. Where have all the memories gone?

I want to suggest nationalism had both an imagination and an imaginary. An imagination is a standard list of possibilities.

An imaginary is a horizon that adds the impossible, the improbable and the probable to the possible. Our nationalisms were a collection of possibilities. Our nation state was an acceptance that the amnesia had begun.

In fact, I want to argue that the nation state as a law and order theory of memory destroyed the future and uprooted memories that could have been the beginning of other possibilities. Communalism is an erasure of memory or a heightening of the artificiality of some memories against others. It is this selective memory of the nation state that makes it genocidal. What begins as amnesia culminates as erasure or genocide.

Consider just the idea of citizenship. The idea of citizenship has no place for the tribe, the nomad, for marginal groups of any kind. Citizenship becomes an authoritarian stencil that erases people who do not fit a standard pattern. Secession, protest and rebellion have to be seen as mnemonic devices reminding the nation state of the worlds it has forgotten.

It is the simplified time of the nation state that creates a form of authoritarianism. I am not saying memory is all about erasure. Memory is also about forgetting. Indian democracy could allow Laldenga to be yesterday's insurgent and then, chief minister of Mizoram. But the memories of today do not know how to forgive. Forgiveness remembers before it claims to forget. Forgiveness never defies justice. It only asks for more than justice.

If you look at the recent adjectives that define us, we tend to associate India with the new, with youth, with innovation. I am not making an argument for tradition but I want to point out that these are signals of erasure. Innovation also creates obsolescence, progress demands amnesia. What we need is a language that allows for a sense of mnemonics, a vocabulary of plurality, heritage, myth, diversity that sees truth as plural and demands that memory need not be one-sided.

There are other forms of erasure present in development. Remember mining is a way of erasing memory. It erases the memory of a landscape. It denies that nature can renew itself.

When you strip-mine an ecology, you destroy its ability to remember, to renew itself. Sustainability can never be complete without a theory of remembering.

This leads me to my last point. The Indian state as a knowledge system emphasizes history, information and science as the three primary modes of learning. But this makes a new generation illiterate, or at least one-sided, in terms of learning. Information is disembedded memory.

It carries no meta-narrative or contexts. History as written memory has little sense of the oral or of myth. Our science follows codes of linearity and progress that have little place for defeated knowledge. The tragedy of the nation state and its sense of history and science is its sense of memory. It is flawed and simplistic. Our sense of civilization, our world of folklore, our multiplicity of dialects as alternative memories must invent a way out of this impasse.

The Asian Age

22 April 2011

A Plea for Memory

One of the paradoxes of our time is that it is in the age of information that memory has become a casualty. Memory is not something stored in a diskette or digitalized in an archive. It is embedded, embodied, lived out. It needs to be told and retold. It is futile to store it because it is invented with every act of storytelling. Memory needs the storyteller more than the museum, more than the network on the archive.

We have to begin by challenging stereotypes of memory which treat it as unreflective expressions of a rote society. Memory then becomes the storage of information we do not fully understand. Such an attitude is unfair, especially to the genius of oral societies.

Memory is not mechanical or repetitive. Our films and documentaries project the stereotype of memory as rote. But rote memory belongs to the printed text. Oral memory was always inventive. Every time you recited a song or legend, you produced variations on the theme. We remember our epics and legends because we constantly improvise on them. This is one reason why there are so many versions of the Ramayana. Diversity is built into the very dynamics of memory. You improvise and invent so that you can remember. Anthropologist

Albert Lord in his great classic *The Singer of Tales* shows that memory is constructed in blocks, and these blocks are shuffled in a variety of ways as we recollect, retell and remember. Memory has a double function: It stores and invents simultaneously so that we may remember.

Memory is embedded and tacit. It involves an ecology of the unsaid and untold woven around an exemplar or practitioner. It has a vitality when it is relived or retold. The richness is lost when you reduce a text to information, and you often bowdlerize it. Our tutorial colleges bowdlerized knowledge; they destroyed the richness of a play by reducing it to formulae. The character of Hamlet is reduced to four points, or Shakespeare's genius listed in three. Information emasculates knowledge by removing its vital flesh, its sense of connectedness to a particular culture.

One has to remember that memory always existed in the plural. There are varieties of memory of which history, genealogy, legend, oral tales are but a few. The ethics of memory in each is different and we need to celebrate this plurality because it shows the past as a diverse universe. We need to relook at the relation between past, present and future. We also need to examine the relations between oral, textual and digital regimes, as the nature of memory in each is different. Each stores knowledge in a different way and each act of storing represents a different philosophy of knowledge.

One of the things modernity does is that it fetishizes progress. Our modern notion of innovation creates obsolescence and erasure. We label something as old or as backward and then proceed to eliminate it. Modern development is based on a destruction of memory. Our ancestors become an embarrassment and we turn our embarrassments into ancestral problems.

The big challenge for information societies is the problem of obsolescence. Obsolescence is often artificial. We label something as outdated and then treat it as irrelevant. An irrelevant society becomes ripe for erasure or elimination. One of the poignant questions one asks is whether obsolescence is tied to the god of information. Is obsolescence the sacrifice this hungry god of the new and the artificially new needs to sustain himself? Most ideas of innovation have little clue as to what to sustain, what to renew. Their search for the new condemns a whole world as useless and old.

Obsolescence allows crafts, industries, skills, cultures to be labelled as outdated and erased, displaced, eliminated or put into a museum. One can shrug off a craft or a tribe as obsolescent. Obsolescence allows for indifference, particularly an indifference to death and disappearance. Storing tribes as information in a museum becomes obscene; it is an act of intellectual rape which denies the right of tribes to exist as living entities.

One has to realize that information is not only about techniques of storage, retrieval and dissemination. One needs an ethics of memory to compensate and complement the more rudimentary ethics of information and innovation. We need, first, an ethics of memory that recognizes that life forms need varieties of memory, given the varieties of information. One needs redundancy, noise and diversity. Ethics has to ask about how one stores the sense of connectivity. Second, memory has to be stored in varieties of time, incorporated into varieties of storytelling. One must redefine terms such as relevance, identity, storage, representation.

I think memory needs the equivalent of hackers. Hackers threaten the security and the pomposity and secrecy of power. We need a set of 'preservers', people whose task is to remember, become repositories of dying or threatened memories, even homes for threatened skills. This is not to create a voyeurism for the past. A voyeurism of this kind culminates in kitsch, where the mass-produced souvenir or the replica displaces the original. A plaster of Paris replica of the Taj Mahal acquires a sentimental or aesthetic equivalence with the original. Tourism as an information system often displays such a tendency.

There is a beautiful story by Ray Bradbury called 'Fahrenheit 451'. It's a tale of a society where books are burned. The ruling regime outlaws the possession of books. A group of dissenters decide to become the memory of the society. Each decides to memorize a great classic and each person is then named after the book, as Hamlet or Rabelais or Don Quixote. Here the person lives out the text and it's such an ethics of memory that an information society needs. Memory is what you live out and in the very act of living out you create a civilization. This is what information societies need to remember.

The Asian Age

29 July 2011

Violence as the Other

A Portrait of the 1970s

There are times when a society abandons its institutions and thinks its way through violence. The 1970s was an era where violence conducted a variety of thought experiments.

Three modes of violence marked this decade. The first was the Emergency, the second was Bollywood and the third was development as violence. The combination of the three created an era where violence became a modern Indian grammar. Only most of India was not born then and what it experiences or recreates now is a vicarious sense of the 1970s.

Naxalbari was almost over and the Indian state thought of its activities as a kind of spring cleaning. The more idealistic of Naxals died in jail and many survivors joined the best social science institutes, perpetuating violence through social science.

But what Naxalism created with such effort, Bollywood created effortlessly. It created the new myth of urbanism and urban violence through an unforgettable hero – Amitabh Bachchan. He represented a generation which saw in violence the ultimate act of problem solving.

Bachchan was the perfect foil to the gentleness of Rajesh

Khanna, a true romantic. Bachchan was the first urban hero. He had no roots in the village and saw himself at home in a slum. He portrayed the true equality of all urban occupations by playing coolie, paanwallah, cop, criminal and smuggler. His was a faith in urban mobility and he had little faith in ordinary goodness. Bachchan represented the poetry of urban violence, the cleansing power of violence as it battled evil.

Bachchan's Bollywood created the myth of violence. Bollywood caught the contradictions between law and family, cop and criminal by showing India had never reconciled the public and private domains in a harmonious way. The good cop destroys a long-wanted criminal only to discover in him a long-lost brother.

The affinity and opposition between law and criminality actually set the base for violence as excess, as the only rhetoric and force that worked. At a time when institutions were sick, when norms were fickle, violence was seen as the only answer. Bachchan was not just the angry young man. He represented a generation which saw in violence the ultimate act of problem solving. But Bachchan's violence was not evil. It could be misunderstood, misused; it could be tragic.

But true evil began with Sanjay Gandhi. He was the architect of the Emergency and a man who single-handedly dissolved the institutional structures around which Nehruvian India was built. Trade unions, courts, universities, the bureaucracy – all dissolved under the corrosive eye of Indira Gandhi's son. He saw himself as Mr Development and used urban and family planning to eliminate the poor as poverty was more difficult to erase.

Tired of the unending talk of democracy, he demanded the silence of submission and dotted politics with illiterate injunctions like 'work more, talk less'. He hated the argumentative Indian.

He created an ultimate circle of sycophancy, and between

sycophancy and fear fabricated India's only period of dictatorship.

The 1970s marked the irony of development as modern technological projects wrecked the countryside – damming rivers, polluting villages, displacing people. The violence of development was disguised by the sanctity we gave to economics as a science. The citizen was no longer a person recognized by the Constitution, he was one who was not vulnerable to development. We were about to create a nation of refugees, ready to convince the world that we were a hard state. Tribes, nomads, slums, pastoral groups were all becoming non-citizens.

In a strange way we live with the decade of the 1970s. The Emergency still exists in some other context. Amitabh survives now in a mellow manner but his message of violence has eaten deep into the psyche of India. Only we label it as globalization. A decade we have forgotten still shapes our unconscious. A Freud of urbanism will have to dig deep into this decade to understand the making of violence in twenty-first-century India.

1970 Operation Flood helps dairy farmers take control of their lives and ushers in the White Revolution.

1971 India, Pakistan fight their second war. Bangladesh is created after Pakistani troops surrender.

1972 Historic Simla Agreement inked between India and Pakistan, forcing them into a reluctant peace.

1974 Under Project Smiling Buddha, India detonates a nuclear weapon on home ground. Over seventeen million Indian Railways workers go on the largest strike ever, demanding a pay hike.

1975 Prime Minister Indira Gandhi declares a state of Emergency in the country. The press is censored, opposition leaders are jailed. Aryabhata, the first Indian satellite, goes into earth's orbit to conduct experiments.

1977 Indira Gandhi lifts the Emergency and releases all political prisoners. Calls for fresh elections which she loses. Thus, the first non-Congress government comes to power with Morarji Desai as the prime minister.

1979 The Morvi Dam bursts in Gujarat, creating the biggest flood-related disaster of independent India. There is massive loss of life.

Hindustan Times
19 July 2012

Allahabad and Kumbh

Where Governance and Illiteracy Meet

Governance is a recently invented term. It was coined by Plato and reinvented by Harlan Cleveland monographs and acquired solidity in World Bank monographs. There is arrogance about its use. World Bank agencies and nation states talk about governance. Multinationals hold seminars on governance, but few look at pilgrimages and sacred complexes as sites for governance.

Kumbh has never received attention from a great urban sociologist of the city or a historian of governance. It is only recently that Harvard University realized what Hindu pilgrims and Mahatma Gandhi knew so well. They emphasized that the Kumbh Mela is not merely a fair or festival. It deals with the governance of instant cities. As Harvard's Tarun Khanna points out, the Kumbh is a city in temporary time where in five weeks a lazy city on the riverbank burgeons into a city of approximately 100 million people. Kumbh becomes one of the great metropolises of modern life. It is a fantastic city as a wonderful swarm, only the swarm is not of insects and birds, but of people as pilgrims.

The mind boggles at the logistics of what is required. It is an experiment in urban planning, law and order and epidemiology. A whole administration has to plan in advance and think on its feet. The number of visitors who attend the Kumbh mela is around 80–90 million. Such a population requires eighty million litres of drinking water, 25,000 tonnes of rice, 35,000 toilets, and a 100 hundred-bed hospitals and twelve smaller health care centres. A local government official states that the food at Kumbh is sold at prices even those below the poverty line can afford. Yet few Indians realize that Kumbh is one of the greatest cities we have created. Enacting the dance of the cosmos, Kumbh should make us proud and, in fact, help us understand that we are masters of governance.

Yet there is an irony. Indians are civic masters at Kumbh and yet seem illiterate outside of it. Think of the accident that happened at Allahabad railway station. The station was far from Kumbh and did not come under the mela's jurisdiction. The railways were in charge. There was a stampede on that day as the railways ran only seventy-five of the 150 trains promised earlier. A huge upsurge of waiting passengers was created. The railway station was like a river overflowing its banks with the platforms packed with people. The overbridge was teeming with pilgrims. The rail authorities stirred up a hornet's nest with a knee-jerk lathi charge, and more than thirty-six people died in the ensuing stampede. The railway station had blocked exit roads and over 6,000 people were trapped on the overbridge. Bodies lay unattended for over three hours. Azam Khan, the senior UP minister, resigned owning moral responsibility for the stampede.

The irony is stark. The difference in the handling of the two events is almost unbelievable. One is masterpiece of governance; the other is a classic case of governmental illiteracy. An Indian journalist confronting the two events will have to ask questions different from the Harvard team. The Harvard team is here to study the Kumbh as a miracle of crowd control, urban complexity and metropolitan behaviour. As its blog claims, it will study everything from public health behaviour, the number of toilets, the nature of information flow. It will eventually produce a classic document on the temporary city.

But Indians confronted with the idiocy of the stampede will have to ask: How do the two events coexist? How is it that Indians can produce a miracle of governance side by side with an illiteracy of civic handling? Harvard Business School claims it is here to ask what the Kumbh can teach it about real estate, infrastructure, civilization and sustainability. A sociologist of our cities will have to ask why we create next to it a complex of illiteracy, bad planning, an indifference to crowds and a complete failure of responsibility. Kumbh and Allahabad railway station appear to be two separate worlds juxtaposed spatially in a world called Uttar Pradesh.

The juxtaposition of the two events almost acquires the status of a fable. Kumbh will join the annals of the great cities of the world and become a classic in religious and urban terms. The railway stampede will pass away as a minor event, shrugged off by all but the survivors. Harvard and America will learn from Kumbh but India never seems to learn from its accidents and disasters. We adore a cosmic churning of life and time at Kumbh but are illiterate about the basics of urban planning outside it. Our IIMs and urban planning institutes will invite Diana Eck and Tarun Khanna to bloat the Indian ego and celebrate our civilizational competence. No one in India will ask if the stampede could have been prevented. Our urbanologists will envy the Harvard study but look with an almost cosmic indifference to the everyday loss of lives in modern India. Indian lives and Indian experiments seem cheap unless Harvard valorizes them.

There is a sadness here which demands more than a religious understanding. In fact, it raises questions. Why is it that religious events work like clockwork while other acts of crowd management bring out the indifference in us? The railway accident at Allahabad station will be dismissed as a footnote but it raises more questions about governance in India than the success of the Kumbh. The Indian mindset sadly produces both the cosmic intensity of the Kumbh and the indifference of the Allahabad station.

Firstpost
12 February 2013

The Tyranny of Mistakes

Many a time, as a commentator or an observer, one watches and listens to India preaching and exhorting itself. I hear Narendra Modi exhorting us to 'Make in India' and I hear Narayana Murthy asking us what India has made which one can find in the streets and markets. The emphasis is on achievement. Success is the currency of the day, the token of esteem.

An observer listening to Modi said, 'What we need to make in India is mistakes.' I realized the wisdom of what he was saying, because without errors, one cannot have a theory of truth as a process. Without mistakes, and the ability to rectify mistakes one cannot have a theory of innovation.

Mistakes in India always have a negative connotation. We associate them with failure. Annual reports of science laboratories rarely list a mistake. Reading the reports, one would think science in India is mistake-free. Our culture has lost its sense of play or even a sense of experiment because neither play nor experiment can take place without mistakes.

Our sense of perfection driven by ranks and the culture of examinations seems to think 100 per cent is the epitome, the hallmark of perfection. I remember two friends at the hostel repeated their maths exam papers because they obtained a 'mere' 97 per cent. They repeated and obtained 100 per cent and went home content in the Tamil Brahmin cosmos. Yet people who get 100 per cent, who 'max marks', as the lingo goes, rarely do research. They are convergent rather than divergent brains, trained for certainty, but uneasy with surprise.

I remember a top scientist, an astronomer at the Raman Institute, Bengaluru, telling me: 'Indians are great summarizers. They can summarize research results better than the original discoverer, but they have little that is original in themselves.'

The scientist seemed to hint that one cannot build a culture of original research or of creative innovation in a society that worships certainty. We lack a subculture that thrives on mistakes, that possesses a culture of storytelling around mistakes, where errors are winnowed out among the productive, the possible and the presently futile. An ethnography of mistakes is an absolute requisite for research cultures. Such cultures create narratives that show mistakes are not fragments of a post-mortem, that analysing a mistake might be one of the best ways of understanding the rituals of the scientific method.

A mistake fine-tunes the researcher's mind. I remember a friend of mine, Dilip Cherian, talking about the late economist, Mrinal Datta Chaudhuri. Mrinal, a superb raconteur, was talking about his days at the Massachusetts Institute of Technology. One day Mrinal wrote an equation on the board which turned out to be a wrong one. He was about to erase it when his professor protested. He said 'Don't wipe it, be proud of it. Von Neumann made the same mistake a few decades ago.' A mistake can be treasured even as nostalgia if it leads to a trail of discovery.

One needs an anthropology of mistakes where mistakes are constructed within an axis of plurality, where not all mistakes are part of misconduct and disaster. Many of our cultures have been formalized into bureaucratic modes of thought. Within a bureaucratic frame, any deviance from habit, routine, protocol becomes a mistake.

A mistake becomes more a form of deviance than a deviation from the norm. It is caught within a moral framework which does not condone such variation. But such an idea of conformity does not allow for research as learning, as play, where truth is not a certainty interpreted by high priests and experts, but something allowing for 'interpretive flexibility'. Such an idea allows for different outcomes and varying interpretations, which also create a culture where marginals, deviants, eccentrics and radicals have a place. Mistakes within a cognitive process then allow for pluralistic cultures.

One has to understand that within the complex cultures of today. Not all mistakes are intentional, mistakes happen despite following a procedure. Fail-safe systems are not always guarantees against disasters. One is reminded of the incident where the plant manager of Union Carbide, on being informed that gas was leaking, claimed, like a habituated technocrat, 'My plant cannot fail.' The informer just asked him to look out of the window.

The culture of mistakes is a complex one, and a field of risk sciences has been developed to understand the relation between mistakes, risks, accidents and responsibility. As a culture, we impose a dictatorship over mistakes demanding the tyranny of the right answer. Knuckles break, egos hurt, as teachers, parents and tutors wield the stick. The right answer in class is the darkness in education.

Because we do not tolerate mistakes, we destroy the sense of play in our culture. We think there is always one answer to every question when a slight change in the angle of the question can bring forth other answers. The bureaucracy of mistakes has to encounter the culture of unanticipated consequences.

In fact, if one looks at the lives of Rousseau, Tolstoy and particularly Gandhi, mistakes were central to their lives. Around mistakes which they saw as experimental, a whole ethical, political universe was created. In fact, in many ways Gandhi's ashrams were centres for making 'mistakes'. Unfortunately, we have bureaucratized our world and we treat mistakes as crimes. Such an attitude does not diminish mistakes, it merely makes us paranoid. We drive the mistake underground and destroy a sense of play and experiment.

I think before we move to the pomposity of innovation and discovery, India needs to be a society more tolerant of mistakes and more sensitive to error. We have to create an ethics responsible and responsive to error. No democracy can survive without it.

Daily O
23 August 2015

Author's Acknowledgements

The essays in this book owe most to Chandrika Parmar, who prodded me to write and then encouraged me to bring out this collection. Chandan Gowda independently proposed the idea of this book and carried it through with patience, creativity and care.

My wonderful bunch of teaching assistants Ranjit Singh, Anushree Goenka, Kritika Gupta, Harshita Gupta, Sania Sabharwal, Lahar Santra and Manasa Kambanna typed incessant drafts of my erratic handwriting with happy ease.

Finally, I must thank Professor Raj Kumar, Vice Chancellor of Jindal Global University for tolerating the erratic behavior of a happy academic.

Editor's Acknowledgements

Shiv Visvanathan invited me to put this book together. I am grateful to him for it.

Chandrika Parmar shared dozens of Visvanathan's articles during the early stage of the book. Amarinder Kaur compiled an extensive database of his articles from various online media sites. I am thankful to them for their keen interest and support.

A few other individuals have extended help in important ways: Vinutha Mallya got the publisher interested in the idea of this book; Keerti Ramachandra and Antony Thomas offered valuable copyediting efforts; Suresh Balatugi procured numerous articles of Visvanathan from the library archives at the Dhirubhai Ambani Institute of Communication and Technology, Ahmedabad; and, Manasa Kambanna obtained copyright permission from various publishing houses. Warm thanks to them all.

To the original publishers of the essays included in this book, I express thanks.

I would also like to thank Megha Divakar, Vikas Kumar and Srikanth Sastry whose enthusiasm and indulgence I freely drew on all along.

Finally, I owe much gratitude to Ajitha G.S., commissioning

editor at HarperCollins, for her warm support, keen involvement and much care in just about every aspect involved in seeing this book through.

About the Author

SHIV VISVANATHAN is Professor, School of Law, Jindal University, Sonepat. Earlier, he was Senior Fellow, Centre for the Study of Developing Societies, Delhi and Professor, Dhirubhai Ambani Institute for Information and Communication Technology, Ahmedabad. His books include *Organizing for Science* and *A Carnival for Science*. Visvanathan is also a columnist for *The Hindu, The Asian Age, Open* magazine, *Sunday Mail* and *Firstpost*.

About the Editor

CHANDAN GOWDA is Professor, School of Development, Azim Premji University, Bengaluru. Besides his academic writings, he has translated Kannada fiction and non-fiction into English, including *Bara*, a novella by U.R. Ananthamurthy, and edited *The Post Office of Abachooru*, a book of short stories by K.P. Purnachandra Tejasvi (forthcoming). He is presently completing a book on the cultural politics of development in the old Mysore state.